The Film Industry in Argentina

The Film Industry in Argentina

An Illustrated Cultural History

JORGE FINKIELMAN

McFarland & Company, Inc., Publishers
Jefferson, North Carolina, and London

LIBRARY OF CONGRESS CATALOGUING-IN-PUBLICATION DATA

Finkielman, Jorge, 1970–
    The film industry in Argentina : an illustrated cultural history
/ Jorge Finkielman.
      p.   cm.
    Includes bibliographical references and index.

    ISBN 0-7864-1628-9 (softcover : 50# alkaline paper)

    1. Motion picture industry — Argentina — History.
2. Motion pictures — Argentina — History. I. Title.
PN1993.5.A7F56   2004
384'.8'0982 — dc22   2003024611

British Library cataloguing data are available

Cover image: Carlos Gardel

Manufactured in the United States of America

*McFarland & Company, Inc., Publishers
  Box 611, Jefferson, North Carolina 28640
    www.mcfarlandpub.com*

To Elaine Mae Woo
My parents
My uncles

CONTENTS

INTRODUCTION

As an artistic and as a commercial spectacle, film — today as in the past — must win the audience's acceptance, move it emotionally, and make it laugh or cry. Public support is never guaranteed; it must always be recaptured with creativity, artistic quality and financial investments on the part of filmmakers, producers, artists, and technicians.

In Argentina, between the first and second decades of the twentieth century, the local film industry lost public support, enduring very difficult years before gaining back popular acceptance. The development of the tango, both as a dance and a music, and that of the broadcasting industry in Argentina, offer significant contrasts between what was actually going on in the country and to what was appearing on the domestic Argentine screen in those days. The big American film companies recognized the need for public support, and they gained it during the days of the silent film. Hollywood was so successful that it was able to gain a control of the market that continues even today.

What distinguished film exhibition in Argentina in the silent film days were the so-called second-line cinemas; the public got into the habit of going "to the movies" for more than merely watching a particular film. In the more expensive first-line halls, there was usually an orchestra that performed music synchronized to the action on the screen. Tango orchestras were in the second-line cinemas, and with their songs, managed to get the public's attention and generate much more enthusiasm than whatever was shown on the screen. It is difficult to imagine today that people went to a very big cinema just to listen to the bandoneon duo of Pedro Maffia and Pedro Laurenz or the Ciriaco Ortiz trio. The theaters didn't have sound amplifiers at the time, so it may be hard to believe today that just a few musicians could get a crowded audience worked up to a frenzy. These events did take place, and fortunately many 78 r.p.m disks which document the music that could be heard in those cinemas have survived. This way of seeing films finally ended in 1931, when theaters in

Argentina resolutely adopted the sound film, causing a terrible crisis for the tango.

The sound film revolution made people think that the dominance of American films would come to an end, due to difficulty accessing countries where people did not speak English. However, Hollywood realized how to reaffirm its worth in these markets. At first, in Argentina, the domestic sound film did not achieve the support it needed because basic problems had not yet been overcome. Businessmen, artists, and technicians finally won the local public's affection after several years of talkies, by the end of the thirties. These films stood next to the best from Hollywood, sweeping away all the troubles that had played Argentine films for years. This popularity of Argentine film coincided with the resurgence of the tango as a popular musical genre.

To describe the aforementioned events today is a heavy and a hard task. The Argentine films produced from 1897 (the year Argentine films were born) to 1940 are, more and more, far removed from public access. For the most part, frankly, the few still available are in terrible condition. This doesn't mean that there are no film collectors or archives with better material. However, the big media enterprises devoted to Argentine films have scant concern for preservation and restoration, and due to deterioration many of the domestic films shown on television in Argentina should not be presented at all. Much of the research for this book was done by examining papers and magazines published at the time of the release and exhibition of the films. These publications can be judged to have a partial view of events in the history of film. Comparing them with what has been written in several books devoted to this subject, the papers leave a favorable and faithful impression of the events. In many cases, they offer much information absent from the books, especially those dealing with the history of American film. It is becoming more and more difficult to find this material today since most of it has been retired from the public libraries where it was available, due to the damage it sustained after many years of being consulted by researchers and the public in general. Many collections are incomplete or are without several pages, probably torn out by some thoughtless person. Anyway, it is necessary to give thanks to the personnel of the Biblioteca del Congreso de la Nación for the excellent work they have been doing for years, and to the personnel of the library of the newspaper *La Prensa*, the most complete collection Argentines can access.

The fate of the Argentine film has almost always followed the path of the tango. The Buenos Aires music has always been better and more profoundly studied than our domestic film industry and allows the understanding many events when the ways of the music and the screen were connected. In this sense I must thank the people of the Internet site "Todo Tango" (http://www.todotango.com) for letting me use lots of their material. Thanks especially to Ricardo García Blaya, Néstor Pinzón, Héctor Lucci, Bruno Cespi, Felipe Van Cauwelaert, and Federico García Blaya for their kindness.

I also must thank collector Samuel Salomón for lending me some bibliographical material and allowing me access to some of the recordings of the orchestras that left 78 r.p.m., from the days of the silent film. Finally, I have to thank the inspiring work of Roberto Di Chiara and his children, Daniel, Luis, and Mariana to preserve and recover most of Argentina's and the world's film heritage, in spite of the economic struggle their "Di Film" archive (http://www.archivodifilm.com) must overcome in order to continue to be the most important of our country. I want to finish this introduction my father, Samuel, and my uncle, Leone Sonnino, for their valuable collaboration and patience in helping me complete this text. Without them this manuscript could have never been written at all. And I must express gratitude to my mother, too, because she had to stand firm against my frustrations and bad humor when I was working.

1

FROM CURIO TO
MASS ENTERTAINMENT

The First Film Exhibitions in Argentina

Argentina was one of the first countries in the world to discover motion pictures. The earliest public exhibition of a film took place on the 18th of July 1896 at the Odeon Theater in the city of Buenos Aires. It was organized by the Odeon's manager, Francisco Pastor, and the journalist Eustaquio Pellicer. The first movies made by the Lumiere brothers were shown. According to the historian Jorge Miguel Couselo, an exhibition of Thomas Alva Edison's "kinetoscope" two years before had gone practically unnoticed by the press. On the 19th of July 1896 the newspaper *La Nación* published an article in the "Theater & Festivities" section describing the extent: "The device that was operated for the first time last night at the Odeon Theater is quite a novelty and is unusually attractive due to the lovely effects of many of its views, in which the movements of people and vehicles are replicated with a such a marvelous degree of realism that it marvels and captivates the viewer, completing the impression of reality produced by the natural size of the pictures shown."

At that time Enrique Lepage, a Belgian, began to look into the possibility of importing film and projection gear in order to enlarge his photographic equipment business. Two of his employees, Eugenio Py, a Frenchman, and Max Glücksmann, an Austrian who was the manager of the Lepage Company, insisted together that their employer should attempt this venture. Max Glücksmann had arrived in Buenos Aires on the 27th of July 1890, a 15-year-old immigrant in search of a future. He arrived in the middle of the revolution that was to topple the government and kill his traveling companion. He managed to find a job in a foundry, but he soon left it to become a photographer's assistant. He began to study photography seriously and started out on his own, earning a modest amount of money before landing a job with M. Lepage. When he started work at

Max Glücksmann

Eugenio Py

Lepage's there were only three employees. Two years later Glücksmann had risen to manager, and after another four years, he became head of the firm when M. Lepage decided to go and live in Europe.

Eugenio Py was a French immigrant, who came to Argentina to work on the railways. He left the trains and established himself as a modest neighborhood photographer; soon after he started working for Lepage, for whom he was to take the first moving pictures of Argentina. The Lepage firm started by producing films using Leon Gaumont's Elgé cameras, which had arrived in Buenos Aires from France in 1897. In 1899 they started recording sound, first on wax cylinders and then on disks. All references agree that the first film made in Argentina was a short (17 meters) movie called *The Argentine Flag*, which showed the Argentine flag flying on a mast in the Plaza de Mayo, in front of the Argentine government building.

Max Glücksmann's commercial instinct anticipated the future of this innovation, and he started to sell projectors and small reels of film. The films were imported, and showed miscellaneous news. According to Couselo the years up to 1900 were years of testing and trials. Argentina cinema in its beginning was not (as in the USA) a source of popular entertainment, but a symbol of European modernism for the rich. The oldest Argentine movie to be preserved is the *Operation on a Hydatid*

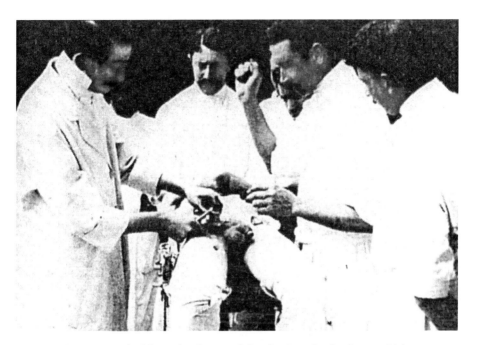

Operation on a Hydatid Cyst by doctor Alejandro Posadas in the amphitheater of the Clinicas Hospital (1898 or 1899).

Cyst, a surgical operation carried out by the young surgeon Alejandro Posadas in the amphitheater of the Clinicas Hospital in 1898 or 1899.

The first newsreels were filmed in the year 1900, and the very first was Dr. Campos Salles' *Journey to Buenos Aires*, shot by Py on the 25th of October 1900. It shows the arrival of the Brazilian President-elect Manoel Ferraz de Campos Salles and his greeting by the president of Argentina, Julio A. Roca. Also in 1900, the first motion picture theater in the city of Buenos Aires opened, the Salón Nacional, managed by Gregorio Ortuño. Movie bars and kinetoscopes followed and then movie theaters started to multiply.

According to journalist Roberto Di Chiara, the Salón Nacional was located at Maipú street between Corrientes and Lavalle streets in downtown Buenos Aires; it had less than three hundred seats, and each film shown lasted between two and three minutes. This cinema later closed, only to reappear nearby as the Porteño. Another theater, the Universal, located at number 442 Suipacha Street, would later be called by the same name as the street. A livery stable in the middle of downtown Buenos Aires (Corrientes Street between Esmeralda and Maipú streets) was converted into one of the best theaters of that time. It was built and managed by Max

Glücksmann. Argentine cinema was growing unnoticed by most and practically ignored by the press. The films were merely newsreels full of society gatherings, lavish parties, military parades, religious celebrations, and important funerals.

The first film to be considered a real documentary was *La Revista de la Escuadra Argentina en Mayo de 1810* (*The Review of the Argentine Naval Squad in May, 1910*), by Eugenio Py, recording the navy's maneuvers. It was first shown on the 7th of June 1901 at the Victoria Theater at a benefit for the Navy Home, and a navy band played appropriate music behind the screen. In 1902 Py captured his own crossing of the Andes Mountains on film. This resulted from a border dispute between Argentina and Chile. He went to film the talks between German general Emilio Koerner, who had reorganized the Chilean army, and colonel Sir Thomas Holdich, commissioned by King Edward VII of England, who had been designated mediator in the dispute. Everything was recorded by Py's camera.

Fiction appeared on film for the first time around 1901, the work of Eugenio A. Cardini, a well-off man who had bought his film equipment from the Lumiere brothers. According to Couselo, Cardini shot *Escenas Callejeras* (*Street Scenes*) and *En Casa del Fotógrafo* (*In the Photographer's House*) with impromptu actors and some simple comic scenes. *El Regimiento Ciclista* (*The Bicycle Regiment*) aspired to the category of urban documentary.

Py and Glücksmann experimented with added sound, lasting the length of a gramophone record, in 1907. They were influenced by similar experiments carried out in Paris by Pathé and Gaumont. A short song, or a short episode from an Argentine or Spanish play or operetta, was played before the cameras. According to historian Pablo Ducrós Hicken, "the actor performed in front of the horn; and once the recording was done, he gestured in front of the camera while listening to the music in the background. Today it is still done in repetitions called playback." According to catalogs from those times you will find, among others, José (Pepito) Petray, Angel Villoldo, Humberto Zurlo and Rosa Bozán, together with theater celebrities such as Eugenio Gerardo López, Alfredo E. Gobbi and his wife Flora Rodríguez. These shorts, all directed by Eugenio Py, were, according to Jorge Couselo, made from the following songs: "Bohemia Criolla," and "El Calotero," by Enrique de María, music by Antonio Reynoso, both from *Bohemia Criolla*; "Pica-Pica el Compadrito," by Miguel F. López; "Los Políticos," by Nemesio Trejo, music by Reynoso; "Abajo la Careta," by Enrique Buttaro, music by Antonio Podestá; "Ensalada Criolla," by Enrique de María, music by Enrique García Lalanne; "Gabino el Mayoral," by Enrique García Velloso, music by García Lalanne in the tango sketch; "El Pechador," "El Soldado de la Independencia," "Los Tocayos," "Mister Whiskey," "Dejá de Jugar, Che, Che," by Angel Villoldo ("Los Carreros" and "El Cochero de Tranvía" were probably also by Villoldo); "La Beata," by Ezequiel Soria, music by Antonio Podestá; "A Palermo" by Agustín Fontanella, music by Antonio Podestá; "Justicia Criolla" by Soria, music by Reynoso; "La Trilla" by Trejo, music by García Lalanne; "Los Escruchantes" by Valaguer and Tubasne. Finally we have to add "El Carro Carbonero," "Ya No Te Acuerdas de Mi," "Gente Buena" and "Guardo Tramway" by unidentified authors.

In 1908 Max Glücksmann took over the Lepage Company and spurred the production, distribution and exhibition of films.

Around 1905 Mario Gallo, a chorus-master from an operetta company, arrived in Argentina. Once in Buenos Aires he became a café pianist. In this job he met another Italian, Atilio Lipizzi, an ex-electrician who projected movies in quick-change artist Leopoldo Fregoly's show. Lipizzi showed Gallo a new movie attraction that was beginning to work in Europe and the USA: characters from fiction, the theater and history recorded on film. Gallo started making films with actors, sets and scripts, leaving behind the documentaries that prevailed at the time. Some of the titles in his filmography are *La Batalla de Maipú*, with actors Eliseo Gutierrez and Enrique de Rosas; *Camila O'Gorman*, with Salvador Rosich and Blanca Podestá; *Güemes y sus Gauchos*; *La Batalla de San Lorenzo* and *La Creación del Himno*. According to journalist Domingo Di Nubila this combination of attractions had such an effect that Gallo was able to create an interest in Argentine movies, laying the foundations upon which the country's cinema industry was to be built.

The first Argentine film with a script was *La Revolución de Mayo*, first shown at the Ateneo Theater on the 22nd of May 1909. It was divided into fifteen parts, of which only nine remain, each preceded by a caption. The movie depicts the events on the 25th of May 1810 (the May revolution) and the days preceding it. This was not only the first fictional film in Argentina, but it is also one of the very few to be conserved from the Argentine silent film era. It has also been established that this was Mario Gallo's first film, and not *El Fusilamiento de Dorrego* as was believed for a long time.

According to Ricardo Manetti, Gallo introduced the first hopeless love affair in *Camila O'Gorman*; which set during the dictatorship of Juan Manuel de Rosas, the film explores the forbidden love between an aristocratic young girl and a Catholic priest, which ends in tragedy. The actors Blanca Podestá and Salvador Rosich played the central characters. That same year, together with journalist, playwright, and later, tango lyricist

José Gonzalez Castillo (who would also translate the films imported by Max Glücksmann into Spanish for the next twelve years), Gallo adapted the novel *Juan Moreira* by Eduardo Gutierrez, giving Enrique Muiño the leading role. He also had the courage to shoot operatic melodramas, such as *Tosca* and *Cavallería Rusticana*. In 1912, he produced Argentina's first full-length feature film, *Tierra Baja*, a film in six acts starring Pablo Podestá, with a script by González Castillo and Camilo Vidal based on a story by Angel Guimará.

Gallo's endeavors took place approximately between 1909 and 1913, but the venture didn't make money and he was to end his days in great poverty. His contemporaries Julio Raúl Alsina and Atilio Lipizzi also made films of the same kind, such as *Avelino Viamonte*, *Facundo Quiroga* and *La Tragedia de los Cuarenta Años*, all made perhaps in 1909 or the year after.

The Uruguayan-born Alsina set up a primitive film studio and lab, the first in Argentina, and in 1910 produced "La Revista del Centenario," a mixture of films made during the celebrations of the centennial of the May 1810 revolution. Some of the professionals who came to film the centennial celebrations ended up remaining in Argentina.

In documentary cinema the work of Italian Federico Valle would be outstanding. He arrived in Argentina in 1911 and set up a lab to translate the captions of foreign movies. According to Di Nubila, Valle had received lessons from Georges Melies himself and had a great deal of experience as a cameraman, having shot images in Europe, Asia Minor and America. After showing films for a time in the city of Mar del Plata, Cinematografía Valle started making industrial films. Although these films were commercial advertising, Valle and his collaborators, especially José Bustamante y Ballivián, infused them with originality and educational values. Some of them were shown hundreds of times, and were requested at times by the audience. Valle's *Film Revista Valle* put into practice a non-conventional treatment of filmed journalism. Just as Py had trained the first camera professionals, Valle was to teach the best camera operators and lab workers.

In 1909 Julián Ajuria founded the Sociedad General Cinematográfica, the firm that was to substitute hiring for the sale of films, and which became for many years one of the most powerful film distributors in the country, along with the Glücksmann Company. Ajuria helped with the funding of various films, such as those made by Mario Gallo, and, later on, the movie *Nobleza Gaucha*.

In 1913, Julio Irigoyen started to produce *Noticiero Buenos Aires* with his brand new company, Buenos Aires Film. His filmography shows a great number of documentaries, newsreels, feature and industrial films. His productions were generally turned down by exhibitors in Buenos Aires, but were well received in the rest of the country. In the following years movie production in Argentina stopped being a family business. Newly companies tried to build the foundations of an industrial system, but silent movie production in Argentina never reached the level of an industry, and remained a craft.

The First Feature Length Films

Around 1914 filmmaking began to grow in importance. In the beginning they seemed a cheap pastime only worth a few pennies, but by 1914 movies were becoming a means of popular education and instruction that responded to the needs of those who wanted entertainment at the end of day. For this reason it is interesting to check some statistics produced by the Buenos Aires theater inspectors in the year 1913:

> *Authorized establishments:* 21 theaters, 130 movie houses, 4 cafés with shows, 35 movie bars, 2 puppet theaters, 5 circuses, 6 open air movie theaters, 2 mutoscopes, 15 merry-go-rounds, 2 skating rinks, 33 societies, 7 dancing academies, 12 varied amusements and 39 premises where music is performed after 12.30 A.M.
>
> *New premises:* 57 movie houses, 10 movie bars, 3 open-air movie theaters, 3 circuses, 2 puppet theaters, 1 mutoscope hall, 4 dance academies, 9 merry-go-rounds, 5 societies, 3 varied amusements and 16 premises where music is performed after 12.30 A.M.

The movie industry had modest beginnings. The first films were very short, showing ordinary scenes taken from everyday life. But the industry grew, invented its own language, created sets and kept its characteristic of being a curious witness. Its development also produced a new way of spreading knowledge. By just viewing a newsreel you could see day-by-day the great events of history and political meetings, strikes, and so on. Short films were joined together and became lengthy, forming, for example, an evening long show. Furthermore, they initiated a new school of acting, taking actions and facial expressions and adapting them to the new media, discarding useless frills more appropriate in the theater. Unfortunately very little is known about the development of film-shows in Argentina in their very beginnings. The few publications from those days still to be found today did not give much space to film reviews. There was an exhibition of scientific 8mm films at the Palace Theater, on April 8, 1914. On the 8th of April there was the premier of the feature *Maldita sea la Guerra* at the Empire Theater, which was sold out to an audience eager to see the horrors of war; next was the first showing of the epic film *Nerón y Agripina* in which 1000 extras and 30 lions took part, accompanied by an orchestra playing appropriate tunes. Finally, on June 23, there was the premier of the second part of the serial *Las Hosannas de Rombadode*, a section called "El Conde Artoff," based on the work by Jonson du Terrail, at the Palace cinema, together with chapters 14 to 40 of *Los Dramas de París*.

A curious episode took place on the 9th of October 1914 in the Argentine Government building. Government ministers, diplomats, high ranking officials and "a small number of ladies" gathered in the conference room of the Sub-secretary of the Ministry of Foreign Relations to view filmed images of the war that was making Europe shudder. The presence of ten automobiles parked outside of the ministry alarmed those passing by, their imagination making them believe anything at all except the fact that the people inside were watching a film projection.

By then World War I was raging. In Buenos Aires, the mayor's office, which had the power of censoring films whenever an exhibition permit was requested, decreed that it was forbidden to show biased films that might provoke demonstrations which would be disagreeable to any of the nations in conflict. These same events were widely reported on in the various newspapers and magazines at that time. Nonetheless, as was stated by the newspaper *La Prensa*, the good judgment of the citizens of Buenos Aires wouldn't allow any demonstrations to take effect when films without any propagandistic or tendentious purpose, but with details of troop movements, defense preparations, fortification works and similar scenes, were shown on the screen.

By 1914 films were already free from the variety performances and other attractions that shared the act when movie shows were beginning. The principal film distributors in Argentina at that time were the Max Glücksmann firm, The Sociedad General Cinematográfica, the Compañia Cinematográfica Argentina, the Casa Edison, the Sociedad Biográfica Americana, the De Ambrosio y Silenzi firm, the Cooperativa Biográfica and Atilio Lipizzi.

Among these companies, Max Glücksmann's was outstanding, and he started to produce feature films of different kinds when he opened his own studios in 1915. The first was *Amalia*, based on José Marmol's novel about the love affair between a young woman and a youthful intellectual who opposed the dictator Juan Manuel de Rosas. The making of this film had special characteristics. It was produced for charity, for the Sociedad del Divino Rostro, a benevolent society founded and led by Angiolina Astengo de Mitre. The script and the direction of the movie were assigned to Enrique García Velloso, who obtained Eugenio Py's collaboration for the cinematography and editing. No trained actors were used, but the cast was made up of prominent members of the local upper crust, such as

Susana Larreta y Quintana in the role of Amalia, Enrique García Lawson as Eduardo Belgrano and Jorge Quintana Unzué playing Daniel Bello. The movie was a careful reconstruction of that period, with much attention given to the details of the sets and wardrobe. According to Jorge Couselo, García Velloso managed to improve on the short films made by Mario Gallo and get around the limitations of his amateur actors. *Amalia* premiered on the 12th of December 1914 at a gala at the Colón Theater, with all the important government authorities in the audience.

This movie was a great achievement, and a few months later Max Glücksmann would reach new heights with his next film *Mariano Moreno y la Revolución de Mayo*. It would introduce national historical themes, more substance, and a larger budget. According to comments made at that time, it was a grand production, faithful to the history of the revolution of 1810, displaying a careful reconstruction of those times. Glücksmann invested a large amount of money to hire a cast of four hundred. The principal roles were played by Pablo Podestá as Mariano Moreno and José J. Podestá as Saavedra, with Camila Quiroga, Juana Conde, Elías Alippi, Julio Escarcela, Alfredo Lliri, César Fiaschi and Héctor G. Quiroga, all of whom were valued actors from the Argentine legitimate theater. Author Horacio Quiroga, under the pen name León de Aldacoa, writing in the magazine *Caras y Caretas* said: "García Velloso, the author of the script, has done a good, patriotic and proper job. Max Glücksmann, as editor, film technician and entrepreneur has accomplished a task which would have made anybody else faint." He also wrote that "the beauty of the cinematography, the quality of the costumes and the acting not only resist comparison with the best films that come from Europe; but there are very few films made in foreign countries which can challenge this great Argentine movie." The newspaper *La Nación* stated that: "The Max Glücksmann Editing Company and its artistic operator Mr. Eugenio Py, have managed to imprint all the scenes with perfect precision in their toning, colors and lighting effects. The work can compare, in this sense, with the movies that come from the great cinematographic workshops of Europe." Furthermore, "Moreno's journey from Buenos Aires to Chuquisaca is meticulously reconstructed in extraordinarily poetic settings. The terrible journey from Luján to Alto Perú comes out of the screen with huge emotional impact." Referring to the reconstruction of the locations, "The Viceroy's office in the fort, the Catalanes café, Rodríguez Peña's house and the red light district have been reconstructed with an impressive thoroughness. The costumes and settings are taken care of, even down to the smallest details." *Mariano Moreno y la Revolución de Mayo* was first shown at the reception hall of the newspaper *La Prensa* the 14th of April 1915, and at movie house six days later. According to this newspaper "the film planned and shaped by Enrique García Velloso is the story of the great orator in action, he whose eloquent speeches electrified the spirit of Argentina at that memorable time. All the great man's life is described according to historical truth, choosing those moments in which his actions were most significant." "The attire, settings, furniture, etc. belong to the time in which those episodes happened. Mr. Max Glücksmann hasn't kept back anything to ensure that the author of the film had all that was necessary to reconstruct each scene with the greatest accuracy." After these films, Max Glücksmann would also make *El Conde Orsini*, possibly the first crime movie, featuring Pedro Gilardoni, Francisco Ducasse, Angelina Pagano, Inés Berrutti and Lina Estévez. According to Roberto Di Chiara this film was successfully released on August 11, 1917. Glücksmann also made *Aventuras de Viruta y Chicharrón* with Celestino Petray, *El Negro Johnson* with the boxer of that name, and *Romance Argentino*, among others. Glücksmann continued to produce documentaries, industrial films and newsreels, all while thriving at the same time as a distributor and exhibitor of foreign films.

The first film made in Hollywood with an Argentine theme, *El Capitán Alvarez* arrived from the United States at the end of April 1915. According to Domingo Di Núbila, Julián Ajuria, its distributor, deemed it an important occurrence and had the film colored by hand. The story was produced by the Vitagraph Company, and featured Edith Storey, William D. Taylor and George E. Stanley, and was directed by Rollin Sturgeon. The plot concerns Robert Wainwright, an American, traveling with his uncle on a business trip to Argentina. He falls in love with Bonita, a niece of don Arana, the minister of foreign affairs to the tyrannical dictator Juan Manuel de Rosas. Bonita is a revolutionary and wins over Wainwright to her cause. Under the alias Capitan Alvarez he fights the despot Rosas, acting as liaison between the revolutionary general Urquiza and don Arana, a secret sympathizer. After a series of revolutionary adventures Wainwright manages to overthrow Rosas, form a new government and join his beloved Bonita. Although the movie had the tempo and the characteristics that were beginning to distinguish Hollywood productions, the mistakes in its setting and its distortion of Argentine history, especially after the release of the film *Mariano Moreno y la Revolución de Mayo*, triggered a great scandal, complete with demands that it be censured and banned. *El Capitán Alvarez* as journalist Diego Curubeto affirms, was probably the first Hollywood film to deal with an Argentine theme, and the first to provoke a scandal. It certainly wouldn't be the last.

By this time two award-winning still photographers, Eduardo

"Nobleza Gaucha," the tango written by Francisco Canaro as the musical theme of the film of the same name.

Martínez de la Pera and Ernesto Gunche, were working in films. They joined forces with Humberto Cairo, program executive at the Sociedad General Cinematográfica, Julian Ajurias's distribution company. From that combination came the film *Nobleza Gaucha*. As Domingo Di Núbila mentions, the film started off badly. The author of the script, José González Castillo, was able to save it with a number of additions and some changes in the captions, using lines that fit the action from José Hernández's epic poem *Martín Fierro*. The movie was an enormous success, unsurpassed in all the history of silent movies in Argentina. It was exhibited simultaneously in twenty-five Buenos Aires theaters, and also shown in Brazil, Spain and other Latin American countries.

Orfilia Rico, María Padín, Julio Escarcela, Arturo Mario and Celestino Petray played the main characters. The plot is fairly simple: a rich landowner abducts a beautiful girl and carries her off to his palace in Buenos Aires. A gaucho who is in love with her goes to her rescue, but is falsely accused of being a cattle rustler by the dastardly landowner. The villain dies in the final scene when he rides over the edge of a precipice while being pursued on horseback by the hero.

The film was very advanced for its time. It featured clear and even exquisite cinematography, with some camera movements and long shots, and even close ups in key situations. While the people of the countryside were shown as being gallant and naïve, the city presented a mundane and slightly (from a rural point of view) sinful image. To this purpose, the movie included some scenes of couples dancing the tango at the Armenonville cabaret in Buenos Aires. The film premiered the 11th of August 1915 in Buenos Aires. *La Prensa*, described it as the most important film yet produced in Argentina. The plot was very simple, and without absurd situations. It showed picturesque authentic scenes about life in an *estancia*. The production showed a moving realism, and the film's development captivated audiences of the time. The actors managed to give their parts great credibility, something absent in the Argentine films released earlier.

Composer Francisco Canaro wrote the score and also recorded it for Atlanta records. Furthermore, Humberto Cairo sold the rights to the name of the film to a merchandise distributor for use with its maté tea. Nobleza Gaucha maté can still be found on the market today.

The huge success of *Nobleza Gaucha*, including its exhibition in foreign countries, led to some thought about the chances of building a national film industry on a firm basis. As Jorge Couselo mentions, the moment was right: World War I had weakened European productions, and American supremacy in Latin American markets was not yet manifest.

What was not perceived with the movie's success was the deficiency of the local market. Once they split with Humberto Cairo, Eduardo Martínez de Le Pera and Ernesto Gunche invested their earnings in the construction of their own studios. They started with *Hasta Después de Muerta*, which was a great success at the time, according to Di Núbila. Florencio Parravicini wrote a script about a young surgeon. A patient that dies under his scalpel during an operation turns out to be the girl he was passionately in love with when he was a student. Parravicini himself (who co-directed with Martínez and Gunche) headed the cast of Orfilia Rico, Silvia Parodi, María Fernanda Ladrón de Guevara, Argentino Gómez and Enrique Serrano.

José González Castillo

Florencio Parravicini also appeared in another 1916 movie, released on the 7th of April *Tierra Argentina*. Co-starring Lola Membrives, the film was originally extremely long, with technical shortcomings and an uninteresting plot. Full of views of the country and scenery that was attractive for promoting tourism, the cast did what it could to overcome the film's problems. By the time it was ready for release many of its problems had been patched up, following the suggestions of the reviewers that had seen the first cut.

Another film that also failed was *Mi Bandera*. The success achieved by some Argentine films stimulated the public's interest, but the low quality of the Argentine film industry and the lack of qualified technicians caused its productions to be defective. For this reason contemporary publications gave little space to the movies made in this country. The film *La Ultima Langosta*, scripted and directed by Enrique E. Millar, opened on August 17, 1916 and showed that Argentina could make films as good as those imported from abroad. This film was awarded a prize in a contest sponsored by the magazine *Fray Mocho*. The daily *La Prensa* compared it to the best foreign films then showing. However, its plot was a bit common showing and conventional, and too simple for a film of its length. Perhaps, due to the fact that the film had to be feature length, Millar filled out the contents of the film, distracting the audience's attention from the principal theme, making the film slow and monotonous. However, the music, specially composed by Osmán Pérez Freire, helped it to obtain a satisfactory result.

A very successful film at that time was *Resaca* which opened on the night of the 24th of August, 1916. It was based on a play by Alberto Weisbach, adapted to the screen by José González Castillo and directed by Atilio Lipizzi for Filmgraf, his own production company. Its cast included Pedro Gilardoni (in the role he had played at the theater), Camila Quiroga, Luis Arata, Marcelo Ruggero, Olinda Bozán, Alfredo Camiña, Eva Franco and Mr. Cordido. The film also included the tango dancer Benito Bianquet (known as "El Cachafaz"), who contributed his unsophisticated choreographic skills, which he was to repeat on other occasions. This film was a great success, having a run of 34 days, with a profit similar to that of *Nobleza Gaucha* the year before. *Resaca* is probably the first Argentine full-length feature whose setting can be considered the tango milieu, that is to say that it is not limited to showing just dance numbers. The critic from *La Prensa* wrote:

> The film's setting, according to the author, take place in a run down Buenos Aires suburb, but in our opinion it could be adapted to any slum background, just by exchanging the tango, maté and guitar for the regional dances, vices and habits of any country.
>
> The film is grotesque due to the crudity and bleakness of most of its episodes. Its plot is based on depravation and vice, and even though there are characters that are decent and redeemable, the whole movie seems to us just a series of adventures of gauchos in the tradition described by (Ricardo) Gutierrez, with the difference that these had noble aspects but in *Resaca* they only have bloodthirsty instincts, and act as if they were wild beasts.
>
> To all this we have to add the exaggerated performing by the actors, with the exception of Mrs. Quiroga and Mr. Cordido, who in our view are those that perform in a more truthful manner.

Lipizzi also shot *Amor de Bombero* (1915), a great success, and *Federación o Muerte*, with Pepito Petray, Ignacio Corsini and others. On this occasion the film was written and directed by Gustavo Caraballo. Di Núbila states that Carballo retired in 1918 after a couple of unsuccessful films (*El Movimiento Continuo* with Roberto Casaux in 1916 and *A las Nueve en el Convento* in 1917). Among his collaborators were two persons who later on were to make their contribution to the cinema: José A. Ferreyra and Edmo Cominetti.

El Crimen de la Calle Suipacha opened on the 15th of November 1916. Retired police inspector Carlos Costa, inspired by a murder case in which he had been involved, made this film. Some facts from the investigation of that crime allowed him to imagine a whole series of scenes, such as the suicide of the chief culprit of the murder and the imprisonment of his accomplices. Carlos Costa also acted the part of the chief detective. On of February 20, 1917, the film *El Alegre Jeremías* was booed by the audience upon its release. Another disappointment was the film *Buenos Aires Tenebroso*, scripted by Manuel Carlés and directed by Carlés, Vicente Marracino and Juan Glize for Cinematográfica Río de la Plata, with the actresses Gema di Guelfo and Vina Velázquez, and actor Pedro Gilardoni. It also included Francisco Izzo and Tita Merello. Its theme music was a tango by Adolfo Avilés. The film purported to show some revolting aspects of low life in Buenos Aires, with the intention of instructing the public about the perils of drug use and abuse. *El Triunfo de las Almas* had better luck. It was shot by Patria Films as "a poem to love and sacrifice" and it featured Camila Quiroga, Eliseo Gutierrez, A. Zama, A. H. Fuentes and Celestino Ferrer. *Santos Vega*, presented in April 1917, was directed by Carlos De Paoli, with a score by Félix Scolatti Almeyda. The cinematography was by Angel Scaglione and Luis Carlos Colombo; Vicente Scaglione, the cinematographer's brother, produced the film. Made to highlight the actor José J. Podestá, it was to give Ignacio Corsini his first opportunity to appear on the silver screen. He had been noticed by the public as a young leading man, but unfortunately the screen was to offer him very few opportunities; he would become, in time, one of the best Argentine singers ever. *La Prensa* had a good impression of *Santos Vega*, praising José J. Podestá in the title role, as well as the work of Susana Vargas, José Rubens and Ignacio Corsini. *Viviana*, by Claudio Miranda, was a fine film first shown on June 17, 1917; a "passionate drama of love and redemption" according to its script:

> The central character is Viviana, a girl caught in the clutches of a white-slaver, who forces her to pretend to be her sister and to seduce Morin, a rich factory owner and partner to Herrera; but Viviana, who still has an honest woman's pure feelings, revolts against the exploiter's plans, especially since her heart is ablaze after crossing looks with Morin, who also responds to the same passion, to the point of proposing marriage to her. The clash that follows between Viviana and Charrel, she defending the man to whom she given her heart, and he defending his miserable plans, completes the plot, that naturally enough ends with the triumph of virtue and the scoundrel's tragical failure.

La Prensa compared *Viviana* to the best films coming from overseas, while noting that the excessive length of some episodes and some out right padding made it a bit boring at times. The reviews were still good. Camila Quiroga distinguished herself in the leading role, and was ably backed up by Julio Escarcela, Eduardo Zucchi and Aurelia Ferrer.

As Jorge Couselo mentions, Federico Valle produced two unusual feature films *El Apóstol* (1917) was a satirical view of the recently elected president, Hipólito Irigoyen. This was an animated film drawn by the artists Quirino Cristiani (whose satirical cartoons used to close the news sequences in the Film Revista Valle) and Diógenes Taborda. *La Carmen Criolla* or *Una Función de Gala en el Colón*, produced by the architect Andrés Ducaud, showed important people caricaturized as puppets. It was established at an animated film festival that took place in Berlin in 1970 that *El Apóstol*, with a script written by Alfonso de Laferrere, is chronologically the first full-length cartoon feature film in the world. As Couselo sustains, *El Apóstol'* preceded Winsor McCay's *The Sinking of the Lusitania*, which took 22 months and five thousand drawings to make. The team that did *El Apóstol* must have been bigger, because in twelve months it did fifty-eight thousand drawings.

Hipólito Irigoyen's government didn't like the release of *El Apóstol* at all, and the Buenos Aires town hall banned its exhibition at the end of June 1917, using the excuse that it was a caricature of the political situation, and threatening to close all the cinemas that disobeyed the order. The next year, Cristiani produced a new cartoon film, released on the 7th of May 1918, called *Sin Dejar Rastros*. He was to continue producing short films, taking advantage of the animated cartoon's capacity for expression. *La Virtud del Ahorro* was a feature planned and acted by the staff of the National Postal Savings Bank, and it premiered on the 2nd of August 1917. It was made to be shown at schools and military barracks in Argentina. It tells the story of a boy who sells newspapers, who, thanks to a gift from his godfather, begins to save money, and manages to put away 150 pesos. His father is an alcoholic; joins a strike and ends up in jail. The child's mother then falls seriously ill and lacks the money necessary for her treatment. Facing this problem the child uses his savings to have his mother cured. After some time the father regains his liberty, but does not dare to come home, because of the shame he has brought upon his family. Then, at the end of the film, when the child is selling his papers in the Palermo neighborhood, he encounters his father, and takes him home. The child, his mother, and his father are reunited.

Francisco Defilippis Novoa's *Flor de Durazno* based on the novel by Hugo Wast (Gustavo Martínez Zuviría) and featured Silvia Parodi, Argentino Gómez, Ilde Pirovano, Celestino Petray and Carlos Gardel in his first screen appearance. The film, shot between June and July 1917 with the backing of the Santa Filomena Association in the same locations as those described by the author, was released on the 29th of September 1917. Carlos Gardel at that time was on the way to becoming the most important Argentine singer of all time, but when he saw himself on the screen in a leading role, he didn't like it at all, because he was overweight.

Flor de Durazno was one of the paramount Argentine movies, having been screened more than 500 times at the cinema where it was released. According to *La Prensa* "the film is an excellent cinematic work, that shows praiseworthy virtues by those who have made it. The principal parts are played to satisfaction, especially miss Ilde Pirovano and Messrs. Diego Figueroa and Celestino Petray, who play, respectively, the parts of Rina, Germán Castillo and don Filemón Cochero. Perhaps somewhat over-dramatic, the novel by Martínez Zuviría has revived."

El Capataz Valderrama or *Carmen la Gitana* opened on the 12th of November 1917, without much success. *La Prensa* noted some technical deficiencies in the camera work and the lab process, but described the films not bad. *La Niña del Bosque* (1917), directed by Emilia Salemy, was a curiosity as it was the first film produced in Argentina especially for children. Salemy would later shoot *El Pañuelo de Clarita* (1919) which, like the former production, was made with child actors taught by the director at her own acting academy (opened in 1915, according to Roberto Di Chiara).

After buying the commercial rights to *Viviana* Camila Quiroga and her husband Héctor started Platense Film. They brought in the French actor and director (since 1906) Paul Capellani and cinematographer George Benoit, around August 1917, to produce *¿Hasta Dónde?* It featured with Capellani himself, Quiroga and her husband Héctor, plus Livia Zapata, Aurelia Ferrer, Celia Podestá, María Combre, Julio Escarcela, Leopoldo Simari, Mariano Galé, Fausto Guerrero and José Prado. The film was finished by the end of 1917. *¿Hasta Dónde?* was a great commercial hit; its first showing was on the 20th of April 1918. Capellani then continued his career in the United States. According to *La Prensa*, the film about the consequences of gambling was well adapted to the Argentine location. Both Camila Quiroga and Pail Capellani distinguished themselves in their parts, especially Capellani who played two roles. *La Prensa* also said that this film "will stand out among the best Argentine films, and can well represent our emerging film industry in foreign countries," and praised "the camera operator for his simply admirable work."

The 1st of March 1918 saw the release of the film version of Darío Nicodemi's comedy *La Enemiga*. The author directed the movie, with Linda Pini in the leading role. The only film produced by the short story author, lawyer and political leader Alcides Greca, *El Ultimo Malón* was also released

Poster announcing *¿Hasta Donde?* (Platense Film, 1918).

that year, in the city of Rosario in the province of Santa Fe. He re-enacted the last Native American rebellion in the country, that of the Mocoví tribe in San Javier, province of Santa Fe, in 1904. The film was shot where the revolt actually happened, and even included some of the people that had taken part in it. According to Roberto Di Chiara it is one of the great rarities in Argentine cinema, because coloring a local film was attempted for the first time. Other movies released that year include *En la Sierra*, released on the 22nd of August, directed by Eduardo Martínez de la Pera and Ernesto Gunche and based on a play by Juana Manuela Gorriti (adapted by Flaminio Pedraza, it created an excellent impression, especially because of the presence of a baby girl only 23 months old); and *El Rosal de las Ruinas* based on a piece by Belisario Roldán. Although the film *El Festín de los Caranchos* was not released commercially, a child prodigy called Ada Falcón, known as "The Argentine Gem" appeared in it. She later became a popular tango singer.

The Platense Film Company became Quiroga-Benoit Film and in 1919 produced one of the most important movies made in the country: *Juan*

"**EN LA SIERRA**"

Verdadera joya de la cinematografía
argentina, presentada por.

MARTINEZ & GUNCHE

Argumento de Flaminio Pedraza, inspirado en
una obra de la patricia Juana Manuela Gorriti

HOY ESTRENO

EN EL SELECT

SUIPACHA 482 – U. T. 7628, Libertad

Mañana 22 en el SELECT, Suipacha 482

y en el SPLENDID THEATRE, Santa Fe 1848

Poster announcing *En La Sierra* (Martinez & Gunche, 1918).

Sin Ropa o La Lucha por la Vida, directed by Georges Benoit from a script by José González Castillo. Given its premier on the 3rd of June 1919, the film starred Camila Quiroga and Hector G. Quiroga. Roberto Di Chiara reminds us that the film was shown in almost all of America and Spain with great success; and was even being projected for King Alfonso VII of Spain in his palace. The script, by José González Castillo, tells the story of the owner of a meatpacking company who is notorious for reducing his worker's wages and for firing them without cause. During a street uprising, the rich businessman's daughter meets a worker who comes from a farm and dreams of union brotherhood and of working out problems between workers and factory owners. As in nearly all early Argentine cinema the contrast between town and country is made evident. The country symbolizes the forthrightness, love of truth and deliverance that the town lacks. The only copy that is preserved, though quite incomplete, was salvaged by the critic Manuel Peña Rodríguez. The film was finished around June 1918. A series of tragic events were expected to take place at the moment when it was released, reminiscent of the events shown in the film.

There are two other films from 1919 which bear mentioning. They are *Lo Que No Se Ve en Delirio de Grandezas* released on the 5th of November, based on a comedy by José Antonio Saldías and performed by the same cast of actors that had performed it at the theater; and *De Vuelta al Pago* released on the 27th of November, written and directed by José A. Ferreyra, with Lidia Liss and Nelo Cosini in the leading roles.

The economist Roberto Guidi, along with Mario V. Ponisio and photographer Alberto J. Biassotti, opened his own film company in 1919 and called it Ariel Film. Guidi's first film was *El Mentir de los Demás* (1919) with Milagros de la Vega, Eloy Alvarez and Felipe Farah. Domingo Di Núbila asserts that Guidi tried to avoid popular conventions of the day, and showed his sense of personality when introducing actors to the cinema, handling them with realism. His films were considered to be technically the best made in Argentina at that time. Guidi retired from films in 1924.

Not all the films made in Argentina in those years were successful. Contemporary publications had very little to say about these failures, and it is very difficult to know exactly what happened. In that sense, the newspaper *La Prensa* published the following editorial on the 18th of May 1916:

> The production of moving pictures started enthusiastically a short time ago by several companies organized with the purpose of developing the industry, which is new to us, has given us a reason to express some slightly unfavorable technical and artistical appraisals. Our criticisms may perhaps have been somewhat harsh, but we have been impelled by the deliberate and wholesome purpose of reaching the desired perfection as soon as possible, and to put ourselves on the same level as the productions that are brought to us from abroad.
>
> Inspired by these intentions, we send a word of support to keep all those concerned from retreating in their struggle, and we will make some suggestions regarding this too. There being firms with enough assets to develop the business, they could well produce something better than what is offered to us, joining together the elements on hand, of which there are plenty, and actors of real merit. We should entirely dispense with those artistically minor elements that, lacking the most elementary knowledge of what is needed to be a good actor, and as a joke, or to earn a few pesos, launch themselves on an adventure harmful to the industry and to the public.
>
> If we take things seriously, as an such an endeavor should, we shall gather excellent fruits. Contrariwise, if we continue organized as before, without marking a clearly defined path, all vigorous and manly energies will be wasted, and large sums of money will be pitifully lost. Let us forget favoritisms and improvisations, which are always self-defeating and let us not forget for one instant that if we want to we can carry out the task, because we have all the necessary elements to do so. Painstaking directors, real artists, not amateurs, authors with discernment: talented and well prepared, all are there to do the work. Each should then take his post, and the Argentine film industry will be a fact. Popular incentive and public favor will not be missing.

The Beginnings of the Recording Industry and the Tango's Popularity

As has already been mentioned, the Lepage Company was the first to start producing films, in 1897, and one of the first films shot there, by Eugenio Py and Max Glücksmann, was *Tango Argentino*. Around 1910, as Jorge Couselo says, tango music would pay tribute to films by way of Angel Villoldo, who composed "Sacame una Película, Gordito" (Shoot Me a Film, Fatty), dedicated to Mario Gallo, the first man to start making films with a story.

Ricardo García Blaya, a journalist and propagator of tango music, states that "the tango is a dance with a rhythm and a musical structure that singles it out among other kinds of music. It was to receive all kinds of influences that accompanied its evolution, which was to happen approximately between 1890 and 1920. The street organs spread it out through different neighborhoods of Buenos Aires and its suburbs, and it was usual to see it danced on the streets, often between men, as women were scarce, due to the immigrants arriving to try to make their fortunes [who] came without their women. The contacts with the opposite sex were at the 'dance academies' or at the brothels."

It is very usual to read and hear that the tango had its origins in the brothels, and this is because nobody has done a serious investigation of its origins. But it is a mistake: there were no musicians at the bordellos. There were only a few places in the provinces, that, appearing to be dance halls, provided a double service, and there they played not only tangos, but also polkas, milongas, cifras, waltzes, and any rhythm capable of cheering up the atmosphere. The rents were very high, there was a large demand, and the loss of money and time entailed by a live band were not justified. The misunderstanding is due to several reasons. Some dance halls or academies did not enjoy a good reputation, and the attendance was varied and at times *non sancta*. There were often hoodlums and loose girls. But this did not make them brothels or anything resembling a brothel. Besides, they did not exclusively dance the tango there. On the other hand, there were also prestigious academies, attended by higher social classes, where the tango was also the most popular dance. Another inexactitude about the tango's origins is that it was forbidden or rejected by the upper levels of Argentine society. It was not so. Some of the most important theaters organized balls where the tango was played, and these were not exactly meant for the poorer classes. By 1910 the tango was already the music of Buenos Aires and the bandoneon had already become a component of all the tango orchestras, giving them their characteristic sound. With the appearance of

Sacáme una Pelicula, Gordito, written by Angel Villoldo and dedicated to Mario Gallo; the very first tango related to films.

the record industry the tango would take another step forward in its evolution. The gramophone record collector Héctor Lucci maintains that, a year after its invention, Thomas Alva Edison's phonograph could already be found in Buenos Aires. It could record sounds and voices on a tin cylinder which could be replayed immediately. After receiving some improvements the first saleable machines arrived in 1891, and in 1899 the Lepage Company started recording commercially for these devices. As it was not possible to record a matrix from which cylinders could be pressed, they had to be recorded one at a time.

In 1888 Emile Berliner patented his own system for recording and reproducing sound. He used a disk on which the sound was recorded by a sideways movement on a flat surface, instead of a winding movement on the side of a cylinder. Berliner called this invention a gramophone. The first gramophones only arrived in Argentina in 1900 and the Lepage Company would also make recordings for this equipment. The great advantage of flat records over cylinders was their lower cost. Thousands could be pressed from one recorded matrix. A substance used to make buttons was found to be just the thing to give industrial support to the recording of sound. After years of lawsuits caused by the use of different systems by major companies, an agreement was reached in 1902 to share their patents.

Argentina had always received recordings made outside of the country, but the record industry established itself here, as Max Glücksmann recalled, when records by popular local artists such as Gabino Ezeiza, Angel Villoldo, Gerardo López, Alfredo E. Gobbi and others started to appear on the market. After acquiring the Lepage Company, Glücksmann would become one of the most important promoters of the industry in this country.

Another man to give momentum to the industry was José Tagini, who was the representative of the Columbia Phonograph Company in Argentina. By 1911 gramophone records had stirred up a great interest in the public, and recordings made in Argentina had a wide acceptance, so Tagini decided to engage an orchestra lead by Vicente Greco to record tangos.

As tango investigator Luis Adolfo Sierra says, "It then became necessary to adopt a term that would identify the music itself. There was a reason. Before the existence of groups that only played tangos, dance-bands and groups of every extraction and assorted repertoire enlivened dances. Polkas, waltzes, schottisches, mazurkas, tarantellas, pasodobles and naturally tangos were performed, but when orchestras that played tangos exclusively became important, and were needed to supply the recording industry, it became imperative to give them a separate identification. And that is what was done. Greco adopted the name Orquesta Típica Criolla, which would later be shortened to Orquesta Típica. It is still applied to tango groups."

The musicians in that memorable group, the first to be known as an *orquesta típica criolla*, were Vicente Greco and Juan Lorenzo Labissier (bandoneons), Francisco Canaro and "Palito" Abatte (violins), Domingo Greco (guitar) and Vicente Pecci (flute). These records were so well received that many tango groups were engaged by other organizations dedicated to sound recording.

Perhaps the most popular of these primitive groups was headed by Juan Maglio, known as Pacho, playing the bandoneon. His group was really a quartet, in which he was accompanied by "Pepino" Bonano (violin), "Hernani" Macchi (flute), and Luciano Ríos (guitar). Pacho would play bandoneon solos that were very popular with live audiences and so they were also recorded, reaching top sales for those times.

There were many record labels in addition to Columbia: Pathé, Marconi, Polyphon, Gloria, Favorita, Cabezas, Gath y Chaves, Tocasolo, Edison, Sonora, Orophon, Atlanta, Era, Sonophono, and more. It was at this time that Carl Lindstrom, who had founded the Parlophone Company in Germany in 1896, gained significance. As Héctor Lucci says, he organized a conglomerate to unite the small companies manufacturing gramophone records. From 1908 to 1914 the recording empire created and managed by Lindstrom, known as Polyphon, was so impressive that there were few cities or towns in the world without German equipment or records. He also searched for those stores that did not have exclusive contracts with other recording companies. To quote Lucci: "The thing was to agree to contract with the store concerned, and having received previous payment, the sale of a certain amount of records. In exchange the store could chose the performer, and if it was desired, the label on the record could display the store's name or trademark."

Present in Argentina since 1911, Lindstrom found in Max Glücksmann a person interested in having the Lindstrom companies manufacture the records that Glücksmann had been recording on an industrial scale since he bought the Lepage Company in 1908. In the beginning the price of records was too high for the general public. Glücksmann understood that the large-scale production of records sold at lower prices would create greater earnings. As a result Glücksmann became the most important record producer in Argentina. On his first records one could see printed "all rights by Max Glücksmann"; due to his agreement with Lindstrom, other records were offered for sale under the names of some of the most famous labels in his domain, especially one called "Odeon." Apart from being the exclusive outlet for these records, Glücksmann also sold the international production from these companies.

In 1913 Glücksmann achieved an important feat in Argentina's recording industry when his company engaged Roberto Firpo. The piano was already the leading instrument *par excellence* in tango orchestras, replacing the guitar. But this was only during live performances, because of the deficiencies of the mechanical or acoustical recording systems of those times. When recording, all the instruments bunched up in front of a huge horn, which was the only sound intake in that primitive procedure as microphones had not yet been invented. The piano always smothered the sounds of the other instruments; therefore pianos could not be used. Roberto Firpo solved this problem, not without difficulty, by using platforms placed at precise distances. Roberto Firpo helped to define the configuration of the *orquesta típica* that was to endure.

In 1917 Glücksmann made the most important decision of his life when he put under contract, with the purpose of cutting some records, a duo of singers named Carlos Gardel and José Razzano. Carlos Gardel was a folk singer who was to appear on the screen for the first time that year in the movie *Flor de Durazno*. He had already formed a popular duo with

Roberto Firpo and his orchestra in the Max Glücksmann recording studios in the days of the acoustic disks.

Razzano. From the first moment of their release these records were very popular. They usually had a song by the duo on one side, and on the other Gardel singing alone (the songs recorded by Razzano alone were very few).

At the end of 1917 Gardel recorded an all-important theme: the tango "Mi Noche Triste." Until then the tango in song form had not been very significant. It was Gardel, the first and greatest tango singer, who set the standard, now and forever, of how the tango should be sung.

The great sales success of this record must have been what persuaded Glücksmann to open the first record factory in Argentina, in June 1919. According to the agreement that he had with Carl Lindman, whose company went under the name "Odeon" in Argentina, the company would now be known as "Disco Nacional-Odeón." On its records you could see printed "Made exclusively for Max Glücksmann by the Argentine Talking Machine Works Buenos Aires." Industrial competition would only come in 1922 when the rival Victor Talking Machine Company was to open its own factory in Argentina, working without middlemen, that is to say, commercializing their records themselves.

Max Glücksmann was at the same time committed to the film industry. As the films produced by him made little profit, he decided to limit his production to industrials and newsreels while continuing to be one of the most important distributors of foreign films. As an exhibitor he controlled up to sixty movie theaters all over Argentina, besides those in Uruguay and Chile; and with the purpose of promoting his records he had all the artists under contract perform on stages all over the country.

Max Glücksmann's first recording studios were in a film storehouse, but they had to be abandoned because of a terrible fire in 1919 caused to the combustion of the cellulose nitrate-based films. The new studios were situated on the upper floors of the building that housed one of his most prestigious movie houses: the Grand Splendid Cinema.

2

THE AMERICAN FILM MOVES AHEAD

Foreign Movies Take Over

From the very beginning of movie history in Argentina, foreign-made films have predominated. Thanks to these films, movies grew extremely popular between 1900 and 1910. Max Glücksmann said that it was due in great part to the work of Charles Pathé, who was the first to produce films in reconstructed settings that were very attractive to the public of those days. Among these films Glücksmann recalled *The Russian-Japanese War*, *Edward VII's Coronation* and *The Anglo-Boer War*. Charles Pathé in France was the first to establish filmmaking on an industrial basis. By 1900 his company had become the most important film producer in the world, which it would continue to be up to World War I. The films had better and better sets, better actors and good means of production. It was only in 1903 that American filmmakers started to challenge European productions. By that time other European countries, such as Italy, Germany, Denmark and others, had started their own film industries, adding to those already existing in France, the United States and Great Britain.

Around 1912, filmmakers were already cutting a scene into a series of takes but they still did not do it like they do now. If this technique is used correctly, the audience quite possibly won't notice that the filmmaker has gone from one take to another. This "invisible" editing was the last step in what could be called *continuity*. The innovators who developed these techniques are unknown today, but their achievements were only reached after much trial and error, and after watching movies made by others, so as to improve their own.

In this manner, producers in America and Europe set out to win over

the public in Argentina and the rest of the world. Audiences would gradually discover a number of actors in certain films, who would later become
their favorites, and they would want to see more films featuring them;
movie stars were born, though they were not yet known by their names.

Much has been written, and very well, about the history of films in
America and Europe. The evolution and development of films have been
very well described, although little has been written about what happened
in other countries. Those who have investigated Argentine cinema have
always emphasized the history of films made in this part of the world over
the films made abroad and shown in this country. At the beginning foreign producers distributed their films through Argentine companies, so
they could only sell their films in one manner: by emphasizing the quality of their productions, which was constantly getting better and better.
These producers had the money to make their films and they discovered
the most talented artists and moviemakers capable of making them. The
success that they were to achieve would shame the Argentine film industry, which would not be capable of competing on the same level.

Sadly, very little can be said about foreign films in our country. Some
of them were advertised in magazines, but very little is known about which
were more successful than others. The unfeasibility of gaining access to
the greater part of the original publications makes the task very difficult,
and the few surviving copies say almost nothing about the point, although
some show advertisements of certain films which in most cases were never
shown again. Some musical scores, directly related to the movies shown
then, survive. The Fox Film Corporation was possibly the first American
company to set up its own distribution organization in Argentina, around
1917. For many years this company also published, a large number of scores,
composed by Argentine musicians, of themes for the films that they distributed. Other film companies did the same (for example, Universal, for
the release of Erich von Stroheim's *Foolish Wives* edited a tango with the
same name composed by Víctor Donato). Carlos Gardel and other artists
and orchestras left many of these versions on records, some of which have
survived.

Looking at advertisements you can see that many foreign artists were
very popular. This can be seen by looking at some advertisements that still
exist for Charlie Chaplin movies, and are very pleasing when seen next to
their better-known contemporaries in English. According to the historian
Jorge Couselo, Chaplin was to inspire a whole series of tangos: "Carlitos"
by José A. Molet, dedicated to Julián Ajuria (who was the first to distribute his films in Argentina); "Max y Carlitos" by D. F. Sclocco, referring to
Max Linder as well; later on Francisco Orefice and Osvaldo Sosa Cordero

Poster announcing *El Pibe* (First National, 1921).

wrote the tango "Luces de la Ciudad," referring to the movie *City Lights*, and much later Alfredo Gobbi wrote "Un Tango para Chaplin."

It is only since 1924 that information related to the movies, in terms recognizable today, started to be available. By then films already had an important role in the Argentine community, and it became necessary for the newspapers and magazines to reflect the fact. What can be affirmed is that the development of the cinema, and the public's habits, were not very different from those in any important city in Europe or America. The few advertisements that survive today give that impression.

The newspapers and *La Prensa* in particular, in those times took little notice of the movies, but if a film was a great success or awakened the public's curiosity they would then evaluate the movie. One example was the Italian movie *Maciste*, released around 1915. *La Prensa* described it as a film "like no other," featuring a muscular hero and in which the action is interspersed with comedy. At the end of that year a popular Italian movie actor, Alberto Capozzi, appeared in Buenos Aires, obtaining success both as a mime and as an actor.

Though the Europeans were the first to know how to exploit their film productions worldwide, by 1916 the United States was beginning to impose its films on Argentina. On Saturday the 22nd of April of that year, *The Birth of a Nation* was released in Buenos Aires. One of the most important films in history, and also one of the most racist ever produced; it demonstrated that American filmmakers could produce a movie with worldwide appeal that would be successful wherever it was shown.

La Prensa, bemoaned the fact that the fictional plot elements detracted from the film's historical aspects, which were the reason the film was made in the first place. The newspaper also said that the plot was well developed, even though it missed part of the truth for the sake of the plot:

> The presentation is splendid, some of the scenes are a real display of cinematographic effects, and the thousands of extras that parade before the audience are directed with great art and success. The war scenes have an admirable realism. As for the rest, we must admit that the film is wearing. The vastness of the plot obliges the audience to make a constant effort with their concentration, and the excessive length of its acts (around an hour and a half each) makes the effort greater. As for the acting, which is good in general, even though there are certain characters, such as Margaret Cameron (played by Miriam Cooper), Flora (Mae Marsh), and Phil Stoneman (Elmer Clifton), who let down the group notably.

After the great success of *The Birth of a Nation* in Buenos Aires, the film was shown in cinemas all over Argentina.

On the 29th of April, a few days later, an English photo-vocal-symphonic show called *The Miracle* was premiered. It would also be a great hit. The actors in the film were the same ones as in the play which was being shown at the Covent Garden Theater in London. It was staged by Max Reinhardt. *La Prensa*, deemed the performances noteworthy, with the actress Florence Winston performing admirably as Margarita. The settings, costumes and staging had a great effect and were exercised with care. The film featured views of the twelfth-century Pechelsdorf Cathedral, shot with the permission of the bishop of the diocese, as well as beautiful scenes of the historical castle of Krentzensten. *La Prensa* described the film's plot:

> The legend that inspired the plot, that is to say, the sinful nun, who escapes from the cloister and is replaced in the convent by the Miraculous Virgin, was very well known in all European countries, taking various forms, such as the Spanish Margarita de Tornera, the Forteresse Beatriz, one of the most modern expressions, and others. Doña Inés herself, seduced by Don Juan, is really the nun of the legend, born probably in Flanders in the central centuries of the Middle Ages. One of the originalities of this production of Volmoeller's play was the making of the embodiment of the Devil visible and sensitive, showing how he seemed to create sin and attract death with music from his flute.

On the 29th of May 1916, *Hypocrites* or *The Naked Truth*, the successful American film written and directed by Lois Weber was released. Modern society, love, politics, matrimony, life in general in all of its different expressions "are present just as truth sees them." The success of this movie seems to have tempted various American writers to work in films. On the 16th of September 1916 the American movie The *Fall of a Nation* was released, based on a novel by Thomas Dixon, who, trying to repeat the success of *The Birth of a Nation*, developed a conflict between natives and immigrants in the United States. He didn't attain it. According to *La Prensa* the film seemed to be made only as an excuse to show battle scenes, shot with all the modern advances available. *La Prensa* praised the film's editing, but described the rest as tiring and very inferior to *The Birth Of A Nation*. The Italian film *La Falena*, based on a play by Henry Bataille, was released on the same day. *La Prensa* praised its leading actress, Lyda Borelli, but described the film as one dominated by sentimentalism.

On the 7th of November of 1916 *Heart* was released very successfully. *La Prensa* reported that the audience followed the sentimental plot, based on the book by Edmondo de Amicis, with great interest, applauding in various parts of the film.

Civilization a new hit from the United States, was released in Argentina the 13th of November 1916. *La Prensa* noted that, despite the films imaginary setting, the audience required it as a thinly veiled commentary on World War I, which was raging at the time, and on the horrors of war in general. In spite of its good intentions, the film failed because of its excessive length.

Another film to show the horrors of World War I was the Italian production *The Conquest of the Adamello*. It was prepared with the authorization of the Italian government and given to the War Committee of Argentina, who presented it on the 9th of May 1917, in aid of the mobilized reservists. *La Prensa* reported that the film left a strong impression about the bitter realities of war by focusing on the conditions that soldiers had to endure.

On the 12th of April 1917 *Soldier Maciste*, also from Italy, was released. The protagonist of this was film was already well known to the Argentine public, having appeared in the very popular movie *Maciste*. Views of the frontier and the Italian army could be seen, and interesting episodes of the war in the craggy regions of the Italian-Austrian frontier. On the 3rd of June, from the United States, came *Joan of Arc*, directed by Cecil B. De Mille with Geraldine Farrar starring, although her name did not appear in the critic published by *La Prensa*:

> The plot of this new production of cinematographic art, in which a very large cast takes part, unwinds on the British front in France, and it combines artistically with a fictional account of the life of Joan of Arc. These episodes make up nearly all the plot of the movie.
>
> The end of the film shows a view of the present war, in which the heroine appears before a dying soldier who has just attacked a trench, rewarding the soldier's bravery with her appearance.
>
> All the progress of the film is followed with a symphonic accompaniment, whose music, adapted to the various dramatic scenes of the film, is a production of the composer Ferst.
>
> The principal settings of this cinematographic work are those that refer to the court of Charles IV, the taking of Orleáns, the triumphant entry to that city and the coronation scene.

The day after *Joan of Arc*'s premier, *The Cheat*, another earlier film by De Mille, was released, achieving a similar success. Fannie Ward and Sessue Hayakawa were in the leading roles. The 23rd of October 1917 the Italian film *Malombra*, with Lyda Borelli starring, was released. *La Prensa* reported that exhibition a private screening two days before provoked a great emotion in the audience, which broke into applause at the end of the projection, and praised for the leading actress' performance.

From 1918, unhappily there is information only about a film made in Chile called *Chilean Soul*. Described by *La Prensa* as a pleasant and entertaining film, it starred María Padín, Carmela García, María Quesada, Arturo Mario, Valerio Bondesio and Carlos Justiniano.

Hearts of the World directed by D. W. Griffith, premiered on the 23rd of March 1919 at the Select and the Splendid theaters. As *La Prensa* said: "The highly favorable and praiseful opinion that a number of American and European personalities had expressed made a large audience come to

"UNA HIJA DE LOS DIOSES" Unica película de un millón de dollars de William Fox.

por ANNETTE KELLERMANN, la mujer más perfecta del mundo

HOY - MAÑANA - PASADO

SPLENDID THEATRE SANTA FE 1848
U. T. 1272, JUNÇAL

Poster announcing *Una Hija de los Dioses* (Fox, 1918).

these cinemas, and their expectations were not defrauded by this new creation by D. W. Griffith." Another film released that year, about which little can be said, was the Italian production *Kelly's Stratagem*. On the 19th of September 1920, the National Feminist Union showed an American film called *The Blue Bird*, based on a play by Maetterlinck. On Saturday the 13th of June, Fox presented *The Love of a Player*, and on the 27th of Decem-

Los Cuatro Jinetes
del Apocalipsis

La magistral novela del celebrado novelista

VICENTE BLASCO IBAÑEZ

ha sido llevada a la pantalla con toda propiedad por la

Metro Pictures Corporation

HOY
—
NOCHE

Unicamente en el

PALACE THEATRE
CORRIENTES 757
DIRECCION: MAX GLUCKSMANN

ber a propaganda film meant to be distributed in the United States to pro-
mote immigration to Argentina was shown.

The 2nd of October 1921 Max Glücksmann presented *The Four Horse-
men of the Apocalypse*, directed by Rex Ingram for Metro, an American
company. The first part of this film takes place in Argentina and is a statement against the horrors of the First World War, but the scenes in which
Rodolfo Valentino dances the tango made him a star worldwide. His gaucho costume was rather absurd, and his dance steps cannot be considered
to be authentic tango. Unfortunately there are no available contemporary
comments of the premier on this film in Buenos Aires.

Jorge Couselo wrote this about Valentino and the tango:

> The image of the Italian leading man, projected from the United States, to the
> rhythm of his fantastic fame, filled the still silent screens all over the world and
> gave the tango an international style, although it was a product of fantasy, "a com-
> bination of rumba, paso doble, cueca and apache dance" as Roberto Guidi
> observed. This happened at the same time as the success of the tango in Paris, the
> appearance of the great Argentine orchestras, and later the voice of Carlos Gardel,
> who would move to films as one of the first conquests of the new talking sound
> films. It could be said that both Valentino and the Argentines committed the same
> sin of dressing as a gaucho to play, dance or sing the tango. In defense of the
> Argentines it must be said that it wasn't a stunt but a way of getting around union
> rules by presenting themselves as "variety artists" which had very flexible rules,
> and did not have to obey the very strict laws against foreign musicians. It is easy
> to imagine that Valentino knew this version in Europe, practiced it as a dancer,
> and exaggerated it in the movies.

The 17th of November 1921, Harrods department store in Buenos
Aires started something new when it opened its own movie theater. The
sculptress Lola Mora de Hernández presented a projector of her own
invention that allowed you to show movies in full daylight without dark-
ening the hall. Various funny films for children were projected, with the
usual illumination and absolute sharpness.

At the end of June, 1922, a film was distributed by Fox Film called
The Mountain Woman, with Pearl White. The musical score composed in
Argentina by Emilio Iribarne and Cancio Millán survives. According to
Miss X, writing in the magazine *Imparcial Film* on the 8th of August of
that year:

> From my point of view this is one of the best films by Pearl White, because the
> plot could not be more appropriate to her conditions as an actress. It is a very

Opposite: Poster announcing *Los Cuatro Jinetes del Apocalipsis* (Metro, 1921).

well made film, original and royally produced and with an excellent photography. It is a pity that logic suffers a bit and that the ending does not correspond at all with the genuine idea behind the film.

This, naturally, is not enough to harm it because it is a film that everybody will like, with well thought out situations, and shot even better.

Around October 1922 *My Boy* was released, and its theme song, written by José Rosito and Eduardo Pereyra, has survived. The magazine *Imparcial Film* commented on the 24th of October that this melodrama was produced starting from a mediocre plot, and made to show off Jackie Coogan, who was a great child star after taking part in Charlie Chaplin's *The Kid* the year before. Beyond Coogan's great merits, the film was pleasant but not extraordinary, as the advertising would have us believe at that time.

At the end of 1922 an Italian film based on Ibsen's *Hedda Gabler* was released, which compared favorably with previous releases. *La Prensa* said on the 9th of December: "There are strange passions in the plot, marked by a sickly modernism, so to say, that leads the protagonist to take the most extraordinary decisions, following an idea that is her supreme reason for existing. There is in an interesting observation of characters in the work that we are referring to, only definable psychologically by an effort that goes beyond the one open to the exhibition of a continuous action, fast and abundant, that is generally the foundation of a cinematographic production, and that is the difference between this film and what is generally offered on screen." This film, directed by Febo Mari, and distributed in Argentina by the Mundial-Film Company, had Italia Almirante Mazzini, Oreste Bilancia and Vittorio Rossi in the leading roles.

There is not much to be said about the year 1923. The Fox Company's films *Nero* and *The Temple of Venus* released around then, seem to have been fated to be forgotten, although the musical themes written for each of them have survived, and better still, were recorded by Carlos Gardel. That year the actor Wallace Reid died due to an addiction to morphine, which was caused by the film company that had him under contract. Roberto Firpo composed an excellent waltz dedicated to Reid, which he played and recorded several times in his career. The original cover of the score shows a photograph of the actor, and the coat of arms of the film company appears twice.

On the 11th of February 1924 the newspaper *Crítica* published professor Lee de Forest's advertisement that asserted with proofs that sound films were a fact, as he had invented a camera specially to make them.

The previous material has been an attempt to document the history of the cinema as it was in Argentina prior to 1924. It can be summed up

"Ranita," a tango written for the film of the same name starring Jackie Coogan.

"Neron," the fox trot that was the theme of the 1922 Fox film of the same name.

with a comment from the newspaper *La Razon* on the 5th of July 1922 about how the United States saw the Argentine film industry:

"Eternamente," a 1923 waltz written by Roberto Firpo in memory of Wallace Reid.

We find a report in a newspaper published in New York which says that according to the statistics collected by the Department of Commerce, the demand for films in Argentina, in proportion to it population, is as large as in any country in the world; and that Buenos Aires has 128 movie theaters which sell 2.250.000 tickets per month. It then says:

The programs in Argentine theaters are much longer than in America. Four films, one American, as the principal attraction, and three European, form the menu served daily to the Argentine public. Admission is paid for only one film or for the entire program. This would appeal greatly to American children who look sadly at the sign "Ten Cents," while they count five or six pennies in their pockets.

Other peculiarities of Argentine movie theaters are the intermissions that are long and frequent, and are a good occasion to greet friends, go and have a smoke or to go and buy chocolates for their girls. This might not find much acceptance in the American public.

The Stagnation of Argentine Cinema

During the second decade of the 20th Century the movies were consolidated, both as an artistic expression and as a show. Producers in Europe and America contributed to their development and conquered the world market, which America would dominate during the next decade. On their part, Argentine filmmakers had a series of successes that managed to rival imported films. But the impact caused by *Nobleza Gaucha* was not equaled by other movies, and as Domingo Di Núbila notes, as the twenties arrived Argentine filmmaking was in a continuous and severe decline, which was

A 1924 Max Glücksmann film advertisement.

to get worse until the appearance of sound and until the industry could establish a systematic activity in the country. According to Jorge Couselo, many of the Argentine silent films, without their directors or scriptwriters confessing it, often stretched out or modified tangos and at times waltzes so as to profit from their popularity.

In the twenties foreign films dominated the market. These films' producers had money, experience and organization. In Argentina there was an excess of enthusiasm but little of the necessary capital and not enough knowledge. Argentine films were produced very modestly, and their producers had to go from movie theater to movie theater begging for an opening to show them. The film producers who managed to last long were those dedicated to lab procedures, advertising productions, and other activities that had nothing to do with fictional films. The important and prestigious persons from the stage, and the authors that were so enthusiastic at the beginning, stopped taking part for many years.

By around 1924 Argentine newspapers already were giving space to both local and foreign films on a regular basis, and protesting voices, demanding good quality Argentine films, were soon heard: On the 29th of March 1924 the newspaper *Crítica* published the following editorial with the title "Argentine Cinematography Plays its Last Card This Year":

This year one can no longer speak of a middling quality Argentine cinema. Either it prevails or it dies.

Its promises are numerous and varied. One could observe an extraordinary amount of activity after the beginning of the year. More than four national productions are completely ready to be presented to the public. Some have been made long ago, but we are not talking of them. The others are a product of the hour, based on observations made on previous occasions and by well-known persons.

The death of our cinematography or at least its protracted paralysis of its most important activities will be inevitable if the public does not find a bigger technical efficiency in Argentine productions.

It must be admitted, to start with, that the competition between producers can mean the ruin of some, those least prepared artistically and those that, even disposing of sufficient financial means, have wasted their assets so as to impress the audience as if they were Americans.

Crítica's attitude to local production is well known for its enthusiasm. Even at the risk of going over the side, it has given its unconditional support, and it must be noted that we have been the only ones to give it the importance that it must have as agents of national prosperity. It is only fair, now that the Argentine film industry has taken a great leap forward, to stop the flow of excessive praise and give each what he deserves, so that judging the values fairly, "the best" be the ones that remain standing, for the better gain of our industry in general and the honor of our art of filmmaking; which up to the present time, and only on a few occasions, has earned the praise "somewhat artistic.

Two years later the crisis in the Argentine movie industry got worse, and the newspaper *La Nación* stated the following:

Judging by this year, and what little it announces, the present season will be exceptionally poor in Argentine films. What we have seen so far is so extraordinarily inferior that it should not be taken into account, and the frustration of the producers is more and more pronounced facing the indifference of the public. That is not more nor less than what should have happened.

Local film production has decreased in values to the point in which not even in second-class theaters, where it is still accepted, does it maintain an appreciable importance. The lack of capital to serve the industry, and also the small artistic significance of the directors and scriptwriters have produced the logical result of a such a poverty in its presentations, that these have turned out to be unendurable to even the best good will of the public and impresarios, especially when they the entrance tickets cost the same, or more, than good American or European productions. While this continues, this sorry state of affairs will get progressively worse and worse for local films.

It is necessary therefore, for a properly established company to try a serious attempt, or that people with real capacity try filming a selected script, to elevate and give stature to the film industry in the country. This will necessarily guarantee good results, for various reasons, because of the love of our public for the movies, which translates into a constant demand for productions, up to the point in which Argentina is one of the world's most important film markets.

This crisis lasted for approximately fourteen years and it would end several years after the introduction of sound films in Argentina. During all that time, American producers managed to fill the void left by Argentine producers, and between 1925 and 1931 they established their own subsidiary branch offices to distribute their films directly.

Nevertheless, the most important film series in those days was the "Film Revista," Valle which appeared weekly (on Thursday afternoons) during ten consecutive years, and which also dedicated frequent extra editions to important goings-on. They were six hundred and fifty-seven editions in all.

According to Domingo Di Núbila, "to make the series, (Federico) Valle had a large and capable team, that grew as the years went by, it included Juan, Arnold and Alberto Etchebehere (or Etcheberre), Antonio Merayo, Francis Boeniger, Roque Funes, Antonio Prieto, Pío Quadro, Alberto and Domingo Sorianello, Fernando and Tulio Chiarini, César Sforza, Andrés Ducaud, Roberto Baldiserotto, Mario Feria, Quirino Cristiani, José Lara, Francisco Escribano, Francisco Mayrhofer and various others that achieved distinguished careers.

"They relied upon the talent and inventiveness of José Bustamante y Balliván for the scripts, and they also counted on the collaboration of Chas de Cruz, Epifanio Aramayo, Luis José Moglia Barth, Eduardo Morera, José Bohr, Miguel Angel Dubini, Carlos Seidel, José Allo, Ricardo Raffo, and Roberto Kulensmidt in other activities and jobs, and many of them were to enjoy long years working for the movies."

"Also according to Di Núbila, 'the Film Revista Valle' had the interest, keenness and insight of the best film journalism, and awoke great interest in the public, surpassing, in a sometimes fierce competition, Glücksmann's newsreels."

Valle's newsreel disappeared in 1931, when Valle lost all his money by investing almost all he had in an ambitious schoolteaching project using films. The authorities brought in by the *coup d'état* of the 6th of September of 1930 cancelled the project.

Federico Valle also produced more than a thousand documentaries, industrial films and several filmed works of fiction. The first one was *Los Hijos de Naides,* premiered on the 27th of August 1921, written by Nelo Cosimi (who also had the leading role) and directed by Edmo Cominetti. Alfredo Zorrilla, Susanne Grandals and Nelly Olmos also took part in *Los Hijos de Naides* in addition to Cosimi and, according to the newspaper *La Epoca,* this film was noteworthy for its technical and artistic qualities, had a thrilling plot, was well staged and was directed with confidence.

The melodramatic plot was described in *La Epoca* as follows:

Pablo Luque, a young man from the South, who is looking for a job, arrives at Los Cardales, Pedro Aguirre's flourishing *estancia*, after seeing his mother die. Aguirre hires Luque and of course Luque's manners awaken Aguirre's and his daughter's curiosity, as they are very different from those of the rest of the farmhands. A few days later, Luque, who was thought a timid lad, proves the value of his fists and his soul. El Quinto, the king of the bulls at Los Cardales, a fearful beast, famous for having killed a handler, escapes and enters one of the fields. Celia is there, and El Quinto, as fast as lightning, charges against her. The cowboys stand looking at the details of the tragic incident, paralyzed by fear. Suddenly Luque jumps off his horse, getting between the girl and El Quinto, and overpowers the beast after a ferocious struggle. The bystanders shout Hurrah, and only Malacara, the foreman stands by, angry and self centered. It is because he his in love with Celia, and he understands that Luque has won over the girl's admiration, seeing the tender and thankful look that she directs at the young laborer. Soon fate faces off the two men. One afternoon Luque is talking to Celia, and Malacara, in a fit of jealousy, orders Luque back to the windmill. Luque obeys, and is on top of the windmill when he sees Malacara trying to kiss Celia. Luque does not hesitate a second, diving off the windmill into the water tank. He has jumped from a height of eighteen meters. With a second prodigious jump he is on land. He runs up to Malacara, fights him, and once he has beaten him, Aguirre arrives, attracted by his daughter's cries. Malacara is fired, and Luque replaces him as foreman, surrounded by the congratulations of his companions, and Celia's tender gazes, that are not unnoticed by Aguirre.

Together with this film Federico Valle presented a documentary on the Nahuel Huapi Lake called *El País Ignorado.*

Valle presented *Milonguita* on April the 25th 1922, written and directed by José Bustamante y Ballivián, based on a tango with the same name written two years before by Samuel Linning and Enrique Delfino. This tango was, according to tango historian José Gobello, the first created as a song; that is to say that Linning wrote the words first and Delfino put them to music. Until then tango songs were musical compositions to which lyrics were added.

The tango "Milonguita" introduces a theme that would become very common in many tango songs: the pretty innocent girl who abandons her neighborhood to come to the center of Buenos Aires and ends up as a prostitute. The tango was a great hit in 1920 and Carlos Gardel recorded it for Max Glücksmann that same year. The film, as journalist Roberto Di Chiara says, was not liked either by the critics or the public and the reports at the time held it to be a great failure. It had María Esther Lerena, Pepe Sassone, Atilio Calandra and Ignacio Corsini (who became famous as a singer when he sang "El Patotero Sentimental" by Manuel Romero and Manuel Joves in Romero's theatrical production *El Bailarín de Cabaret*).

On the 4th of July 1922 the Tylca Company presented *La Muchacha del Arrabal,* written (with Leopoldo Torres Ríos) and directed by José A. Ferreyra. According to *La Razon,* the plot of this film involves a young painter bent on showing the misery of workers in the vaudeville theaters and cabarets. He defends a young girl from the clutches of a pimp, nobly offering her refuge in his own studio. They fall in love, but the pimp, who has managed to escape from jail, returns to reclaim his victim. She pretends to follow him willingly, but the pimp becomes a victim of his own evil deeds. The comic performance of Carlos Dux was described as outstanding.

Ferreyra had the intention of synchronizing the action with sound from records. It turned out to be impossible, and Roberto Firpo's tango orchestra accompanied the exhibition of the film. Firpo also composed the theme song, with lyrics by Ferreyra and Torres Ríos. The tango "La Muchacha del Arrabal" was later recorded by Carlos Gardel.

The documentary in three acts *La Argentina* by Renée Oro was released in October 1922; it was a commercial about Argentina, and had already been shown outside of the country. On the 3rd of November 1922 Eduardo Martínez de la Pera and Ernesto Gunche presented their film *Fausto,* based on a poem in gaucho style by Estanislao del Campo.

According to *La Prensa* the narration in verse would have been enough to follow the picturesque action, considering that the film is a transcription, eliminating very few lines of the poem. The principal value of the film was in the way the country scenes were shown and the characteristic settings, and in the organization of the moments that evoked the times of the story, such as the entrance to the old Colón Theater, the carriages, and all the other details—especially considering what could be expected after all the changes in the architecture, which did not allow faithful reproductions of the old building. The actors, described as good in general, included Blonda Vivente (Margarita), Delia Codebo (Siebel), Carlos Varela (Mefistófeles-Laguna), Carlos Rohmer (Anastasio el Pollo), Rodolfo Vismara (Fausto-Ramón Beltrán), and Valentín Silverio (Pablo Amiral). At the end of November 1922, Colón Film presented, without success, *La Chica de la Calle Florida,* written and directed by José A. Ferreyra, with Lidia Liss and Jorge Lafuente in the leading roles. According to *La Prensa,* the idea had already been exhausted in popular novels, and nearly so in the short history of film. The movie tells the story of a salesgirl in a shop who is hounded by the manager; he has already victimized other girls among her shop mates.

On the 26th of February 1923 the Compañía Cinematográfica Buenos Aires, owned by Julio Yrigoyen, published the following advertisement in *La Prensa:*

The Buenos Aires Film Company has completed the edition of three new films with Argentine plots, directed by Mr. Julio Yrigoyen.
The titles of the films are: *La Aventura del Pasaje Güemes* written by Mr. Alberto Weisbach, starring Mrs. Neubour, Rodolfo Vismara and Matías A. de Torres. *De Nuestras Pampas* script by Leopoldo Torres Ríos, starring Blanca Olivier, Rodolfo Vismara and César Rocha; and *El Guapo del Arrabal* written by Leopoldo Torres Ríos and starring Rodolfo Vismara, Matías A. de Torres and Luis Poublan.
The same firm is preparing a fourth movie called *Alma Maleva,* by Mr. Marcel Peyret, making a total of five films, that it proposes to release every year.

La Prensa published the following announcement by the Tylca Company on the 23rd of March 1923:

The Tylca Company of Argentina will show its first production of the year at the end of the month. Its title is *Midinettes Porteñas.* The script of this film is by Mr. Rafael Parodi, who has been in charge of the artistic direction in the production of the film mentioned.
The technical aspect has been directed by Mr. Andres Ducaud.
The players in *Midinettes Porteñas* are the artistes Amelia Mirel, María Delelis, María Spinelli, Aquiles Marchesi, Carlos Dux and Angel Boyano.

La Prensa noted the release of a series of documentaries on the 1st of July: *El Desfile de Rodados, La Rioja, un Bello Rincón de la Argentina,* and *Del Atlántico a Los Andes.*
El Desfile de Rodados was a Touring Club Argentino film, which showed some historical vehicles such as the stagecoach in which Facundo Quiroga was murdered, as well as means of transportation, from early vehicles up to trains without rails and the most expensive automobiles of the time.
La Rioja, un Bello Rincón de la Argentina was a documentary about the North-Western Province, showing the cable car from Chilecito to La Mejicana station as it passed through valleys and reached great heights. The film also showed the mining industry in the region.
Del Atlántico a los Andes was a documentary on the province of Río Negro. At the beginning the film also presented some paragraphs by the writer Ada M. Efflein, taken from her play *Pasajes Cordilleranos,* in which the territory is described and its natural beauties praised. The film showed a sea lion hunt at Quinta Bermejo, on the Atlantic; the building of the railroad, dams and embankments on the Neuquén River at Contralmirante Cordero; and finally, the mountain region and the Nahuel Huapi lake. This film was presented with dyed colors.
Two films were offered in August 1923. One was *La Casa de los Cuervos* by Gustavo Martínez Zuviría, based on his own novel; the other was *El Matrero* directed by Edmo Comminetti and produced by Federico Valle.

La Casa de los Cuervos was faithful to the original novel, and was shot at the locations indicated by the book. It showed Colonial buildings corresponding to the time that the action took place.

El Matrero had a skillfully developed and dramatized plot, in which the hero, a doctor, must resolve the dilemma of choosing between his mother, whose life can only be saved by an urgent operation, and that of his wife, exposed to the passion of a morbid character who the doctor has to help.

The last Argentine film of 1923 was *El Escándalo a Media Noche*, produced by Zenit Film and directed by Roberto Guidi. At the start of 1924 Corbicier y Cía announced the signing up of Leopoldo Torres Ríos and Nelo Cosimi, with the purpose of making six films per year. According to the newspaper *Crítica* the film *Buenos Aires Bohemio*, by Leopoldo Torres Ríos, more than demonstrated the excellent work that the director could accomplish in Argentina. "In his work we have always seen his power of observation, he is a man who tends to get better and better."

One of the first Argentine films in 1924 was a documentary on the annual voyage of the training sail ship, the frigate Sarmiento. *La Prensa*, on January 27th noted that the film roused a great interest in the audience, and that it showed several aspects of life on board, the crew's maneuvers, and later showed scenes from different moments of the voyage. It was described as an interesting exhibition of the voyage's more attractive aspects, which follows the interests of a young sailor completing his education. His education on the voyage is both technical, and in the observation of the phenomena, facts, and works he will encounter.

The 31st of March 1924, the film *El Ultimo Gaucho* was premiered at a private showing. It was directed by Julio Irigoyen who wrote the script together with Leopoldo Torres Ríos. Cinematography was by Roberto Irigoyen. The film's leading parts were played by Diego Fernández, Ada Cornaro, Matías A. de Torres, Totón Podestá, Justina Leonor, Lía Dalvi, Arturo Sánchez and Aparicio Podestá. According to the daily newspaper *Crítica*, it was a simple melodrama, and the actress Lía Dalvi, making her debut, was the best thing in the film. The paper also said "our audience needs these simple films to learn how to appreciate our domestic productions, and more so, considering that in *El Ultimo Gaucho* the technical efficiency in tying opposite situations together, and framing the actors' action in beautiful natural backgrounds is already evident."

El Ultimo Centauro, from the Lautaro Film Company, was a film version of Ricardo Gutierrez's work *Juan Moreira* with a script and direction by Enrique Queirolo, with Angela Quesada, Carlos Perelli and Pedro Costanzo in the leading roles. *La Nación* observed that the action developed according to the novel, but created a series of new situations with the intention of making the character Juan Moreira more interesting. The 10th of April 1924 saw the release of what was possibly the best Argentine film of that year: *El Consultorio de Mme. Renée*. Produced by the Mundial Film Productores Company, it was written and directed by the Italian director Carlo (or Carlos) Campogagliani. Acting in the film were Letizia Quaranta, Augusto Gonçalvez, Ada Comaro, Angel Boyano and Magdalena Gutierrez. The script allowed the director to show unknown corners of Palermo, aerial scenes of Mar del Plata, and a car race that took place in that city, in which Campogagliani himself took part. According to the review for *Crítica*: "It is the first time that this critic has gone home completely satisfied by what he has seen done, after seeing the exhibition of a film by an Argentine producer.

"We now believe that there are people among us who are capable of understanding perfectly the way of routing the domestic film production, and it is to Mr. Alejandro F. Gómez that the local film industry owes its first triumph and its first legitimate glory."

La Loba by Francisco Defilippis Novoa, was a failure; it opened on the 14th of April 1924. Produced by the Compañía Cinematográfica Selección Nacional, its leading actors were Argentino Gómez, Gloria Ferrandiz, Consuelo Abad and Nelly Olmos. It was a melodrama about a woman whose life is blown into a thousand pieces after the death of her son. Its great defect, according to *Crítica*, was that it was a bad instance of theater shot on film: "It is even more certain that the actors are not at fault, they have stuck to their roles as stage actors; the blame, if it exists, belongs to the artistic director, if he existed."

On Tuesday the 29th of April *La Cieguita de la Avenida Alvear* was released. Produced by Buenos Aires Film, it was written and directed by Julio Irigoyen. Eva Franco, Elsa Conti, Diego Figueroa, Ada Cornaro, Adolfo D. Torres, Aparicio and Totón Podestá played its leading roles. But this film had no significance. The deficient acting, direction, production and photography were on the same level as that found in other Argentine films released at the time, both by this producer and others.

An oddity from the 18th of May 1924 was the scientific film *La Rinoplastia Argentina*. Colón Film produced it to demonstrate the surgical technique of Dr. Oscar Ivanissevich. On the 28th of May 1924 *Donde el Nahuel Huapi es Rey* was released. The next day said:

The local production company Cinematografía Argentina Federico Valle premiered *Where the Nahuel Huapi is King* yesterday. It is an Argentine film that is lovely because of the framework in which the action develops: the Nahuel Huapi Lake District.

A simple plot, with tidy storylines and violent passions unfolds through the acting of Amelia Mirel, Raquel Marín, Nelo Cosimi and Arauco Radal, who have all taken part in other films that the producers have shot in Patagonia, and are capable members of our cinema.

The Federico Valle Company has not spared any effort or money to lead their company in the patriotic task of showing these remote Argentine territories.

On the other hand, *La Prensa* published the following remarks on the 1st of June:

As a young industry, Argentine films only produce movies based on national characteristics from time to time, always inspired by the praiseworthy purpose of showing the savage natural beauties of our country, or the progress of our capital city. These pictures have the forgivable faults to be found in all works that are just beginning, and that will be corrected step by step, but it is also necessary to remember that Argentine film industry has produced films of some merit. We must therefore expect the new productions to show some progress. If we do not forget films produced in this country in recent times, worthy of praise and encouragement, we must admit that the new recently released production *Donde el Nahuel Huapi es Rey*, cannot compare to them and adds nothing of value to the silent art.

The plot is a legend of love, hate, and death, but it is so poor, its structure is so weak that the action that is developed in six short acts could have been completed in two. The legend is neither original nor interesting. The only worthwhile things are the panoramic views, for they are situated in the picturesque and fertile region of the beautiful Nahuel Huapi Lake, showing pretty vistas although some are very dark. The acting is correct, with the actor Arauco Radal outstanding, who shows conditions and skills worth mentioning for acting in films. The photography has moments of high quality in certain close ups and in some wide angle shots, even though they have refrained from putting on film some of the richest natural motifs in the Patagonian Cordillera.

The Corbicier Film Company released *El Arriero de Yacanto*, directed by José A. Ferreyra, on the 6th of June 1924. Its leading actors were Yolanda Labarden, Nelo Cosimi and Héctor Míguez. The film was produced in the Córdoba hills; it had flaws in its photography and was poorly staged. *La Epoca* described the plot of this production, a quite conventional melodrama, is as follows:

A virile young cattle drover, hardened in the vigorous and healthy way of life of the country, arrives at Yacanto, in the Province of Córdoba. Chance puts him in contact with a woman of sickly beauty, who has arrived there to recover her strength, lost in the depraved Buenos Aires nights. He feels attracted to the visitor's strange beauty, and becomes a plaything in her hands and those of her companion, a loose-living parasite, often to be found with that kind of woman.... The couple attracts him to a gambling table, and there, the good gaucho loses the proceeds of his last livestock sale. The faithful lad, who has followed and watched over his boss, tells him how he has been cleverly cheated out of his money by those people. In the knowledge that he has been cheated, the cattle drover attacks the pair of adventurers furiously with his fists, and abducts the woman, hiding in a corner of the hills, meaning to show her how he earns the money that they tried to steal from him. The city woman who is used to living by night does not understand that primitive way of living. The hardships of the rustic lifestyle exasperate her and her hatred of the strong drover increases. On the other hand he feels love and contempt for her; nevertheless, he care for her with great attention. The days go by and the woman starts to go through a change of opinion. Little by little she begins to admire the man's primitive virtues: when her companion in mischief comes searching for her together with folks from the town, she confesses her love for the drover, and blames her former companion for stealing from those who are now his companions. These react and seize the card sharp, while the woman, formerly dragged down by city low-life begins to redo her life, sincerely loving the good drover."

Criollo Viejo was presented on June 1924 by Tylca Film. Directed by Rafael Parodi, its actors were Amelia Mirel, María Navarro, Francisca Baratti, Diego Figueroa, Felipe Farah, Augusto Gonçalves, Alvaro Escobar and Julio Donadille, all of whom performed well. Produced in the province of Córdoba, the film had very good production values, although the action at the beginning was very slow. The plot of this melodrama was simple, but the film, ably directed by Parodi, had thrilling moments. The verdant Córdoba hill country served as the beautiful background to the action. In the film, Don Armando de la Peña owns an *estancia* (ranch) in a picturesque angle of the plain. The ranch is managed by Pedro Orias, who is loyal and fair, the model of an old *criollo*. Orias lives with his wife and his children, Juan, Carlos, and María. The first of his sons, Juan, worries his father because he is lazy, hot-tempered, and a gambler. On the other hand, Carlos has inherited his father's virtues. The *estancia* owner's family is different. Don Armando's offspring do not make their happy. Mercedes, her father's favorite, likes the life of the big city, and continues her lifestyle in the country. She is flirtatious and vain, and despises Carlos, the manager's son. Her feelings towards Carlos do not change, even after he saves her life. Mercedes' opposition hides her budding love for him. The son of the rancher also likes the vice of the city, and continues to behave badly in the country. One day, Juan, the son of the *criollo*, wounds a gambling companion at the local general store, and his father turns him over to the authorities, to ensure that justice is served. Carlos, the young man from the city, used to easy conquests, surprises the beautiful and humble María, the old *criollo*'s daughter, and tries to force her to kiss him. Without knowing who the girl's offender is, Maria's brother, Carlos, fights the other Carlos.

The inevitable soon happens; the boss hears a different version of events and makes the his manager's son leave the house. In a faraway cabin he will look after the flocks. Inspired by the quiet surroundings, Carlos remembers the dear image of the owner's daughter, Mercedes. A red glow in the distance warns him of a fire at the *estancia*. The flames have started to take hold of the buildings, and Don Armando is helped out of the rooms by the faithful *criollo viejo*, and Carlos saves Mercedes. De la Peña's son Carlos dies among the rubble. Later on, Mercedes learns the truth about the episode between her late brother and her rescuer. She asks his forgiveness, and they begin a love affair. Pedro Orias' happiness is complete when the prodigal son, Juan, returns from jail, rehabilitated.

Por los Mares del Sur was from late June 1924. It was a documentary shot during the voyage of the ship *Guardia Nacional* to the South Orkney Islands Observatory, and showed, besides the beauty of the region, scenes of life on board, including whale and seal hunts.

Nelo Cosimi directed and starred in *Carne de Presidio* from his own script, for the producer Corbicier y Cía. It was released at the end of August 1924. The plot tells the story of a crook, El Ladeao, who is transformed by the love of a blind girl, played by Amelia Mirel. The blind girl regains her sight thanks to an operation by a neighboring surgeon, and only awaits the return of her loved one. But when El Ladeao leaves jail the girl discovers that her hero is pathetic, and keeps her sadness to herself. The man then understands the state of affairs, and commits suicide. According to *La Prensa Carne de Presidio* would have been a better film if the view of the sad background where El Ladeao moves had not been shown in such somber tones, and if the disgusting realism had been excluded. "As it is, it is commonplace film, without importance in the local cinematography. We can only point out as good the performance by Mr. Nelo Cosimi. He shows in every film performance qualities as an artist of character, and he possesses, among others, the rare quality of being able to give his character originality. The actress Amelia Mirel also achieves an outstanding performance in *Carne de Presidio*, in her short role as the blind girl."

A local release that took place in the middle of September 1924 was that of *El Poncho del Olvido*, produced by Cinematografía Curell, with Mary Clay, Felipe Farah, and José Plá in the leading roles. Its director was Ricardo Villarán, and Enrique Maroni and Adolfo Avilés wrote a tango as the theme song. It was not exactly the typical story of an innocent neighborhood girl who ends up as a prostitute in a cabaret in the Buenos Aires downtown. Forced to abandon her humble home and the man she loves, fearing not being able to resist the coming poverty (the result of a sudden change of fortune that condemns her to destitution) the heroine discovers in the downtown cabarets the bitter and real contrast between the women of pleasure who seek a false future, and those who make hard choices in order to have a life in common with those they love. The outcome, however, is conventional.

Valle Negro premiered on the 11th of September 1924. It had Mary Clay in the leading role, and, according to Domingo Di Núbila, its director was called Martinelli. It was based on a novel by Gustavo Marínez Zuviría, who (under the pseudonym Hugo Wast) produced the film with the Atlanta Company. *La Prensa* reported that the film was well received by the audience, and beyond some trivialities, showed a technical progress comparable to the foreign films from those times.

The documentary *Por Tierras Misioneras* was first shown near the end of September 1924. The film showed many of the natural attractions of the region, including the Iguazú Falls, shown from dangerous points of view, and the cultivation and production of maté tea.

On the 16th of September 1924, Buenos Aires Film presented *Los Misterios del Turf Argentino*, directed by Julio Irigoyen and shot during the month of May. Its leading actors were Manolita Poli, Lilian Olivilla, Lía Balvi, Arturo Sánchez, Totón Podestá, Augusto Gonçalves, Adolfo Torres, Aparicio Podestá, Julio Andrada and Oscar Caprarella. It was a conventional melodrama about a girl in love with a humble jockey, and ended with a very well shot race at the Hipódromo Argentino racetrack.

There were also other Argentine films made in 1924, but there is very little information about them. *Pata de Zorro* from Hugo Wast Film and the Atlanta Company, was based on a story by Gregorio Martínez Zuviría written especially for the screen. We know only that *Capital y Trabajo*, from the Cooperativa Biográfica, was about a social problem.

Colón Film also released two films that year: *Las Bestias Tienen Sed*, produced by Angel Boyano and directed by Jorge Lafuente, with technical direction by the brothers Luis Angel and Vicente Scaglione. The script was by Manuel Lema Sánchez, and its outdoor scenes were shot in the Córdoba mountains. María Delelis de Boyano, Ema Jones, Jorge Ravel, José Pla, Julio Donadille, Herminio Barbiccino and Héctor Menéndez played its main characters. The other film, directed by José A. Romeu, was *Historia de un Gaucho Viejo*, seven acts long, also with technical direction by the Scaglione brothers. Shot at San Rafael, in the province of Mendoza, it was acted in its principal roles by the selfsame Romeu, Mycha Flores, Néstor Chepary and Marco Ombú, all amateur actors from San Rafael.

The first film from 1925 was a documentary shown in private in April, *A Través de los Andes Fueguinos*. The film showed different aspects of life in Tierra del Fuego, and showed a forest fire in one of the great local woods,

INO ES UNA MAS!
No es otra película nacional,
es una gran producción de
HUGO WAST FILM
Estreno Martes 9   Callao y Petit Splendid

Poster announcing *Valle Negro* (Hugo Wast, 1924).

the hunt for five escaped convicts from the prison, and the life and habits of the Ona and Yaguan native Americans. The Sociedad General Cinematográfica released *El Caballero de la Rambla*, filmed as *El Caballero de la Capa Perfumada*, on the last days of April 1925. Its director was the novice Francisco P. Donadio, who had excelled as an actor in Italian films. The cast was made up of Emilia Vidal, Olga Casares Pearson, Mario Parpagnoli, Angel Walk, José Plá, María Spinelli, Severo Fernández and César Fiaschi. The story was about a girl who loved to read pulp fiction.

According to Roberto Di Chiara, Buenos Aires Films presented *Tu Cuna Fue un Conventillo* directed by Julio Irigoyen, in May 1925. It was adapted from a play by Alberto Vaccarezza, with a script written by the author himself. Not much is known about this film; it had María Esther Podestá, Ada Falcón, Consuelo Velásquez, A. Camiña, Juan Portal, José Ramírez, Diego Figueroa and Julio Torres in the leading roles.

Y en una Tarde de Carnaval ..., directed by Enzo Longhi, was released in June 1925. It was based on a story by Alfredo Méndez Caldeira. Lidia Liss, María Spinelli, and Nelo Cosimi stood out in a cast that also included Ida Gordini, Sara Belmonte, Jorge Lafuente, César Robles, Rafael de los Llanos, Alvaro Escobar and José Plá. The plot involves a villain who is turned down by the girl that he loves. The villain, for revenge, tries to destroy her relationship with another man. He has his rival fired from his job, causing the family t go hungry and aggravating the illness of a child. The villain sends the woman's husband into the arms of a loose woman, causing him to forget his duties to his family. Still, the young wife's dedication to her husband is strong. The villain then manages to take the husband to his former employer's home in order to burglarize it. A picture on a wall next to the strong-box reminds him of the home that he has abandoned, and the worker escapes the trap and rejoins the family that he loves.

At the end of June 1925 *Cuando Buenos Aires Duerme…*, written and directed by José A. Ferreyra, premiered. The actors were Mary Clay, Delfa Hernández, Carmen Martínez, Auguston Gonçalves, Oscar Murria, Julio Donadille and A. Morena. Its production and acting were good, but its plot was weak: another melodrama with the usual underworld scenes, and the cabaret that appeared so often in Argentine films in those days.

Carlo Campogagliani directed *La Esposa del Soltero*, its title was changed to *La Mujer de Medianoche* when it was released in October 1925. Campogagliani and his wife, Letizia Quaranta, were in the leading roles of this film, together with Julio Donadille. It was produced by Federico Valle and Paulo Benedetti in Argentina and Brazil, It was a simple and slightly naïve comedy that took place in Buenos Aires and Rio de Janeiro, with very good photography. An invention called "cinematrofonía" was used in this film; it allowed the orchestra in the pit to play the score, which appeared in subtitles on the screen. According to Roberto Di Chiara, this system had already been used by Benedetti in Brazilian productions. Among the musical themes included in *La Dama de Medianoche* could be found the tango "Buenos Aires," by Manuel Jovés and Manuel Romero, recorded by Gardel two years before.

Manuelita Rosas, based on a work by E. Rossi, was directed by Ricardo Villarán, and its cast included Blanca Podestá, Miguel Faust Rocha, Nelo Cosimi (as Juan Manuel de Rosas), Amelia Senisterra, Alberto Ballerini, Ricardo Passano and Blanca Vidal. To recall Rosas and his times was very difficult due to the complexity of his character, although the film was a very good effort, with excellent photography by Alberto Biasotti. Except for Nelo Cosimi as Rosas, the rest of the cast suffered from their lack of experience facing the cameras. The great problem with this film, however, was Blanca Podestá's performance as Manuelita Rosas, as she was too old for the part.

On the 27th of September 1925, Federico Valle presented a film called *Argentina* in the ceremonial hall of the newspaper *La Prensa*. Directed by Valle himself (together with Arnold Etchebehere), this film was produced at the request of the Ministry of Foreign Relations for the purpose of adver-

«M A N U E L I T A   R O Z A S»   E N   E L   C I N E

Blanca Podestá en el papel principal.

Faust Rocha, en el galán de la obra.

Nelo Cossimi, encarnando a Rozas.

Ricardo Passano, en el jefe de la Mazorca.

The principal cast of *Manuelita Rosas* (1925).

tising the country in the principal cities of Europe. This film was divided into seven acts and a prologue.

The last film released in 1925 was *Muñecos de Cera* produced by the Tylca Company. Written and directed by Rafael Parodi, it had Amelia Mirel and Felipe Farah as its principal actors. During its production the year before, *La Epoca* remarked on the 21st of August 1924 that "although the film is highly dramatic, it doesn't lack funny parts. It also has a powerful attraction: Prince Umberto, Alvear, Yrigoyen and many other personalities in it, even though none of them have posed for the film."

Another film from 1925 release date unknown was *Padre Nuestro* directed by Julio Irigoyen for the Buenos Aires Film Company. According to Roberto Di Chiara it was co-produced with a Spanish company, with Susana Alvear and Jaime Devesa in the leading roles. While the film's subject is unknown, it was probably taken from the tango the same name by Alberto Vaccarezza and Endique Delfino, with the intention of repeating on the screen the success of the recording by Azucena Maizani.

Chichilo y Carmelita en Buenos Aires was probably released in 1925. It was produced at the end of the preceding year by Ariel, directed by Mario Parpagnoli and photographed by Alberto Biasotti. Apparently it was the first tragicomical film made in Argentina, with Emilia Vidal, Carlos Dux, Alfredo Santerini and Alfredo Faita in the leading roles. Unfortunately little more is known about this film. Among the films from 1925 about which there is little available data, there is one which stands out: *El Organito de la Tarde*. It was directed by José A. Ferreyra and starred María Turgenova, Julio Donadille, Mecha Cobos and Arturo Forte. This film arose from the popularity of its namesake, the tango composed by Cátulo Castillo the year before. As it was a hit, Jose Gonzalez Castillo, the composer's father, wrote the lyrics so that Azucena Maizani could sing it. González Castillo was a journalist and a man of the theater, as well as a pioneer in Argentine cinema. Around 1922, after the success of his tango "Sobre el Pucho" he added the writing of lyrics for tangos to his other artistic activities.

The journalist Julio Nudler says that González Castillo, the author of countless plays, converted many of his tango lyrics into theatrical pieces. He also converted them to film melodramas. With his son Cátulo he formed the only father-son duo of tango creators. Nevertheless the lyrics of "Organito de la Tarde," written after the music, sound quite forced, as does the story of the old organ grinder and the death of his daughter, and a lame man and the loss of his leg. The music is much better than the words, but José A. Ferreyra based his film of the same name on these lyrics. For this film Ferreyra also wrote "El Alma de la Calle" or "Callecita de Sub-

"El Alma de la Calle," the tango by Raül de los Hoyos and José A. Ferreyra written for Ferreyra's production *El Organito de la Tarde* (1925).

urbio" with music by Raúl de los Hoyos. The results must not have been memorable as there are no reviews on the release of this film.

The first Argentine film released in 1926 was *La Vuelta del Toro Salvaje*, directed by Carlo Campogagliani, for Federico Valle, in the month of April. As *La Prensa* sustained on the 14th of April, the boxer Luis Angel Firpo played himself on screen. Presenting Firpo as an actor on screen (he had already appeared before in his fights on film) produced only average results. The film showed his abilities as a boxer, but not as an actor.

Based on a play by Armando Discépolo, *Mateo* was a tremendous failure when it was released in May 1926. María Esther Podestá de Pomar was the heroine of this film, and she performed well in a worthless film. The film was a comedy about horse-cab driver whose daughter leaves him for a criminal. But in the epilogue the crook lets her go and the father regains his daughter.

Around June 1926, *Bajo la Mirada de Dios* directed by Edmo Cominetti, with cinematography by Alberto Biasotti and sets by Rafael Manzini, was premiered. Its leading actors were Julio Andrada as El Tape, Mary Clay as Susana, Augusto Zama as the priest, Angel Boyano, and Eduardo Morera. The film and the actors were praised by the press at the time. This film was shown abroad before being released in Buenos Aires, and was reportedly a success in the city of New York. The story was a melodrama set in the north of Argentina (although it had more universal than local characteristics), showing beautiful Colonial architecture, and involving subjects that had never been broached in Argentina's cinema.

One of the most important actors in the history of Argentine films, Florentino (later Floren) Delbene, appeared for the first time on the big screen in the film *El Lobo de la Ribera* directed by and starring Nelo Cosimi and released in October 1926. The actress Chita Foras also took part in this film, and even Antonio Prieto, its cinematographer, took part as an actor. Although its plot was common and insignificant, its production was good, showing riverside street scenes near the Riachuelo in a realistic manner.

Any discussion of 1926 requires mention of a catastrophic event that occurred on the 14th of April. After a loud explosion, heard many blocks away, Federico Valle's facilities in downtown Buenos Aires caught fire. In monetary terms, Valle's losses were total. Many films were lost forever. *La Vanguardia* published the following on the 8th of April:

> Our readers have surely not forgotten the fire that occurred in the laboratories and offices of the Cinematografía Valle some months ago and which caused, along with other damages, the loss of the film archive, in which all the social, political and economic aspects of the country were recorded.
> However just a few months have been sufficient to fill the gap, improving when-

Estado en que quedó el archivo de la empresa cinematográfica Valle Film, después del violento incendio.

El incendio en la "Valle Film"

E N contadas ocasiones los incendios locales provocan tanto pánico. El fuego cortó la salida a los vecinos que ocupaban el mismo edificio, causando el espanto consiguiente, que no adquirió graves proporciones, debido a la oportuna acción de los bomberos y a su tarea de salvamento, que dió lugar a episodios emocionantes.

Numerosas mujeres y niños fueron librados de una muerte segura y espantosa por los bomberos.

Aspecto que presentaba el patio de la casa después que fué aplacado el siniestro.

The fire at the Federico Valle company in 1927.

ever possible on the destroyed archive, by means of the technical advances of these last few years as well as by the capacity accumulated by the experience of long years of continuous labor.

A dozen camera operators have been covering the different geographical zones of our country during the last six months, obtaining advantageous results, because there is no interesting characteristic or potentiality or progress that has not been reproduced by the cameras operated by the employees of that production company.

It is only fair to hope that Cinematografía Valle will continue with that work of information and promotion.

One of few Argentine films released in 1927 of which there is a record was *Federales y Unitarios*, directed by Nelo Cosimi, who also played the leading role. By then local productions had been reduced to a few films, as there was not enough money to make them. *Federales y Untarios* was a pretentious film, and the work of Nelo Cosimi proved that reasonable results could be obtained with very few means, including showing the atmosphere of the past with accuracy. The subjects shown were well known: Rosas' tyranny and doomed love affairs, cursed by the division between "Federales" and "Unitarios."

It is quite possible that the tango "Federación," by Francisco Canaro and Luis Riccardi, with lyrics by Juan Andrés Caruso, was composed as the theme song for this film. Apart from Canaro, both Carlos Gardel and Enrique Delfino recorded this song for Max Glücksmann. Another 1927 movie about which little is known, other than the information supplied by Domingo Di Núbila and Roberto Di Chiara, is *Perdón Viejita* which premiered in December at the opening of the Hindú Palace Theater. José A. Ferreyra wrote and directed this film, based on the tango with the same name by José Antonio Saldías, with music by Osvaldo Fresedo. The composer recorded this tango three times for Max Glücksmann: first with Carlos Gardel singing, then an instrumental version, and again without vocals on the occasion of the release of this film. The actors were María Turgenova, Stella Maris, Florencia Vidal, Alvaro Escobar and the bandoneon player Luis Moresco in the part of the villain.

The first film released in 1928 was *Regeneración*, also directed by Nelo Cosimi, who performed in it together with Chita Foras and Emilio Firpo. It was released in the cities of Remedios de Escalada and Pergamino on the 15th of January, and shown in Buenos Aires on the 17th of that month. *Regeneración* was produced by La Fraternidad, the locomotive engineer's trade union, and has, according to *La Vanguardia*, the following plot:

Alfredo and Francisco are boiler stokers; both work at the Remedios de Escalada Depot, Southern Railroad. While Francisco is a good worker and shows that he is a real man in all he does, Alfredo abandons himself to vice, dragged down by a faithless friend who does not leave him even for an instant.

Esteban, another railroad worker, is the foreman of the locomotive depot at Remedios de Escalada, where he has earned the respect of both his superiors and his subordinates due to his decency and honesty. He is a widower, and feels a deep affection for his two daughters, Dora and Lola, both of whom he wants to set on the right path.

Francisco is promoted to engineer, and sets up a home with Lola; he is always seen to behave properly Alfredo follows the wrong path, after everybody becomes fed up with him he is fired for being drunk on the job. His friend convinces him to abduct Dora, Esteban's other daughter, to avenge his being fired from his job.

After three years have passed, Alfredo's home is in a shambles, the consequence of the abuse of alcohol, showing how low a drunk can get.

Francisco's home is the other side of the coin; he lives happily with his wife and little boy, but he suffers now, because his child is ill, and in his saddest hour he must leave him in the hands of the doctors since his duty as a worker calls him to his locomotive to do his job.

Alfredo mistreats Dora because she cannot find him enough money to satisfy his evil instincts, but by means of Francisco and at Lola's request he manages to take some money home. His evil friend takes advantage of the circumstance to goad him on, saying that Dora cheats on him with his brother-in-law Francisco. Alfredo, mesmerized by his friend, believes all this, and a lot more besides, and on an occasion actually slaps Francisco, but Francisco's calm appearance, his admonishments and his good advice touch Alfredo's heart.

He is given back his old job, after the pleas made on his behalf by his old comrades and his engineer, Emilio. Once restored to his job, and with everybody's forgiveness, even Esteban's, there is only one thing to make him unhappy: the recollection of his faithless friend, who, lost to the world, continues to drag around his misery. But one night, knowing that Alfredo must drive his train, number 323, the so-called pal, aware that his friend is away from home, goes there with evil intensions, but drunk as ever he does not notice the proximity of a train when he crosses the track, and he is killed by the locomotive that by coincidence is driven by his former friend Alfredo.

Alfredo has been redeemed, the obstacle has disappeared, the faithless friend that had tried to sink both homes into the abyss has gone, and new and promising horizons open up for both stokers: work and honesty are back in command, and Alfredo has become a man who is good for both humanity and progress.

On the 23rd of June Federico Valle presented the documentary *Entre los Hielos de las Orcadas del Sur*, recorded by the camera operator Juan Carlos Moneta on the annual expedition to the observatory on those islands. This film was originally shot in 1925, but that first version was lost in the fire at the Valle Company in 1926. For that reason Valle had to wait a full year to be able to send a camera to the southern part of the country. The results, both from a commercial and a film point of view, were excellent, and José Bustamante y Ballivián managed to pair all the images shown to the audience with explanatory captions. Besides showing different aspects of the expedition and its work, the film showed expeditions and hunts organized by the expedition in its time off. *La Prensa* made the following comment on the 25th of June 1926: "They leave on a dogsled, and danger is always lying in waiting for them. The ice-cap is not dependable. If it breaks, it will swallow up the trusting man who has miss-stepped. But once the obstacle is overcome the expedition continues. Sea leopards and sea elephants offer original views of the polar fauna. And further on, seals and petrels, and in a region that seems made for them, of penguins. The lives of the different species of penguins, the funny aspects of their lives, happiness and sadness, idylls and tiffs, are the most interesting chapter, both witty and lively, of the film."

Maipo Film presented *La Borrachera del Tango* on the 27th of August 1928. Based on a popular play by Elías Alippi and Carlos Schaeffer Gallo, directed by Edmo Cominetti and photographed by Alberto Biasotti, its actors (some appearing for the first time in films) were Nedda Francy, Eduardo Morera, Felipe Farah, Carlos Dux, Siches de Alarcón, Elena Guido, Alicia Vignoli y Elena and Haydee Bozán. A tango with the same name (surely the film's musical theme) was recorded by Carlos Gardel.

Unlike *Bajo la Mirada de Dios*, done by the same producer, *La Borrachera del Tango*, which that was a hit on stage in 1921, was one of the greatest failures ever produced in Argentina, and it was removed from distribution after its release. The film showed a series of accessory and useless scenes and the plot was confusing, monotonous, and lacking harmony. According to Jorge Couselo, its theme was the negative influence of the tango on traditional family structures. The results on screen were so boring, and so bad, that the film was a colossal failure. On the 11th of October *El 90* was released; it was based on the revolution that took place in Argentina in 1890. It was directed by L. J. Maglia Barth and based on a story by E. Gouchon Cané, and it was another failure. It was a disaster, in spite of an interesting theme. This was due in large part to a childish production technique, and uncooperative actors and camera operators.

A film made by amateurs called *La Tragedia de Wanda Wladimiro* was premiered in the first days of November 1928. While a film with this characteristic cannot be judged with the same approach as normal commercial productions, the makers of the film earned praise for their effort in this enterprise, which they under took with few resources and little knowledge. Wanda Giovanelli, in the leading role, and Aurora O. Torrico, Metilde de Belle, Víctor Pereyra, Alex Wassilieff, Roberto Tellarini, Horacio Balza, and Juan Lichesich, in other roles, were adequate in their acting.

Nelo Cosimi, Chita Foras, Florentino (later Floren) Delbene, Esteban Berría and José Piña played the leading parts in *La Mujer y La Bestia*, directed by Cosimi and released on the 21st of November 1928. It was the first film produced by a new company, the Sociedad Anónima Cinematográfica Hispano Argentina Manzanera, or S.A.C.H.A. Manzanera. It told the story of a tracker and guide, Aniceto, who lives with his young wife, Margarita, in a picturesque valley near the Córdoba mountains. Their landlord, Rolón, is a brutal terror, and there is little work in the area. Aniceto manages to get hired by an English expedition that wants to explore the region, and he leaves for the mountains with them. Rolón, discovers Margarita bathing in a creek in the hills and molests her. Rolón has further plans for Aniceto: he follows the expedition cuts the rope that one of the explorers is using to descend into a ravine. That night Aniceto is hauled in front of the authorities accused of the crime.

El Carancho, another character who has been abused by Rolón, wants revenge and helps Aniceto to escape from prison. Aniceto escapes, goes to the shack where Rolón is hiding and frees Margarita. There is a short fight between the villain and Aniceto; Aniceto kills Rolón and burns down his shack. *La Mujer y la Bestia* managed to stand out among Argentine films from those times. Cosimi's work as the director and actor (in the role of the villain, Rolón) was excellent, and the entire film managed to hold the audience's interest. Worth mentioning in this film is the scene in which Cosimi surprises Chita Foras (playing Margarita) bathing in a creek. According to *El Diario*, it never went beyond the limits of morality, because it was done with prudence and good taste. Apart from Cosimi's good performance, the performances by Chita Foras, and Florentino (Floren) Delbene (as Aniceto) were well done.

At the beginning of 1929 Julio Irigoyen presented his film called *La Casa del Placer*. The results were regrettable and scandalous, so he stopped producing fictional films for a number of years. The huge failure of this production was reflected well in *La Prensa*, in its edition of the 15th of January:

> Its exhibition is announced as "a realistic work, not suitable for the under-aged." And in this sense it could be said that it is the first time that our dawning local production ventures into subjects so lacking in dignity. They have tried to show a number of well-known artists from the local stage in a salacious story easily able to awaken an unhealthy interest in the public for an essentially materialistic reason. If that has been the intention of its directors we have to admit that they have also failed. *La Casa del Placer* is not convincing even as a dirty film with pornographic scenes. It has neither a well-developed story nor does it have good technique to give the film some value. In short, it gives the idea of something merely sketched, inspired in vulgar themes, fit for pulp novels, with no real emotion.
>
> The saddest thing is that they have caught up a qualified group of artists in the venture. The leading character is played by the celebrated singer Azuzena Maizani in an unworthy role. Those who appreciate the artist's celebrated virtues as a genuine creator of tangos have seen her dignity tarnished. The same can be said of the young actress Carmen Valdez, seen lately as a valuable actress in the theater, and of Ada Cornaro who is a tradition on the local stage. It is really hard to believe that these good actors have agreed to take part in such an unseemly production, utterly outside our country's film production.

On the 27th of March 1929, S.A.C.H.A. Manzanera produced *La Quena de la Muerte*, directed by Nelo Cosimi. Its leading actors were Cosimi,

Nelo Cosimi and Chita Foras in *La Quena de la Muerte* (S.A.C.H.A. Manzanera, 1928).

Chita Foras, Leonor Alvear, Florentino (Floren) Delbene and Antonio Prieto, who was also responsible for the camera, both here and in other films from this director. The theme of the film, treated with sincerity and ability, comes from the contrast between the feelings and habits of two half-breeds and those of a rich, city-bred heir and his wife. Nelo Cosimi had a new success with this film.

Aventuras de Pancho Talero was based on a comic strip by Arturo Lanteri, and it was one of the few successful Argentine films of 1929. Directed and photographed by Alberto J. Biasotti, its stars were José Petray and Carlos Dux. The characters from the comic strips managed to pass onto the screen without losing their wit, very well embodied by local artists, and the outcome was good.

The 1st of June 1929 S.A.C.H.A. Manzanera presented a new film by Nelo Cosimi: *Corazón Ante la Ley*. Besides Cosimi, its leading actors were Olga Casares Pearson, Victoria Real, Edith De Rosa, Florentino (Floren) Delbene, Alvaro Escobar, Miguel Gómez Bao, Esteban Berría, Francisco

Walther, Ricardo Passano and Julio Andrada. For the first time an Argentine film obtained the Army's collaboration. Almost all the film takes place in the San Martín courtyards and exercise fields, and its cadets do their maneuvers specially for the camera, and parade in a ceremony that was never really performed: the degrading of an officer. This participation by the Army enhances the value of the film, and above all, it allows a glimpse of future and better contributions to Argentine Cinema.

Nelo Cosimi directed and had the leading role in this melodramatic story of intrigue, in which an officer is accused of being a traitor due to the disappearance of certain secret plans, and unjustly condemned, until the confusion is cleared up and he is exonerated.

Alma en Pena, was inspired by a tango by Anselmo Aieta with words by Francisco García Jiménez. The tango was recorded both by Carlos Gardel and by Ignacio Corsini, and the film had María Esther Podestá, Segundo Pomar (Podestá's husband) and Alvaro Escobar in the leading roles. The last silent film directed by Julio Irigoyen it premiered on the 30th of June 1929 was it another failure for Argentine films. The story told of the tribulations of a poor woman, whose husband is a crook who dies while trying to seduce a girl who is later recognized as his daughter. The facts appeared without much action, in a disorderly manner, and with the exceptions of María Esther Podestá and Segundo Pomar, the acting was bad.

The last fictional film to be released in 1929 was *Destinos*, produced by the Ariel Company. It was directed by Edmo Cominetti and photographed by Alberto Biasotti, who found redemption for their failure in *La Borrachera del Tango*. Its actors were Felipe Farah (Carlos), Eva Bettoni (Inés), Carlos Dux, Siches de Alarcón, Antonio Ber Ciani, Julio Bunge, Lucy Cortés, Hilda Alsina and J. de Emerici. *Destinos* starts out as a story of the behavior of students in a boarding house, who know more about love affairs and parties than studying. Then there is a sudden change of tone, from comic to dramatic, when the lads have to face the reality of everyday life in pursuit of their goals. Towards the end the plot gets complicated, with an incestuous marriage that later proves to not be so; the protagonists can go on loving each other, as there is no blood relationship. The film ends with some comic scenes.

The production of the film was good. The outdoor scenes were shot in different parts of Buenos Aires, and the night scenes in lighted streets, especially Corrientes Street, showed pretty and original effects. The indoor scenes were equally good. The actors distinguished themselves in their parts.

Destinos virtually closes the silent film period in Argentina. From

June 1929 forward, sound movies began to be shown, and local productions had to adapt to the new situation. At the end of the year *La Prensa* summed up our industry's production:

> Argentine film production continues to advance with hesitating steps. It lacks directors, and above all, money. As an industry it still does not inspire trust. We have been repeating it since we started reviewing the few local releases that there were in 1929. Local production will continue to vegetate until it involves qualified persons in these activities. There have been it is true, two serious attempts last year; they are no more than good intentions: *Destinos* by the director Cominetti demonstrated some directorial virtues, as well as the acting. Manzanera's *Corazón Ante la Ley* also showed progress in multiple aspects.
>
> We shall have to wait for the arrival of better intentions. When the country's exhibitors make up their minds to take local production seriously, when the entrepreneurs start taking risks, and when, at last we obtain the collaboration of conscientious directors and writers, then we shall begin to be proud of our country's movie industry. That will be the moment to enact laws to protect it. Until then we will have to wait.... Local industry continues, for now, to be a promise.

Looking back on the period of silent films, a touch of sadness tinges all that refers to Argentine productions. Not all the films from the time are indicated here, because of the impossibility of obtaining precise facts about their respective releases. The newspapers gave very little space to films before 1924, and even less to local productions.

The Argentine silent movie period was very unsatisfactory, according to film critics' reviews of the period, some of which have been reproduced literally here. Most of the films have been forgotten, and most of them are lost forever. The great majority never managed to please the audience. This sad truth was reflected very well in the editorial "Dificultades que se oponen al desarrollo de la cinematografía nacional" (Difficulties that oppose the development of an Argentine film industry) published in *El Diario* the 17th of April, 1929, a few months before the beginning of the sound movie revolution.

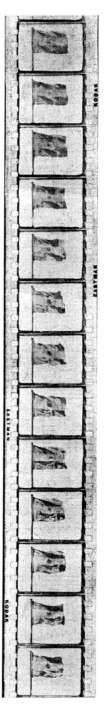

Histograms from *Corazón Ante la Ley*

The creation and development of the cinema art and industry, where so many diverse factors must unite to obtain a triumph, is a gigantic labor that can only be achieved through strength of will, enthusiasm, and constant labor. Those who have never approached the backstage of films cannot have an idea, not even a glimpse of the difficulties, almost insurmountable difficulties, both material and moral, that face the producer. The former are easier to resolve than the latter. The financing; the acquisition of artists and directors; the purchase and upgrading of all kinds of things: photography, sets, wardrobes, etc.; moving the production to remote places; the organization of a vast system of promotion to attract the world's attention onto a producer, a film or an artist; all these are a series of obstacles than can be overcome with zeal, hard work and intelligence. But it is not enough.

We all admire the work done by the United States in a little over twenty years. When they started to shoot the first movies in California — we still haven't forgotten them — they achieved marvelous results. They were the first steps in a new art and a new industry, and they put all their will in their growth and perfection; from the men who had the future of the cinema in their hands, to the most modest of spectators. This firm support for their films by the American people was, without doubt, the decisive factor for the fast and widespread triumph of the film industry of the United States of America.

It is precisely what is missing in Argentina. There is a general skepticism about all that the country produces, be it industrial, commercial or artistic. There is a public that does not seem to understand the effort that sustaining and developing our film industry means. It is a lack of trust in our country, of enthusiasm and also of patriotism. The producer thus trips up on moral difficulties after having overcome the material obstacles.

It is quite true that our public has good reasons to have a certain distrust of Argentine films. There has been an abuse of realistic films that are really only examples of the lowest kind of pornography. But their conscience and their discernment must lead them to distinguish between this crude and inferior production and the (modest, of course) well directed, worthy, patriotic efforts that are made to contribute to the progress of Argentine film-making, in which we should all be involved: the Argentines for patriotic reasons, the foreigners for gratitude to the country. This triumph will bring Argentina both moral and material benefits. It will be a faithful advertisement for the country abroad and it will create an unbounded source of riches.

To reach such a success it is necessary to have everybody's support. A calm judgment, always relative, because it is not possible to measure with the same stick first attempts and works done after a long experience; a timely applause, constant support sincerely leaving aside all malice are necessary.

We must all give our help. The public (better than any strict law) can choose between productions, demanding films made with dignity and good intent; it must demand programs that include our films, and the exhibitors must also submit to them with pleasure, choosing them, on their part, so that the fine efforts in pro of our local cinema are not lost by indifference and misunderstanding.

In this way, the Argentine Republic will have, one day, a powerful film industry.

American Companies Launch Subsidiaries to Commercialize Their Own Films

When Julián Ajuria founded the Sociedad General Cinematográfica in 1912, film producers from all over the world stopped selling their films and started renting them to local exhibitors. Throughout the first decade of the century producers from different countries tried to captivate the Argentine public with their productions.

After the beginning of their second decade Argentine films suffered a crisis, losing audiences, while American and European producers won over the viewers. The Fox Film Corporation was possibly the first American company to establish a subsidiary in Buenos Aires to sell their films, eliminating the need for distributors. At the same time, some companies exclusively devoted to importing films from Europe were launched.

If the big Hollywood studios only started commercializing their films themselves in the middle twenties up to 1931, why were these films successful in Argentina, and why couldn't local producers ever manage to prevail in all this period of time? The answer is that the Americans succeeded because of the great quality of their productions. It was necessary to have time and money, as well as an evolution and standardization of production and distribution methods.

As they did not have control over the market, American film companies needed something else that was missing in Argentine films at the time: invariable quality. The films could be good or not; what set them apart was that they were generally enjoyable, and they had performers that the audience could identify with: the first great film stars.

The real history of silent films in Argentina is not very different from what can be found in books on the subject that have often been badly translated to Spanish. However, since they have always been researched in the United States and Europe, there are facts that those books never described.

According to *La Vanguardia*, Emile E. Shauer, director and treasurer of the Famous Players–Lasky Corporation (Paramount) came to Argentina on the 26th of February 1924, to "personally study the Argentine market conditions, and to bring back a direct impression of the tastes and needs of our audience." A year later, in 1925, Paramount opened it subsidiary in Argentina.

The American companies introduced an industrial method of marketing that is still in use today: films are produced for the domestic market and perhaps for some European countries; once the film is made it is forced onto the rest of the world. When the time comes to show a film in another country the best commercial opportunity is chosen; sometimes the films are shown a few months after their release, but at others years may pass before a film sees foreign distribution. What is shown in the films generally has little or nothing to do with what happens in similar circumstances in other countries, but they are imposed upon the market all the same.

Various European countries also tried to win over the audience. They never managed to remove Hollywood from popular taste, nor from its power over of the screens, but they always managed to occupy an important space in public preferences.

In 1926 Argentina ranked in third as a buyer of films from Hollywood. The official numbers from the American Secretary of Commerce (according to *La Prensa* in the edition of the 7th of June 1928) reached their highest point since 1919, in spite of the joint efforts by buyers from other nations, backed at times by their own governments.

It is worthwhile to comment upon some on American movies released in Buenos Aires between 1924 and 1929, and to mention some additional nearly forgotten film news.

On the 15th of April 1924 *Donde el Norte Empieza* (*Where the North Begins*) was released. The attraction of this Warner Bros. Studios release, set in regions that are perpetually ice-bound, was the dog Rin Tin Tin. The film was a great success with the public.

El Ladrón de Bagdad (*The Thief of Baghdad*) was released in Argentina on the 16th of August 1924. Although the plot was childish, the film possessed an emotional and captivating charm. In *El Ladrón de Bagdad* an unreal world appeared before the eyes of the spectator, full of strange elements. Many scenes were surprising, and altogether, the film produced the same feeling as an exotic novel. The actors' performances were good, with Douglas Fairbanks outstanding in the leading role.

A few days before, *La Prensa* published this forgotten curiosity:

A few days ago, at a scientific session that took place at the Coliseo Theater, an original invention related to films was shown for the first time. The inventor is Mr. Carlos Anselmi. It is a refrigerated film projector, that allows the film to be stopped in front of the aperture, as was definitely demonstrated at the time, without the 150 amp arc light burning it. The new device offers many advantages; the most worthwhile mentioning is that it completely removes the dangers of fire inside the projection room, because the films are cooled by compressed air when projected, by a special refrigerating system.

The inventor, Mr. Anselmi, is an expert mechanic, who knows all the secrets enclosed in a good film projection device. He has finished his invention after long years of patient toil, and as he easily demonstrates in all the experiments shown, it is a singularly useful one.

The release of *The White Sister* (*La Monsita*) in September 1924, gave Dionisio Lofredo a reason to compose a foxtrot with the same name, and to dedicate it to the film's star, Lillian Gish. The story was touching, and notable for its simplicity. A cast of the Italian actors backed up Lilian Gish with noteworthy performances. Gish, the actress of *Corazones del Mundo* (*Hearts of the World*), *Intolerancia* (*Intolerance*), and *Pimpollos Rotos* (*Broken Blossoms*) achieved a notable artistic success, as did the film's director, Henry King.

Siegfried, directed by Fritz Lang, was one of the great successes of the time, and was released in Buenos Aires on the 25th of October 1924. A noteworthy occurrence associated with this German film happened some months after, when the audience in the Cine Teatro Colón in Curuzú Cuatiá (province of Corrientes) forced the management to repeat the dragon scene, which was received with uproarious applause of approval.

The Moon of Israel, released on May 1925, was an Austrian film, directed by Michael Curtiz. Adelqui Miller, the leading actor, would leave his mark in Argentina many years later. The exodus of the Jews from Egypt was the theme of this beautiful film, which was very well produced, with an interesting way of showing a plot that was very difficult to shoot. Its impressive settings revealed a great effort.

One of the first films exhibited in Argentina made by what was then the new company MGM was *Revelation*, which premiered in July 1925. Directed by George D. Baker, it was a beautiful production thanks to its settings, the photography, and the performances of Viola Dana, Monte Blue, Lew Cody, Frank Courier, Edward Conolly and Marjory Daw.

In April 1926, two years after its American release, the Fox Film Corporation presented *The Iron Horse* directed by John Ford. In its way it was a superior film. Set in 1869 and based upon the construction of the American transcontinental railroad, the film had many good scenes and a plot full of emotional, tender, painful and happy situations. Madge Bellamy and George O'Brien headed a good cast that also included Francis Powers, J. Farrel MacDonald, Gladys Hulette, and Ciril Chadwick.

On the 18th of April, Universal presented *The Phantom of the Opera*. The studio achieved a success with this film comparable to the one that it had achieved two years before with *El Jorobado de Notre Dame* (*The Hunchback of Notre Dame*). Lon Chaney, the hero of both movies, obtained a great triumph with his characterization of the Phantom, although the character did not allow him to fully express his artistic temperament. Mary Philbin, Norman Kerry, Arthur Edmund Carew and Gibson Gowland filled the other main roles the film.

One of the most important films of all time, *The Battleship Potemkin*, was released in Argentina on the 21st of October 1926. The film lacks an exceptional plot, although it shows some well-illustrated episodes of the revolt of the crew on board the *Potemkin* in June 1905. According to the newspapers from that time the reconstruction of those episodes did not justify a film of the length of *El Acorazado Potemkin*, although it is undeniable that there are outstanding scenes. The film's action, overloaded with unnecessary, often repetitious scenes, is monotonous and tiring until it reaches its epilogue, when it becomes really intense.

Based on Emile Zola's novel, *Nana* directed by Jean Renoir, was released on the 10th of November 1926. The film was not successful, in spite of the effort put into it by its makers. This version of the well-known novel would have left a better impression and would have been more convincing if the actress Catherine Hessing, playing Naná, had not acted in such an extravagant fashion.

Codicia (*Greed*) premiered in Buenos Aires on the 24th of December 1926. Its director was Erich von Stroheim, who presented an interesting leading character in this film: a woman who is good at the beginning, but who becomes a miserly shrew because of her unlimited passion for gold. The film offered some noteworthy scenes, where the study of the details, from a photographic point of view, reached superior heights. *La Prensa* noted that the film was not flawless: "However, as its most outstanding fault, one can point out its disproportionate length, a circumstance that is stressed by the director, in his desire to add new secondary situations, in his search for details. That is why *Greed* is a bit monotonous in its development, notwithstanding the director's technical originality, displayed in emotionally overflowing scenes."

The film is about a noble single man's vain attempts to transform his greedy wife. Zasu Pitts was extraordinary in her role. Her work had great dramatic force. Gibson Gowland was good as the husband, a simple man, whose life is ruined by the all-consuming greed of his wife.

In 1927, on the 30th of March, with the release of *Bardelys, the Magnificent*, Metro-Goldwyn-Mayer started the direct distribution of its films in Argentina, together with those of the First National Company. Until then, Max Glücksmann had been the distributor of the films of these American companies, and he would continue to be their principal exhibitor.

On the 31st of March 1927 an old character from the American cinema appeared on a Buenos Aires stage for the first time: Eddie Polo. *La Prensa* referred to the event thus:

> More than ten years ago American distributors imported an artist with extraordinary strength and appeal with his incredible adventures, and his absurd cowboy movies. It was Eddie Polo. One film above all gave him great fame. It was called *The Broken Coin*. Grace Cunard, a star who shone in days gone be, and works

little today in the Northern studios, surprised everyone together with Polo with their extraordinary actions in the face of death. Little by little the reputation of the artist, clever at switching hands with a revolver, a master of the art of imposing his will with his fists on ten or fifteen enemies, an expert with the lasso, grew among the cinema fans. In truth Eddie Polo deserved the admiration. He had won it putting his life on the line day after day, in a continuous display of recklessness and of the power of his fists.

Last night, at the Gran Cine Florida the audience met the flesh and blood Eddie Polo. The artist was presented in a sketch called *In a Tavern in Paris*. He was received with a warm ovation. But once that they had seen the hero of those terrifying adventures, as seen in serial films, from nearby, the public wanted to see something more from Eddie Polo. And in this sense the show was a failure. The artist only did a scene from many in his film repertoire: in an unequal fight, he easily overcame a bunch of rivals. Nothing else. That is why the exhibition turned out to be slightly feeble. They should have mixed the short appearance of the actor on stage with an appropriate addition of cheerful and entertaining variety numbers. As was demonstrated last night, Eddie Polo is at the top of his physical powers, but the exhibition of punches only is by no means a complete show. The audience, which gave its applause to their old acquaintance, and even made him speak, understood that it was so.

The Lost World was released on the 15th of June 1927. Based on Conan Doyle's novel, the First National Company achieved a noteworthy version, overcoming all the obstacles associated with the evocation of the time of the dinosaurs and other monsters. The film's characters were played by Lloyd Hughes, Bessie Love, Lewis Stone and Wallace Beery.

By September 1927, *Sparrows*, with Mary Pickford in the leading role, was a great success. She was preceded by a very well founded popularity, won by playing good and noble girls, a type of role she perfected to the point that American movies in those days had practically no other actress capable of playing that kind of character. Her performance as Mother Mollie in *Sparrows* captivated the audience from the first scenes.

With Jean Coquelin in the leading role, the French film *Father Constantin* was released at the end of September 1927. The nub of the plot concerned a village priest, a simple man, austere, piously devoted to his mission, played by Coquelin. His adventures, grief, and happiness make up all that is interesting in the film and contribute a natural note, with magnificent picturesque settings that were unmistakably French.

The great silent film *Napoleon*, by Abel Gance, was released in April 1928, and it was an unexpected event and a great box office success. The film was approved by such demanding audiences as those in Paris, London, Berlin, and other European capitals. From the moment of its release it was always shown to sold out audiences; the theaters were always filled, and many people were turned away. Few times had there been such a success as *Napoleon*. The public followed it with great respect, with growing interest as the film developed, and few spectators left the hall before "The End" appeared on screen. *Napoleon* marked an epoch in the development of the film as art and industry.

Not all silent films were that important. A good example, appearing on the 28th of June 1928, was the MGM film *Adam and Evil*, with Aileen Pringle and Lew Cody in the leading roles. It was a commonplace production based on a silly script about two husbands trying to show who is more stupid.

Steamboat Bill, Jr., the last Buster Keaton produced by his own film company for United Artists, before he moved to MGM and lost his artistic independence, worked better in Argentina than in the United States. The action took place in a provincial setting, and the comedian went from humor to sentimental sketches with equal success. His customary seriousness, the source of his original board of humor, moved everybody to laughter. Ernest Torrence and Marion Byron were remarkable in the film as well.

A well-loved Argentine actress, Mona Maris, appeared for the first time on the screen in a German film, *Los Esclavos del Volga*. She would become famous in Germany, and would later try her luck in Hollywood. The film was directed by Richard Eichberg; in *Los Esclavos del Volga*, Mona Maris proved to be a very sensitive actress. Her portrayal of the character Tatiana showed that she was an actress who could be expected to turn out noteworthy performances.

A famous silent Russian film, *October* was released on the 4th of April 1929. If they had not gone too far in the use of captions, mostly useless, the film would have been much better. Furthermore, the work of the director, Sergei Eisenstein, tired the audience at times. This reproduction of the October Revolution was presented by eyewitnesses and directed by people who took part in the events depicted;. that is why the appearance of the principal protagonists of the revolution, especially Lenin, was so convincing.

A few days later, on the 13th of April 1929, another great film had its premier, *The Passion of Joan of Arc*. Its director, Carl T. Dreyer, based the film on a story that he had written with Joseph Delteil. There were notably successful portions, and others that were rather boring. The film is famous for its early, striking use of closeups. The procedure, while very useful in displaying the smallest features of the actors, was wearing, even tiring the audience's eyesight with the continuous coming and going of the camera. Silvain, Schultz, Rayet and Berley joined Maria Falconetti as Joan of Arc as the principal members of the cast of this drama.

On the 10th of May 1929, MGM presented *Mr. Wu*, a film that was known beforehand due to its previous appearance as a stage production. Its leading actors were Lon Chaney, Renée Adorée and Anna May Wong. The plot concerns Mandarin, who, faithful to his traditions, kills his daughter after she is raped by a westerner. The film is a drama about love and revenge. Anna Way Wong was outstanding in this film, but Lon Chaney was not the right man to play the role of Western man for which he was cast. The conventional presentation of the Chinese setting puts it among the ordinary films of the time.

On the 12th of June 1929 Max Glücksmann presented the First National Pictures film *The Divine Lady* at the Gran Splendid, and on the 28th of June the Paramount film *The Wedding March*, directed by Erich von Stroheim, at the Palace. Although both films were essentially silent, they were the first films with a sound track shown in Argentina. With the release of MGM's *The Broadway Melody* on the 29th of August, Glücksmann started the sound movie revolution.

In contrast with what happened with Argentine films of the same period, many of the foreign silent movies, whether mentioned here or not, have kept the same status that they enjoyed in their time, while others gained a greater reputation many years later when they were shown at film clubs. Strangely enough, the first film club in Argentina started to operate around this time, and its purpose, besides reviewing the history of films, was to show all those films that were not brought into the country for market reasons.

On the 23rd of June 1929, after a trip to Europe and the United States to study the progress of films, Max Glücksmann stated the following, as reported in *La Prensa*:

> I believe, and I am convinced of this, that films are going through one of their most important periods. There is a worldwide interest in their improvement. That is why the essential object of my trip has been limited to talking films and sound movies, whose progress in the United States has reached a high level, but which without doubt pales, when compared with what it will be in the future. In the United States, in the first place, and in Europe after, the interest that there is for the new show is all embracing. It could be said that in the Republic of the North there is a real army of wise people dedicated only to perfecting sound films, and only one enterprise has allotted millions of dollars to these studies. There are great surprises awaiting us, and we must expect sensational and unexpected things from them.

The Films by Jose A. Ferreyra and Nelo Cosimi

As the silent movie era came to a close, it would only be a few years before Americans would dominate the screens, with Europe trying to compete. There were films for all tastes, and great artists both in front of and behind the cameras.

For Argentine films, the decade of the twenties was the worst in their history, with their crisis getting worse and worse. Those who ventured into film production had to learn the craft from watching foreign films. Furthermore the producers had to struggle to get their films shown. They had to know everything, both in front and behind of the cameras, and personally take charge of the advertising. According to Antonio Ber Ciani, who had a part in the film *Destinos*, they all had to do several jobs at the same time, because they worked as they had in the theater, that is to say, as a cooperative.

As there was no money, working conditions were very deficient. To quote Ber Ciani: "There was only one camera to shoot everything, with only two lenses, and nothing else. They were defective, and so was the lighting. We had to work in the sunlight, with hand reflectors for the sun. It was really a tremendous effort. The editing was done by hand, without a moviola. We looked at the film against the light and cut it with a pair of scissors in certain places. We knew what scene it was because we had the slate, and after that we spliced it. It was the same with the wardrobe and with the sets likewise: we did everything ourselves, we even borrowed clothes from the neighbors."

In this context there was one producer who managed to stand out, even though his films practically never had an impact in the press at the time: José A. Ferreyra. Son of an Afro-Argentine woman who was descended from slaves, he was educated in the best schools, and at the beginning his work in film was as a painter and set designer.

According to Jorge Couselo, Ferreyra conceived the plots of his films without writing a script; he developed the story while he shot. His

José A. Ferreyra

silent films were about the suburbs, the lives of the poor and people and situations taken from tangos. His first film was *Una noche de Garufa* from 1915, about which there is little information; it was inspired by Eduardo Arolas' tango of the same name.

His next film, called *El Tango de la Muerte* (1917), starred Nelo Cosimi. Both Couselo and Domingo Di Nubila consider it the first film with a story totally inspired by a tango. As Couselo says, "It sketches particular people (the girl from the edge of town who leaves home to live a life of sin, the seducer, the thug), and puts the action in a low-life riverside café, attended by complacent waitresses." He writes the captions— unavoidable elements in a silent film– in almost *canyengue* verse form.

Palomas Rubias, a comedy of student life based on a story by Leopoldo Torres Ríos, with Lidia Liss and Jorge Lafuente, was considered to be his first really accomplished film, although he later preferred to shoot melodramas.

Practically all of Ferreyra's later films would be extensions and enlargements of tango lyrics: *De Vuelta al Pago* (1919, with Nelo Cosimi and Lidia Liss), *La Muchacha del Arrabal* (1923, with Lidia Liss), *Melenita de Oro* (1923, with Lidia Liss, José Pla and Alvaro Escobar), *Corazón de Criolla* (1923), *La Maleva* (1923), *Mientras Buenos Aires Duerme* (1924, with Julio Donadille, Nora Montalbán and Elena Guido), *Mi Ultimo Tango* (1925, with Nora Montalván), *El Organito de la Tarde* (1925), *La Costurerita Que Dió Aquel Mal Paso* (1926), *Muchachita de Chiclana* (1926, with María Turgenova, Florentino Delbene, Arturo Forte, Ermete Mediante and Alvaro Escobar), *La Vuelta al Bulín* (1926) and *Perdón Viejita* (1927). He also made films about country life, such as *Campo Ajuera* (1918, with Nelo Cosimi, Lidia Liss and Yolanda Labardén), *La Gaucha* (1921, with Jorge Lafuente), *La Leyenda del Puente Inca* (1923), *El Arriero de Yacanto* (1924, with Nelo Cosimi and Yolanda Labardén) and *Odio Serrano* (1924) that, according to Couselo, do not have the naturalness of those that have to do with tangos.

Regrettably, these films had practically no repercussions and received virtually no space in the press at the time. Ferreyra also wrote lyrics for tangos (several were recorded by Gardel) that were always used as themes for his movies. For *La Costurerita Que Dió Aquel Mal Paso* which could be translated as *The Seamstress Who Went Wrong* (with María Turgenova, Felipe Farah, Celso Palumbo and Arturo Forte in the leading roles), a film based on a poem by Evaristo Carriego in which the entire plot is contained in the title, he wrote the following tango with Leopoldo Torres Ríos, with music by Gullermo del Ciancio; its title was reduced to *La Costurerita*. It began with the following stanza, which sums up the plot:

¿Que tenés, costurerita,	*What's wrong, little seamstress,*
que no cantas como antes	*That you sing don't sing as before,*
al llegar la tardecita?	*When evening comes?*
Que tenés, costurerita?	*What's wrong little seamstress?*
Acaso el muchacho aquel	*Has that young lad*
que ya no viene a la puerta	*Who used to call at your door*
te ha dejado el alma yerta?	*Left your soul ice-cold?*
¿Acaso el muchacho aquel?	*Has that young lad...?*

For the showing of *La Muchacha del Arrabal* he had the support of Roberto Firpo's tango orchestra, which played the tango of the same name composed by both of them together with Torres Ríos. Their original intention, according to Firpo, was to use records, but it was not possible. The actress Maria Turgenova, the director's wife, was the star of several of these films, and she used to sing the musical theme of each one in person, in the theaters where they were premiered.

As a film director, Ferreyra was not in favor of adapting great literary works. It was his point of view that their value is literary, and on screen they lost almost all they had of value, as the images needed a physical continuity, while in literature the action was imagined by the reader.

After producing *Perdón Viejita* (according to Couselo, Di Núbila and Roberto Di Chiara) Ferreyra went on tour with María Turgenova and some of his films looking for new markets. After leaving the United States he went to Spain, where he managed to get some exhibitions for his films, but the trip ended in total financial ruin and disenchantment. He was sent home by his friends in 1930. Outside of the country he had heard the advice of those who warned him of the coming of sound, and once back in Argentina, Ferreyra was to start a new phase in his career.

If José A. Ferreyra's silent films received little notice, those by Nelo Cosimi had fairly favorable reviews at the time. Casimi was born in Italy in 1894 and had lived in Argentina since the age of four. After working in films as an actor he started to write scripts and after 1922 he became a director. As a director Cosimi is probably the most interesting of the silent film period. He tried not to limit his activity to tango films and directed all kinds of movies.

When Cosimi's company merged with the S.A.C.H.A. Manzanera Company his films started to have a much more solid base than previous Argentine films, as well as intelligent promotions during the production (including information not necessarily related to them — for example the news of his marriage to the actress Chita Foras during the filming of *Corazón Ante la Ley*). Antonio Manzanera's company, within the limited resources of the Argentine film industry of the times, established the basis of the real industrialization of Argentine films, and in 1930 would successfully set in motion the Argentine sound film industry.

Una Nueva y Gloriosa Nación

From 1915 on, Hollywood studios sometimes made films that took place in Argentina. Many great stars took part in those productions, but in general the outcome left much to be desired. American films generally showed a superficial and false view of the country, and these productions normally did not do well in Argentina. The film producer Julián Ajuria tried to convince the big Hollywood studios to make a film with a credible and convincing Argentine theme. His attempts had no favorable reply, so he decided to finance the production himself in the United States, and use big movie stars. The film, to be called *Una Nueva y Gloriosa Nación*, had Francis X. Bushman in the leading role as Manuel Belgrano, in a story about the May 1810 Revolution. Its director was Albert Kelly, photography by Nicholas Musuraca and Georges Benôit, who had already done the photography for *¿Hasta Dónde?* and directed *Juan Sin Ropa* in Argentina. Of course the news reached the newspapers, which looked at it with total skepticism, as this commentary, published in *La Vanguardia* on the 7th of September 1927 shows:

> We do not expect much good from this film. We already know that the Yankees don't fool around with business of recreating period settings. And, above all, if its action should take place in Buenos Aires, capital of the Republic of Rio de Janeiro, you can imagine if there is room enough for the whims of a director's fantasy.

Months before the release of *Una Nueva y Gloriosa Nación*, once the press had access to the finished film, comments like the above disappeared — especially after the highest government authorities, including the president of the country, Marcelo T. de Alvear, had access to it. The exhibition was greeted favorably, and the film was praised both for the emotion that the work projected and for the educational value of its historical point of view. Julián Ajuria commissioned several Argentine intellectuals to design precisely and accurately, period costume. Museums and archives were consulted frequently to assure authenticity and the early criticism soon faded in the face of Ajuria's careful study and dedication to accuracy. The newspaper *La Vanguardia* published the following article on the 26th of April 1928, which reproduces a complete scene from the film:

> One of the most emotional scenes in the film is when we catch Belgano and Cisneros in a game of chess that could very well be symbolic, because they would

Poster announcing *Una Nueva y Gloriosa Nación* (Sociedad General Cine-matográfica, 1928).

meet again a short time after in the great revolutionary contest.

Belgrano, as a representative of Buenos Aires, and a great influence among the Creoles, was well received at the Viceroy's residence, who however did not know that he was one of the most ardent disseminators of revolutionary fire. Ideological enemies, they proceeded, however, with due caution, even though their apparently subtle conversations would reveal hidden intentions. "As you see, Belgrano" Cisneros would say during a game of chess, "...As soon as my king makes another move ... all your pawns will be defenseless."

"If my pawns were a people, they would need no more than this motion to finish the king!..." and underlining the phrase with a strong gesture, Belgrano answered the meaningful words of the Viceroy as he knew how, who, in truth, had meant to refer to the "pawns" of the revolution that was just beginning to take shape in those days.

This scene, described succinctly, from one of the situations at the beginning of the drama, easily lets you imagine the degree of interest that it acquires as the May revolution approaches.

These historical evocations, when mixed in with the romantic scenes in which Belgrano is the focal point, make up the plot of *Una Nueva y Gloriosa Nación*, show once again, how much can be expected from the screen in its reconstructive phase. Without doubt there is nothing as noble or worthy of public gratitude as recalling to mind in such a vivid manner the memory of our glorious past, of the days of rejoicing for the country and its immortal heroes.

The day before the film's release, the esteemed Argentine historian Ricardo Rojas wrote the following commentary:

The film called *Una Nueva y Gloriosa Nación* is one of the noblest efforts of the film industry, and perhaps the most interesting for our country. I have spoken out against the so-called "silent art" many times, but only because of the misuse that is done with it, with a repertoire that is generally corrupting of the people's moral and esthetic sensitivity. We are far from such a danger with this film, sober in its fanciful intrigue and serious in its patriotic episodes. Perhaps we could object to some details of historical value, but I will abstain from doing so in deference to the general merit of the work, and I pray that it starts a run of films of the same kind, for there are plenty of appropriate stories in Argentine tradition.

The private showing that took place a few days ago was an undeniable success, as we said at the time, The principal characters, Belgrano, Moreno, Castelli, Saavedra, Juan Balcarce, Alberti, Rodríguez Peña and other members of the first Junta are notably well characterized. Belgrano is outstanding, played with great dignity, ease and efficiency by the well-known actor Francis. X. Bushman. Jaqueline Logan, another actress well known to our audience, precisely acts as Monica, the heroine of the romance. The Cabildo, the old covered market, the Fort, are accurately reproduced. Among the spectacular scenes there is the battle of Salta, a charge of Güemes' gauchos, the creation of the flag at the river cliffs of Rosario, and others.

Una Nueva y Gloriosa Nación is a film that deserves a frank and outspoken encouragement for the effort that it meant, and for the movie itself.

The public finally knew *Una Nueva y Gloriosa Nación* on the 10th of March 1928 at the Cervantes Theater. The showing was accompanied by an orchestra of fifty musicians and a mixed choir with 30 voices playing a specially adapted score. With this film, Julián Ajuria, in his own words, wanted to "contribute to the popularization and greatness of Argentina," and also to stimulate the Argentine film industry to the prosperity he believed it would one day attain.

One of the principal merits of *Una Nueva y Gloriosa Nación* was the accurate reconstruction of the past, above all the scenes of the ball at the Fort, the meeting of the First Junta, at the Cabildo; and the Cabildo's façade and the old covered passage. The scene of the creation of and pledging to the flag, and the battle of Salta, with its formidable attack by the great gauchos, were moving but didn't pander to sentimental nationalism. The emotion flowed naturally.

Francis X. Bushman played a virile and handsome Belgrano, always in the role of the hero, sober and energetic. Jacqueline Logan played Mónica appropriately. Charles Hill Mailes managed to recreate the persona of Cornelio Saavedra with notable success. The Argentine actor Paul Ellis, whose real name was Benjamín Ingénito, played the part of the gaucho Juan Balcarce very well. At times he was placed too prominently in front in the group scenes, for example the meetings in front of the Cabildo, but for the large part his character was quite convincing. *Una Nueva y Gloriosa Nación* was not meant as an exact re-creation of the past, although it incorporated well-known historical facts. On the other hand, the romance between Belbrano and Mónica, was a careful and respectful fantasy.

FBO Pictures distributed the film in the United States. The title in English was *The Charge of the Gauchos*. The film company was in the process of changing into RKO Radio Pictures and sound films were starting; the film was cut and shown at double feature programs, and without a promotion effort similar to the one in Argentina it was not a success. In Argentina, *Una Nueva y Gloriosa Nación* was the most successful silent film of all. It was exhibited for two years, but the year after, the sound film revolution began and the film was removed from circulation for several years. Today, unfortunately, this film is lost. Most Argentine silent films suffered the same fate as *Una Nueva y Gloriosa Nación*. Almost all were lost, and the very few that survive are incomplete copies in very bad condition.

Julian Ajuria's purpose with *Una Nueva y Gloriosa Nación* was to stimulate the creation of an Argentine film industry. But it was not the time yet. Radio was developing breathtakingly, and before the silent film era ended people often went to the movies to hear their favorite orchestras rather than to see the film.

Although Hollywood films still dominated the market, everything would change with sound movies.

3

THE CINEMA ORCHESTRAS

Background Music for Silent Movies

Even though they had no sound, silent movies were never shown in silence. According to Roberto Di Chiara, the idea of accompanying films with music first appeared in bars and restaurants in Argentina when many of these establishments decided to install a screen in the back, and a projector next to the tables. There was generally a piano. The piano player, who looked at the film from one side, had a different and appropriate theme for each scene. For love scenes he played a waltz, for emotion a milonga and for drama a tango. Some more modest establishments did not have a piano, and the audience had to be satisfied with a violin. Curiously in the center of the city the musicians were men, while in the suburbs they were mostly women.

With the evolution of movies, the musical accompaniment also changed. Big scores were composed for big films. When the films were adapted from musical compositions, fragments of the original pieces of music were always included.

How was the music for films created? The film was simply projected in front of a musician who made a note of the different scenes to create a suitable background. He could end up with new, original themes, or the adaptation of popular themes. The big American and European film companies would soon distribute a series of instructions together with the rolls of film for the projectionists and musical directors of the cinemas, telling them how to put music to each scene. Furthermore, music editors always tried to include some theme or song with commercial potential, hoping to spur the sale of sheet music and records. In some cases the themes would

86

be composed in Argentina, and at times they were tangos. The cinemas in various countries did not necessarily follow the instructions of the film studios, and each theater could provide its own musical accompaniment, from a symphony orchestra and impressive choirs to an organ or a simple piano.

Only the most important cinemas of each city presented the films with a synchronized musical background. The rest, those with cheaper prices and generally far from the town center, were not so structured. Many of the greatest Argentine musicians would first appear in this capacity. Jorge Couselo says: "The story must have started with a piano, and it is not difficult to imagine contradictory things arising from the pranks of a musician bored stiff by routine. Oral tradition says that El Entrerriano may have been the background music of an Italian melodrama with Francesca Bertini, and La Cumparsita could have accompanied Tom Mix shootouts in the American Far-West. Foolishness like that contributed to the charm of mythological evenings at the cinema, till the prank got established, and the tango melodies even gained their independence from the fable that the beam of light projected onto the screen."

Enrique Delfino is possibly the most important Argentine composer of all time and not simply of tangos. He was the son of a concessionaire of a café in a theater, he showed musical talent from a young age, and when he was fifteen he landed a job as a pianist in a cinema, around 1909 or 1910 Delfino said. "I liked that job just fine, it allowed me to improvise all that I wanted at the piano. I was already a composer without knowing it. You had to shed light on what was happening on the screen, adding the appropriate music. In those days the audience wasn't demanding. You had to cover up the monotonous little noise, rather like a sewing machine, made by the projector as the film passed through. You had to hide it, fill it in with your own things. That's when I started to realize that I was an improviser."

During the silent movie period Enrique Delfino made a name for himself as a pianist in movie houses. People went to see him and not the movies; in his shows he combined humor, improvisation, and his own inborn talent as a tango player and composer. In 1919 Delfino started the great discography that would stretch the last days of his life. Among his other activities were compositions for plays and the music of fourteen Argentine films.

In 1917, when he was 14 years old, Sebastian Piana made his debut as a pianist in a cinema at Villa del Parque, a Buenos Aires neighborhood, to help his parents out financially and further his musical education. As there still was no official music conservatoire, Piana had to do what was

Enrique Delfino

called "orchestral practice" at the Cine-Teatro Mitre, in the Villa Crespo neighborhood. Besides films, *tonadilleras* (female Spanish popular-song singers), comic-musical duets, couples and trios of Spanish dancers, and more appeared there.

By way of José González Castillo, who was a friend of his father, Sebastian Piana was presented to the cellist Carlos Marchal, who was in charge of all the orchestras in Max Glücksmann's movie theaters. He was assigned to the Cine Park in the Palermo neighborhood to play the harmonium; all the Glücksmann orchestras used them because they could replace several wind instruments. According to Piana: "I earned a certain standing as a player of that instrument, especially because of my harmonic intuition; that is to say: as not all the arrangements had parts for the harmonium, I was obliged to replace them with a clarinet, saxophone, trombone, or any other instrument part. Since these were melodic, it was necessary to add the harmony to justify the character of that, by definition, harmonic instrument. My ease in enriching these parts made me stand out among my colleagues. One night the Maestro Ferruccio La Stella, a clarinetist and at the same time secretary to the Maestro Carlos Marchal, who as we know was in charge of the company's orchestras, turned up to inform me that I had been transferred to one of the company's most important theaters, the Palace Theater. It was in the seven hundreds of Corrientes Avenue, and together with the Grand Splendid, was one of their principal cinemas. I was a year at the Palace, and then I was sent to the Cine Electric."

There were not only pianists in the cinemas; there were also players of other instruments. The bandoneon player Federico Scorticati said that the musicians did not want to play in cabarets since these were the hardest jobs; they required the most effort and paid the least. According to the tango historian Luis Adolfo Sierra, the pianos that accompanied the movies in the Buenos Aires cinemas were gradually exchanged for the more popular and more highly valued tango orchestras: "Each orchestra had its redoubt in a certain cinema, where groups of fans, called 'barras' went daily — to listen to and to applaud their favorite musicians. The cinemas in the center of town attracted numerous and enthusiastic audiences with their orchestra programs, who paid less attention to the screen than to the way the music was played by the musical groups. But this new stage did not remove the tango from the Buenos Aires cafés and cabarets that had always enjoyed the presence of the essential tango orchestras, called 'orquestas típicas.'

Roberto Firpo and Francisco Canaro

Like any other music, the tango grew, leaving its primitive style behind. There are a large number of recordings in existence from the late teens to around 1920 but the different groups still did not have their own distinctive styles.

Orchestras began developing their own styles of playing tangos around the beginning of the twenties. According to Luis Adolfo Sierra: "The shape of the 'orquesta típica' had reached its definite form with what was commonly called the 'sexteto típico.' This group of two bandoneons, two violins, piano and double bass turned out to be the best and most representative musical group for this kind of music. And it was not an isolated occurrence, or the result of the musicians' determination, but they found in that combination of sounds the best musical format in which to propose all the different ways of playing the tango."

Two artists who gave definite shape to the tango orchestra were Roberto Firpo and Francisco Canaro. Firpo had added a piano to his 1913 recordings, and around 1917 Canaro brought the double bass into the orquesta típica.

Both musicians had an abundant recording history with the Max Glücksmann label, and also played in his cinemas. After playing in all the Glücksmann cinemas in Argentina and Uruguay, Firpo settled down in the Florida cinema, right in the center of Buenos Aires. Canaro, although he never played during the film projections, recorded several musical themes from them, and was a pioneer Argentine movie composer. He composed the theme for the film *Nobleza Gaucha* and in 1925 inaugurated the Paramount Cinema in the city of New York. Francisco Canaro was also dedicated to supporting the tango, largely by means of his union activities. He was a tenacious businessman, and later in his career a film producer.

Canaro and Firpo performed their music in styles based on their different personalities. They started to establish different approaches, the fore-
runners of the different styles that would be important in the twenties.
Instead of the rigid traditional scheme of playing with essentially simple
harmonies and an emphasized rhythm, other ideas appeared, inspired by
the wish to achieve more musicality in tango playing, enriching its technical and expressive possibilities.
    According to Sierra:

> Francisco Canaro never worried about the harmonic resources of his orchestras,
> he gave the groups that he directed a markedly accentuated rhythm, although
> with a denser sound and a faster beat than in primitive tangos; the undisputed
> originator of what is known as a square beat, sacrificing even the melody's pos-
> sibility of being sung in a flowing manner. All this was in an essentially dance-
> able concept of tango music, once that the original rhythmical division of the
> music of two by four (mistaken designation that still prevails in tango literature)
> had been changed to the correct four by eight time. With Robert Firpo, to the
> contrary, there was always a strong tendency towards essentially melodic forms
> of expression; the definitive inclusion and systematization of a piano in tango
> orchestras is owed to his wish to renew the esthetic concept of the music. He
> introduced a solid rhythmic base, flexible, agile, and soft, with a deliberate accen-
> tuation and taking great care of the balance of the sound, without loud and anti-
> musical and flashy resources. He gave special attention to the elegant use of
> nuances, on the basis of subtle intentions in impeccable good taste; a pre-emi-
> nence of singing strings and a legato sound, and an image of an orchestra with a
> permanently compact sound, although perfectly good for dancing to.

    Both Roberto Firpo and Francisco Canaro had many musicians in
their orchestras who would, simultaneously or at a later time, form their
own orchestras. Another thing that distinguished both of them was that
they were the first to give their solo instruments the chance to display
themselves.
    The Carnival celebrations gave dance orchestras the opportunity to
shine, and during these festivities many theaters and cinemas stopped
showing films; the seats were removed and the cinemas were converted
into dance halls. These dances were in fact annual tango festivals, and the
authors kept the introduction of their best compositions for these occasions, when they would receive enormous popular exposure. The 1917 carnival dances in the Colón Theater in the city of Rosario joined the
orchestras of Roberto Firpo and Francisco Canaro in what was, in those
times, a giant group. Among its members were Osvaldo Fresedo, Tito Roc-
catagliata, Agesilao Ferrazano, Juan Carlos Bazán, José Martínez, Leopoldo
Thompson, Cayetano Puglisi, Alejandro Michetti, Pedro Polito, Juan

Bautista Deambrogio (Bachicha) and Alejandro Scotti, besides the directors. This assembly was one of the first predecessors of the future great tango orchestras that would be created to play at the Carnival dances in Buenos Aires theaters and cinemas, and which sometimes had up to fifty musicians.

Osvaldo Fresedo, who was among the musicians who played at the 1917 carnival dances, grew in importance two years later, when he formed his first orchestra. Always sensitive to all kinds of improvements, he grew with the times without ever losing his unmistakable style and sound. Fresedo continuously managed to stand out during the musical transformation of the tango as a real leader in each stage of its development. Fresedo's first records are from 1917, and his last from 1980.

According to Luis Adolfo Sierra:

> From the initial stages of his first orchestra, around 1919, you could already notice the musical quality and the balance of sound that was going to prevail as the unmistakable and dominant mark of his professional career. He introduced interesting effects, such as very soft "staccatos," "legato crescendos" and attractive syncopated effects in a constant array of tints in a varied display of musical colors. He also gave his musicians more opportunities to shine, introducing eight bar piano solos and placing the violin "contracantos" (normally incorrectly called "harmonies") in the foreground with more expressive autonomy, and at the same time renewing the expressive and sober phrasing of the left hand on the bandoneon. Fresedo even allowed himself the luxury of introducing in his more advanced orchestras some instrumental timbres that were not traditional in the tango, all in an orchestral context of perfect synchronization and refined good taste. And of course, keeping the intact rhythmic and melodic concepts that are the very essence of our tango. That is to say, the attractions of its musical beauty intelligently combined with the unmistakable truthfulness of an eminently popular artistic expression.

Fresedo's popularity was such that for a time (between 1925 and 1928, when he went on tour in the United States) he had four orchestras playing at the same time: the official one that made his recordings, another at the Fénix cinema (with pianist Carlos Di Sarli in charge), the third in a bar that he owned and a fourth in a cabaret. The director passed a short time with each, going from one to the other, so as to be present at all in person.

Juan Carlos Cobián was a pianist who appeared with Fresedo and who had started out accompanying films in a neighborhood cinema a great composer, he introduced several ideas that he had previously put in his scores into the music of Buenos Aires, freeing it from its musical primitivism. As a leader he introduced substantial variations in the use of the piano as the principal instrument in the orchestra, using the "arpeggioed tenth" in the left hand, and he adopted the method of filling in the space in the melodies; up to then its principal function was rhythmical. He also introduced short instrumental solos for the violin, the bandoneon and the piano. His first orchestra played for a short time at the Abdullah Club in 1923 and recorded a series of records for the Victor Company. It disbanded when the composer decided to go to the United States. Nevertheless, his influence would be fundamental to the musical development of the tango.

The Impact of Julio De Caro and His Orchestra

Julio De Caro, who had been one of Cobian's violinists, reunited some of the members of Juan Carlos Cobián's orchestra, heading a group with a distinctive style and creating a school of music ahead of its times. It would be the most important movement for change in the history of the tango.

According to Luis Adolfo Sierra and other tango historians, and judging by his recordings for the Victor Company (which had him under contract from 1924 to 1928), the Julio De Caro orchestra marked a real revolution in tango playing. The orchestra incorporated new musical techniques, especially in harmony and counterpoint, without debasing the tango's own rhythmical and melodic essence. The harmonized piano accompaniment, the variations and the phrasing of the bandoneons, the contracantos of the fiddles weaving melodies in pleasing contrast to the central theme, and the piano and bandoneon solos, which had a harmonic and tonal richness unknown until then, were some of the contributions that Julio De Caro's musicians brought into tango playing. Added to them was a rhythmical richness, in which the difference in each of the instrumental sections could be perceived as an attractive background, while the violins and the bandoneons sang in front.

As Luis Adolfo Sierra observes:

> Buenos Aires was going through the moment of great success of tango orchestras in the silent screen cinema halls. And the impresario August Alvarez offered Julio De Caro a contract for an unimaginable sum of money for those times, to perform at the Select Lavalle with a great promotion and an assured repercussion, artistically speaking. The audience went there exclusively to listen to the orchestra, without bothering at all about the film projection. Nobody bothered to find out what film they were projecting. And seeing the very widespread slogan "the genuine porteño melody orchestra" printed on the programs of the Select Lavalle, it can be admitted that the work of Julio De Caro's orchestra was already a true tango school. The front rows were invariably occupied by musicians and young

The Julio De Caro orchestra in a 1926 Victor advertisement.

future tango lovers that absorbed his style and formed their esthetic background so as to add their creative talents later to the ideas and forms first revealed by those admirable and very original musicians. Many great tango players that appeared after the Julio De Caro orchestra cinema period have confessed their emphatic conviction that if they had not been nurtured by the essence of that pioneering band of tango players, very possibly their musical destiny would have been very different, and perhaps having nothing to do with the tango.

In 1928, while also conducting tours in Argentina and Brazil, the orchestra left the Select Lavalle to go briefly to the Petit Splendid, and spent the rest of the year at the Renacimiento cinema. In 1929 the orchestra changed cinemas for the last time when it went to the Real Cine, as

Julio and Francisco De Caro

well as changing their recording company from Victor to the new Brunswick label.

Orchestras and Musicians from Those Times

During 1924, a cinema in the Constitución neighborhood decided to exchange the pianist for an orchestra directed by Enrique (Minotto) Di Cicco (one of many instances in which he left Francisco Canaro's orchestra, where he was the first bandoneon from 1920 to 1956, for a time). The experiment was such a success that soon many cinemas in Buenos Aires were striving to employ the most famous tango orchestras, and this went on until the firm establishment of sound films in 1930. There was no synchronization between music and image: the audience went to hear its favorite orchestras and not to see the films. With very few exceptions the musicians that belonged to those groups would also play in others, which they sometimes conducted, or in recording sessions. The most important group that did not share its musicians was conducted by the fiddler Julio De Caro.

The appearance of the Julio De Caro Orchestra at the Select Lavalle in 1926 began a trend of placing the orchestras in the most important cinemas in downtown Buenos Aires, located mainly on Lavalle Street between Carlos Pellegrini and Florida and on the surrounding streets. The exhibitors sought to attract the public with different orchestras and soon a whole number of musicians managed to stand out; some even left recordings as evidence of those times.

Luis Adolfo Sierra describes two opposing ways of playing the tango. On one side was the "evolutionary" tendency, started by Juan Carlos Cobián, Osvaldo Fresedo, and Julio De Caro. According to the newspapers from the time it was more a concert music than dance music. On the other was the "traditional" tendency, attached to the old ways of playing, that is to say with an evident predominance of the rhythm (conventionally accepted as the most danceable form) over all harmonic concerns. However this separation is arbitrary. All the orchestras soaked up Julio De Caro's ideas. Roberto Firpo always sought musical improvement and had very distinguished musicians in his various groups, even letting other and better pianists with a superior technique than his lead them occasionally, while always keeping a carefully arranged interpretative structure and a notable tuning of the whole.

Francisco Canaro, feeling De Caro's impact, decided to make a series of recordings for Max Glücksmann called Serie Sinfónica (Symphonic Series) starting in 1928. Without giving up his traditional characteristic rhythm, he presented elaborate musical arrangements played by a larger group of instruments, obtaining some of his most important artistic triumphs. The Serie Sinfónica was discontinued in 1933; Canaro had adopted its structure for all his public performances and recordings. Another musician, under contract to Glücksmann, Juan Maglio "Pacho," who was still as popular as in 1912 (although he no longer played the bandoneon) applied many of the concepts introduced by De Caro in the group that he led in those days.

Pedro Maffia and Pedro Laurenz had been an unforgettable pair of bandoneons in Julio De Caro's orchestra, enjoyed by all those who went to the Select Lavalle in 1926. (Fortunately, ten recordings were made for the Victor Company [RCA Victor since 1929].) At the end of 1926 Maffia created his own orchestra; it had its debut in March 1927, at the Electric Palace Cinema, and then moved to the Hindu Cinema in 1929 and started to record for Brunswick. Maffia assumed a style that was a replica of De Caro's, which he had helped to create. His orchestra had a more muted sound and he always followed an unalterable stylistic line, stressing the quality of his versions and his complementary choice of collaborators.

When he started recording for Brunswick he included a cello, giving his group a more velvety sound. Pedro Maffia performed bandoneon duets with Alfredo De Franco (recording four tunes for Max Glücksmann in 1927); Pedro Laurenz, his ex-partner in the Julio De Caro Orchestra, did the same with Armando Blasco (making a recording in 1926 for RCA).

After thirteen years with Roberto Firpo and, almost simultaneously, ten, with Francisco Canaro as first violin, Cayetano Puglisi decided to form his own orchestra to explore ideas for renewal of his musical expression. These included a very deliberate rhythmical accent, with a purposeful and appropriate instrumental display by each of the soloists. By doing this,

Cayetano Puglisi's orchestra

Sierra observes, Puglisi was: "Creating a concept of such quality in tango playing that several decades from his fleeting and temporary recording period — a series of 32 recordings for RCA Victor — those recordings prove that at the end of the twenties all the conditions were given for the evolution of the instrumental configuration of the tango, confirming the truth that nothing new was missing in the most genuine tango formations that laid down the permanent and inalterable essence of our instrumental tango."

Luis Petrucelli was an excellent bandoneon player with a delicate sensitivity in line with Pedro Maffia; they were in the Julio De Caro Orchestra together. After playing in several orchestras, he formed his own in 1927 to play at the American Palace, and the following year he signed a contract with RCA Victor, where he recorded some excellent records.

Carlos Marcucci was one of the most prestigious and admired bandoneon players in tango history and, according to Luis Adolfo Sierra, one of the Argentine musicians most artistically relevant. His 1927 orchestra was one of the best of the period; after working in theaters and cafés he was signed up by the Metropol Cinema, and in 1929 left a short series of excellent recordings for RCA. Marcucci's musical talent allowed him to perform some admirable bandoneon solos and duos with Salvador Grupillo that have, fortunately, been preserved on disks.

Carlos Marcucci's orchestra

The orchestra conducted by the fiddler Agesilao Ferrazano and the pianist Julio Fava Pollero also had an important part to play in the cabarets and cinemas of the time. When they were signed up to record for RCA Victor, according to Raúl Lafuente, they were made to look as if they were separate; they were billed as Ogesilao Ferrazana and his orquesta tipica, or Julio Pollero and his orquesta típica, but it was actually the same band.

Ciraico Ortíz was one of the best-loved bandoneon players; his phrasing was unmistakable, whatever orchestra he was playing in. After passing through Roberto Firpo's and Francisco Canaro's orchestra in 1925 he became an established musician at RCA Victor, and also presented his first orchestra at the Gaumont, near to the National Congress Building. Two years later, at the same cinema, he appeared in a trio with the guitar players Vicente Spina and Ramón Méndez. The Ciriaco Ortíz Trio was one of the most successful Argentine music groups of all time, asserting the role of the guitar, which had been displaced to a secondary role of simply accompanying singers. Ortíz later had an important part to play with different groups that were conducted by Ortiz himself at times. Besides conducting he always played himself, and was outstanding leading his trio, starting an abundant series of recordings in 1929 playing tangos and folk tunes, that went on till the end of his days.

Anselmo Aieta, one of the most celebrated bandoneon players, was a longtime performer in the downtown Buenos Aires cafés, and in the Hindú Cinema. He was also the author of some very important tangos, headed a group with a very simple musical concept, and left a series of recordings for the Columbia label. Another bandoneon player, Juan Bautista Guido (el Lecherito, the little milkman) headed an orchestra whose style was the heavily based on rhythm, generally accepted as the best style for dancing. He performed at the Real Cine and left a series of Victor records. Francisco Pracánico, who today is best remembered as a composer, made his debut as a pianist at a cinema in the city of San Fernando at the age of 13. As leader of his own orchestra he was in line with those that put the accent on rhythm, and not melody; he recorded for the Electra Company in 1926 and 1927.

Among the orchestras dedicated to a dance style of music, there was one lead by the pianist and composer Francisco Lomuto. His popularity rivaled that of his great friend Francisco Canaro, also his rival as an entrepreneur. Signed up by Max Glücksmann, he started his recording activity by recording eight piano duets with Héctor Quesada in 1921 that are unfortunately lost today. He formed his own orchestra in 1923, with which he continued to record for Nacional-Odeon, providing it with an instantly recognizable color and a zesty and fast rhythm. In 1926 he had his first appearance at the Petit Splendid Cinema, and finally moved on to the Select Suipacha, where Lomuto had a great acceptance among the audience, increasing his popularity as a composer. According to Oscar Zucchi: "His orchestra had a very definite personality, good rhythm, and was stylistically orthodox, and not in a creative quest, but rather looking for an adequate sound for dancing, pleasant to the ear. In another order of things, he was noticeable for his strange finales, with a diminished seventh as a signature."

When the Select Lavalle lost the Julio De Caro Orchestra around the end of 1927, the exhibitor Augusto Alvarez hired another that was headed by the fiddlers Edgardo Donato and Roberto Zerrillo. They were so successful that the next year the cinema programs announced them as the "Típica Criolla Donato-Cerrillo, 'The 9 Tango Aces,' the most formidable typical Creole orchestra ever heard," and at the foot of the page it said: "9 — outstanding musicians and maestros — 9."

In 1929 this orchestra had its recording debut for the Brunswick label. Around 1930 the society had a friendly parting of ways, and Donato continued to lead the orchestra alone. Oscar Zucchi says that while they were together the orchestra was contained, with a deliberate rhythm and few moments for displaying soloists in the different instrumental parts. When Donato started his career as an independent leader, you could perceive a more dynamic phrasing, with a clear preeminence of the bandoneons, the inclusion of some brief cello and piano solos and frequent participations of the director playing pizzicatos. Towards the end of the silent movie era, in 1930. Edgardo Donato and his orchestra inaugurated the Broadway Cinema.

Among the tango orchestras that performed in the silent movie cinemas, two others would deservedly reach success several years later. The violin player Juan D'Arienzo headed a group that played at the opening of the Hindú Cinema in 1927, earning enough popularity to allow him to make a series of sixty records for the Electra label between 1928 and 1929, when the record company closed down. It had a style that was exactly the opposite of the one that he would make famous a few years later: a calm rhythm, with a tendency to legatos, an abundance of solo instruments and no piano accents.

The pianist Carlos Di Sarli grew in stature and popularity towards the end of the thirties. All the characteristics that would distinguish his later orchestra were already present in his first orchestra; that orchestra played at the Renacimiento cinema and left fifty excellent recordings for RCA Victor, between 1928 and 1931, that were appreciated by the critics of the time. According to Luis Adolfo Sierra, "The Di Sarli style, which has remained unaltered since its beginnings back in 1926, is essentially similar to that of the early Osvaldo Fresedo. Without major harmonic worries, the Carlos Di Sarli orchestra versions are invariably tied to an established format, whose interest is achieved by way of a very precise range of hues, alternating in very successful contrasts the 'staccatos' with the 'legatos,' and the 'crescendos' with the 'pianissimos.' The use of the strings in unison, almost always leaving out the bandoneons as the first voices, and the permanent presence of Di Sarli with his inimitable leading on the piano, as well as the 'contracantos' of the first violin, give the group its characteristic color."

Argentine Jazz

The tango was the favorite music of Argentina when the twenties started, although it had not displaced the folk music that could still be heard in country's cinemas. Jazz also became popular in those days.

While it is true that the big recording companies made most of their money with records made by popular local artists, they also imported records. Jazz had appeared in the United States, and a market opened up for the sale of this music, which was played by local musicians and orchestras who would alternate with their tango colleagues in the cinemas.

The jazz pioneer in Argentina was Adolfo Carabelli. His musical origins were classical, however. He was talented enough to play concerts in the most important halls of Buenos Aires when he was a child. When he was fifteen he went to study in Italy at the Milan conservatoire. He returned to Argentina when the First World War was declared, around November 1914, offering a concert at the reception hall of the newspaper *La Prensa*. On that occasion he showed his talent both as a performer of the classical repertoire and as a composer. Around 1917 Carabelli began to play jazz, after meeting a pianist, Lipoff, who came to the country as an accompanist to the celebrated ballerina Anna Pavlova and played in the same program as Canabelli. He formed his first jazz band, the River Band, with the idea of progressing in this new style. By 1922 he already had a band in his name that was the most popular of its time. The band, which was known for the variety and quality of its musicians, who in many cases came from the tango, played all the foreign novelties for the first time in Argentina. After recording for Electra, he transferred to Victor, where he was also taken on as artistic manager. A short time after, Carabelli was leading his band at the Gran Cine Florida, sharing the billboard with Roberto Firpo and the organist Julio Perceval. In this manner, as Sebastián Piana remembered, the cinemas broke new ground regarding orchestras.

They had no longer one, but three: one that played classical music, one that played tangos, and another that played jazz.

Although there is not much written about the jazz bands that had a parallel history to that of their tango colleagues, we can mention that Pedro Maffia shared the billboard of the Electric Palace with the Eleuterio Irribarren band. This band had a very long recording history with the Max Glücksmann Company, recording from 1922 until the end of the silent movie period. Cayetano Puglisi also shared the billboard of the Paramount Cinema with a jazz band lead by Gordon Stretton.

Adolfo R. Avilés also deserves mention; he was a very good composer of folk and tango tunes, but he was

Adolfo Carabelli

only successful playing jazz at the Paris Cinema. He left a series of recordings for Max Glücksmann, starting in 1925.

Other popular jazz bands in those times were the González Jazz Band, which recorded for Electra; the band lead by the banjo player Nicolás Verona; Henri Binstock's group; and Eduardo Armani's band. While they were all successful; they could not be compared to their American colleagues.

The impact and popularity of these bands led several prestigious tango musicians, such as Francisco Canaro, Roberto Firpo and Francisco Lomuto, to play jazz and even compose it. This happened between 1922 and 1923. At first they used instruments that had nothing to do with the tango, such as drums, trumpets, and other instruments, exclusively for the recording of fox trots and shimmies. Little by little these instruments joined the bandoneons in all their recordings. That is how Francisco Canaro (who was admired by American musicians) used a trumpet or a Hawaiian guitar intelligently in his tango recordings, just as Roberto Firpo was to use a trumpet or Francisco Lomuto a clarinet. Lomuto in particular stood out in the world of jazz, and his fox trot "Hay que Aprender a Bailar" from 1931 was favorably compared to the best from outside the country.

Fortunately, many of these orchestras cut disks for the recording companies, leaving documentary evidence of the period. RCA Victor, under the management of Adolfo Carabelli, managed to popularize many tango musicians, and challenge Disco Nacional-Odeón. However, the artistic manager of this company, Mauricio Godard, had the most popular artists of the time, putting the accent on jazz and folk music. The bandoneonist Rafael Rossi, who was signed by Max Glücksmann in 1927 to record folk tunes (although he later included tangos), became the most successful artist in the company and stayed there until 1980. Glücksmann's company, Nacional-Odeón was among the conglomerate of recording companies that made up Polyphone (later was called Gramophone). The different record labels that made up Gramophone had many Argentine groups in Europe under contract for the purpose of recording tangos. But these groups, which were distributed by Glücksmann in Argentina, never managed to become popular in at home.

It is not possible to end this examination of the silent movie musicians without mentioning the Orquesta Típica Victor, created exclusively for recording tangos. This orchestra was born in 1925, by the initiative of Adolfo Carabelli (who had never been devoted to the tango until then), to fill the vacancy left by the Osvaldo Fresedo orchestra when it left Victor to go to Disco Nacional-Odeón. Carabelli wanted an attraction with the same prestige and quality, and he found it. Its musicians were taken from the cinemas where they headed their own groups. The Orquesta Típica Victor was so successful that a few years later Brunswick and Columbia would create their own similar groups, the first conducted by Pedro Maffia and later Juan Polito, and the second by Alberto Castellano, although neither reached the popularity of the RCA Victor orchestra.

The orchestra's personnel changed a lot, but the departing musicians were always replaced by others of excellent quality, and it was able to endure throughout the thirties, ending in 1944. Besides tangos and folk themes, the Orquesta Típica Victor recorded several fox trots. The orchestra left more than three hundred recordings, with a style that held closely to the original score, with well-adjusted instruments, an essentially danceable rhythm, and an adequate display of the numerous soloists that successively played in it. Among the musicians that took part we can find Luis Petrucelli, Nicolás Primiani, Ciriaco Ortiz, Vicente Gorrese (Kalisay), Agesilao Ferrazano, Manlio Francia, Eugenio Romano, Humberto Constanzo, Elvino Vardaro, Cayetano Puglisi, Federico Scorticati, Bernardo Germino, Fausto Frontera, Eduardo Armani, Orlando Carabelli, Carlos Marcucci, Eugenio Nóbile, Jaime Gosis, Pedro Laurenz, Antonio Buglione, Aníbal Troilo and others.

Film Exhibitions in the Silent Movie Period

As Julio Nuder said, during the silent movie period the public cared little about the movie, but wanted an orchestra. The audience showed their approval with their applause (to the great disgust of the movie actors) while the exhibitors gauged the degree of acceptance of the musicians with a stopwatch and considered whether it was worthwhile to add a new section. The films did not have a standard projection speed, and the way that they were presented was based upon the commercial interests of each cinema.

Even though they went to listen to the orchestras, the public always realized what the situation with the film was, and made itself heard with its protests. As the films were not shown at the right speed, the details were lost, and the copies ended up by being ruined. So, around 1924, Max Glücksmann decided to give each of the exhibitors of his films a list with the exact length of each and the approximate projection time, at a normal speed. Nothing seemed to end the problem, and the cinemas' projectionists were unfairly blamed by the audience. When the films were shown too fast — it was always the management's decision or due to the need to keep to a timetable — or when the films were in bad shape, the audience always ended up insulting the operator.

These operators surely deserved more respect than they received from the audience on those occasions, as they themselves were victims of the situation. Furthermore, they had to do a really difficult job. According to *La Vanguardia*, on the 22nd of June 1927, no projection room in Buenos Aires the conditions stipulated by the law. Also, none was in an adequate condition to ensure the health of the workers who had to do their job there.

By the end of the silent period, it was evident that the cinemas had done practically nothing to solve these problems. Buenos Aires City Hall had also done nothing to stop films from being shown faster than the right speed. So, the cinemas managed to present four shows instead of three. The problem was more evident in the cinemas on Lavalle Street, and on others nearby. The large number of theaters in this small radius allowed the public to choose the show that attracted them most in a few minutes. The audience's complaints were never acknowledged by the powers that be, and the public was forced to pay high prices for films that could not be appreciated properly, due to the high speed at which they were shown.

4

BROADCASTING IN ARGENTINA

The Beginnings

There was reason for celebration in Argentina on the 27th of August 1924: the wireless radio celebrated its fourth year, and during that period it had developed extraordinarily fast. On its fourth anniversary all the radio stations in the country joined together to honor the day, commemorating the original transmission in 1920. On that occasion, Miguel Mugica, Enrique T. Susini, César Guerrico, and Luis Romero Carranza transmitted a complete opera, Wagner's *Parsifal*, from the Coliseo Theater in Buenos Aires. To duplicate that transmission, all the radio stations of the country stopped broadcasting for 30 minutes, and they used the same transmitter used four years earlier.

The original transmission on the 27th of August 1920 was the first broadcast in the world, meant for the public in general, and it was meant to be continued despite its experimental character.

According to the radio historian Eduardo Blanco, the broadcast made the people responsible insist on continuing their work, always seeking improvement. "Almost without trying," Sussini said, "we inaugurated broadcasting in the world, as only two months after our broadcast was a similar one done in the United States, and a year passed before they started to transmit programs like the ones we were doing." The success of the 1920 transmission was reflected in a comment published by *La Razon* the next day:

> It is possible for a lot of people to ignore something at the same time simple and marvelous. Hidden between chimneys, ventilation tubes, telephone and power poles, spreading over the roofs of the houses of the sensitive and alert city, there

Enrique T. Susini

are a good number of radio antennas. They correspond to an equal number of transmitters and receivers, belonging to the Order of Marconi, for private use and all authorized.

Somebody had the happy idea of putting a powerful microphone high up in the Coliseo Theater. And last night, a sound wave snaked, worm-like, from 9 P.M. to midnight through space, as if covering the whole city in subtle clouds of harmonies: the most capricious, rich and charged with noble emotions.

And for three hours, and not only those secret pioneers, but all those who by reason of their trade, or by chance — sailors on ships with radios, operators of radio electric stations, all slaves to listening, had the present of *Parsifal*, Wagner's masterpiece, that was being performed in the above mentioned theater.

Good sowers, they threw fistfuls of emotion into space to be picked by all that hungered and thirsted for them. And I declare that those benefiting could have believed that those divine notes came from heaven....

During 1921 Radio Argentina grew in various ways: the Ministry of the Navy gave it an identifying sign, L.O.R., in an attempt to organize a growth that was already beginning to be both explosive and chaotic, and its transmitting power was multiplied fourfold, allowing better reception. Besides the operas from the Coliseo Theater, to which were later added those from the Colón and Cervantes theaters, transmissions of more popular music were organized. On the 12th of October 1922, Marcelo T. de Alvear, on his inauguration, became the first Argentine president to speak using the new means of communication. Following business logic, the merchants that already sold radio receivers thought it necessary to install new transmitting stations, so by the end of 1922 Radio Cultura, Radio, Sudamérica and Radio Brusa appeared. The important thing was to keep up regular transmissions, and that the signal should not cut off suddenly.

By 1923 there were approximately 150,000 radio receivers in the country, each serving two or more persons. The radio programs transmitted were by then almost all made in Argentina. By the next year broadcasting had become even more important. The La Plata University opened its own radio station on the 5th of April with the idea of broadcasting the popular lectures given in its halls so that they could be heard with the most rudimentary receivers in the country.

More time was to pass before rules were set for the operation of the broadcasters.

The Rapid Development of the Broadcasting Industry Compared to Argentine Cinema

When the twenties started it seemed as if Argentine cinema was heading for fame. Between then and the advent of sound movies it lost much ground that it would find hard to recover. Without popular artists, its absence of industrial foresight caused it to lose viewers.

On the other hand, in the years between 1920 and 1924 broadcasting had an extremely fast development, becoming an important element of everyday life. Theater and music entered the home by way of the different radio stations, and received a massive and sympathetic support. The live performances of the artists who also performed on the radio were helped by the publicity that the radio gave them. Merchants discovered in radio the best way to advertise their merchandise, and they often paid with goods instead of money, starting a habit that still goes on today, with artists and technicians taking home cans of oil, soap, coffee, and other products.

The most famous orchestras from the cinemas and cabarets, and the most popular artists of the times, did not perform on the radios then. Nobody could pay them the money they wanted. What is more, almost all of them were under contract with recording companies, and were forbidden to perform on the radio, which was seen as a competitor.

The radios, then, had to find their own artists, small groups that passed the time of day going from one broadcaster to another, accompanying singers in international or criollo themes. Some of the musicians who led these groups were Cátulo Castillo, Antonio Sureda, Ricardo Brignolo, Francisco Pracánico and Antonio Polito.

The radio is a means of communication for those who can imagine characters, situations, views, without seeing them. The first news programs consisted of reading the principal Buenos Aires newspapers. As many stations were in theaters, they adapted a theatrical structure to their needs, giving birth to the radio-play. According to Enrique Bravo "The radio-plays, as has been rightly said before, inherited from the newspaper serial its exuberant action, full of changing options, comings and goings, quick

decisions, dramatic outcomes, cut off just when the half-hour assigned to each episode was finishing. Some plays reached a length of an hour and a half."

According to Elena dos Santos:

A concomitant phenomenon was the proliferation of artists. All those having a penchant for music or the stage, very difficult to carry out in the years before, had the radio at the reach of his hand and of his desires of progress and fulfillment. The artistic circuit grew surprisingly. More devotees and more listeners demanded more artists. The first to answer was the great city, then the cities inland, and finally the whole country. The dream of being an artist was a fever that caught men and women, young and old alike.

Buenos Aires broadcasting stations started to sprout like mushrooms in a favorable rainy season, until there were more than fifteen. These radios (Cultura, Callao, Prieto, París, Naciónal, etc.) were like family homes. The radio threw out the solemnity of the theater, stage, lights, the distance from the character who was up there onstage, and the audience down here, in the stalls. The radio made people feel that to be an artist was not something strange, but something simple and easy to reach. Even the radio owners had artistic whims. Señor Teodoro Prieto, owner of the station called after himself, and a radio receiver seller, closed the circuit playing leading man in a radio troupe, together with the actress and singer Herminia Velich.

However, the most popular artists still did not have access to the radios. That only happened after 1924, when the recording industry understood the importance of radio broadcasting for the diffusion of its products before a growing massive audience.

The First Transmissions of Official Ceremonies, Sports, and Other Events

The development of Argentine radio broadcasting was not without its ups and downs. But from these drawbacks came the necessary solutions that would turn the radio into a powerful means of communication in the country. Argentine cinema never achieved successes similar to those of radio broadcasting in those days.

With the transmission of the Firpo vs. Dempsey boxing match in 1923, radio found a show with which to attract a large audience to the radio sets, anxious to follow the details of the events. A year later, on the 28th of September 1924, a milestone was reached with the first transmission of a football match, a sport that was to reign over many radio stations from that point forward.

Opposite: A 1923 broadcasting advertisement

In that first match, the Argentine national team faced Uruguay. The journalist Aldo Rossi was in charge of the transmission. As there still was no experience in transmitting football matches by radio, the audience had to have a plan of the football field, divided into numbered squares, and the speaker had to say in what part of the field the ball was and where the action was occurring. This system turned out to be too complicated and was discarded a short time later.

Both the match and the transmission were interrupted due to incidents caused by the public in the stadium, which were also transmitted over the radio. Several days later, on the 3rd of October 1924, the game was continued, and its details were broadcast again.

Federico Valle had the historic soccer match filmed, and made into a movie that reflected the occasion with a noteworthy sharpness, according to the newspaper *La Razon*, and without missing any of its most interesting details. The film was presented a week after the match.

On the 19th of July 1925 a series of gym classes were started on L.O.X. Radio Cultura, backed by the YMCA, and with the pianist and composer Adolfo R. Avilés (who played jazz at the París Cinema, leading his orchestra) played the musical accompaniment of the classes.

In 1925 the radios also started to broadcast the official time. The pioneer was L.O.V. Radio Brusa, and *La Prensa* printed the following on the 28th of October:

> Adopting a procedure put into practice in the United States by some broadcasters that re-transmit on their respective wavelengths the signals that the department of the Navy of that Republic emits daily through their powerful radio station N.A.A., in Arlington, near Washington, the broadcasting station L.O.V. that works from our metropolis has started to re-transmit the hourly "beeps" that the Ministry of the Navy transmits to the navigators, every day except Sundays, up to 10 P.M., using the radio station L.I.H. at Dársena Norte.
>
> With that in mind, a receiver has been placed at the L.O.V. station on the same wavelength as L.I.H. to pick up its time signals, and re-transmit them after amplifying them conveniently, passing them on to the microphone circuit of L.O.V., so that the re-transmission is simultaneous, and therefore without error.
>
> The hourly "beeps" of L.I.H. are five, as is well known, each of which is preceded by other "beeps" at one second intervals, but so as not to tire its audience the station L.O.V. only re-transmits during the minute before the last "beep" that marks 10 o'clock sharp, and is announced by 11 "beeps," followed after 24 seconds of silence by the "beep" indicating 10 P.M.

From the beginning, the radio stations read the news directly from the Buenos Aires papers. The first case of a printed media going on the air took place when L.O.Z. Radio La Nación went over the airwaves for the first time in November 1925. The daily newspaper of the same name was the owner of the broadcaster, and the brackets under that name lasted exactly ten years, when they became Radio Mitre.

The first opera and concert transmissions from the Colón Theater were in 1923, but the next year the broadcasts were suspended because they interfered with those from the Navy Ministry. This ministry was originally the one that controlled the broadcasting stations until the responsibility was transferred later to the Secretaría de Correos y Telégrafos, sección Radiocomunicaciones (Mail and Telegraph Secretariat, Radio Communications section).

Once the technical hurdle was resolved another appeared. This time it had to do with money. As the fee demanded by the theater for the transmissions was prohibitive, several broadcasters decided to transmit operas from other theaters. The public protested about the impossibility of enjoying transmissions from the Colón Theater, and around 1925 the Municipality of the City of Buenos Aires decided to set up its own station for that purpose. It would also be used for Government for the broadcasting of official ceremonies. The 23rd of May 1927 L.O.S. (later L.S.1) Radio Municipal was on the air from the Colón Theater.

On the 13th of February 1928 something happened that would have wide effects: L.O.O. Radio Prieto started to transmit the news between 8 A.M. and 9 A.M., highlighting the most important information in the morning papers. From then on, practically all the stations would have news broadcasts.

When 1928 arrived, radio broadcasting in Argentina was a powerful business when compared to the local film industry, and the sound movie revolution was still a year away. But, how powerful was it? With the change of national authorities, in October, the new government discovered that most of the stations did not occupy the space assigned them, causing overcrowding among the broadcasters. The state itself was responsible for the congestion because it had the power of granting the corresponding licenses, and it decided to establish a timetable from 8 A.M. to 4 P.M. and another between 4 P.M. and 12 P.M. to be distributed alternately between stations in such a way as to avoid superimposition of spaces. The resolution was to go into effect in 24 hours starting from the 15th of November.

Facing this situation all the broadcasting stations stopped transmitting all that day. The stations could not obey that resolution when they had signed contracts with artists, advertising agencies and technicians. The next day the broadcasters started transmitting again, and the government agreed to negotiate. Because of this conflict all radio stations united in the Asociación Nacional de Broadcasters, with the purpose of defending their interests.

The Alliance Between the Record Industry and Broadcasting

In the beginning, radio consisted of the live transmission of events. The technical difficulties, both in transmission and in reception, made the use of records difficult, and the big recording companies had in the beginning forbidden the reproduction of their records by the broadcasters. The artists under contract with these companies were also forbidden to perform at the radio stations.

The recording companies did not take long to discover the usefulness of radio in promoting their productions and making them known, and in time the use of records was regulated. But the public prefered to listen to its favorite artists live.

Max Glücksmann, who had the license to exclusively commercialize the Naciónal-Odeón records, decided to join Antonio Devoto and Benjamín Gache in 1922 to set up an experimental broadcasting station, originally called TFF Radio Grand Splendid, in the same building as the cinema with the same name. In those first years of trials the orchestra from the cinema and the one from next door (Capitol, also belonging to Glücksmann) took part in the station's programs.

On the 9th of July 1924 L.O.Y. Radio Naciónal (later L.R.3 Radio Belgrano) started transmitting. With this event the alliance between the broadcasting and recording industries became effective, when Rosita Quiroga, a singer under contract with Victor Talking Machine, was presented in its transmissions. Victor was Max Glücksmann's greatest rival, but until then it had never been able to compete with his control over the most admired figures in popular music. From then on many artists who performed for L.O.Y. were called on to record. Among these the most distinguished was Agustín Magaldi, who also took part in the opening transmission of Radio Naciónal, and who, only a few months after, started a successful career on records singing duos with Pedro Noda and as soloist. Perhaps other artists did not have the same success, but at least they left some recordings that are testimonials of this period of the beginnings of Argentine broadcasting. But not all of the most popular artists of the future RCA Victor performed on the radio: the company's most popular orchestra, Osvaldo Fresedo's, did not do anything except record until the 26th of October 1925, when he left the company in disagreement over money, going over to Disco Naciónal-Odeón, where Glücksmann made him perform before the microphones at Splendid. One of the first tangos that he made known then was "Perdón Viejita"; it was sufficiently popular to be made into a film by José A. Ferreyra.

The appearance of the Victor Company's artists on the radio surely made things happen with a rush, and only two months later TFF became L.O.W. Radio Grand Splendid (later LR4 Radio Splendid). Wishing to place itself among the most important broadcasters of the country from the very first day of its official launching, on the 6th of September 1924, it started with the most prestigious artists under contract with Max Glücksmann: Carlos Gardel, Roberto Firpo, Francisco Canaro, Adolfo R. Avilés, Enrique Delfino and others were presented over its wavelength. The artistic director of the station was Mauricio Godard, who also had the same responsibility in the recording company. At the beginning, both Radio Splendid and the future Radio Belgrano had to combine their transmission schedules so as not to overlap, due to the technical problems that existed in those days. Once those problems were solved, the two stations became the most powerful broadcasters in Argentina. L.R.1 Radio El Mundo, after its opening in 1935, would overshadow all Argentine broadcasting, opening the first broadcasting studio with an auditorium for the public. Until then when a radio station wanted to transmit an artistic event live, it did it from a cinema or a theater.

Each recording company's artists appeared only on certain radio stations, but after a time agreements were reached to remove this limitation. Record companies found the best promotion came through the radio stations, and they lent them their artists. Artists did not charge the broadcasters for their work and considered the gain in sales of their records sufficient pay, though they were sometimes paid with goods or food. But when Rosita Quiroga's musicians, who did not gain anything from the sale of records or promotion, revolted, they started to receive money for their work. A short time after employment practices were normalized, and they started to receive salaries, although they sometimes had to be satisfied with goods supplied by the advertisers, such as soap, cans of edible oil, etc.

The great event that marked the beginning of the relationship between recordings and the radio happened a few weeks after the launching of Radio Splendid, when the first Disco Naciónal-Odeón contest took place and the broadcaster transmitted all its sessions. For the first time the audience could go to an auditorium (in this case the Grand Splendid Cinema) to listen to its favorite radio artists. They sought the best tangos, which were voted for by the audience in the cinema, and besides prize money, they guaranteed the songs a widespread audience. In the final round the musical performances were entrusted to the Roberto Firpo Orchestra, and the winning tango was "Sentimiento Gaucho" by Rafael Canaro (Francisco Canaro was to add his name to it later on). The Roberto Firpo Orchestra immediately recorded all the prizewinning tangos, and words

SENTIMIENTO GAUCHO

Tango de R. CANARO
PRIMER PREMIO

DEL

GRAN CONCURSO DE TANGOS

DEL

DISCO DOBLE "NACIONAL"

REALIZADO EN EL

GRAND SPLENDID THEATRE

DISCOS DOBLES "NACIONAL"
25 centimetros a $ 3.—

Por la Orquesta ROBERTO FIRPO

6310 — Sentimiento gaucho, Tango. R. Canaro.
El sabio, Tango, J. Canaro.

Por la Orquesta FRANCISCO CANARO

4035 — Sentimiento gaucho, Tango. Típica, R. Canaro.
Yo tuve un amorcito, Fox-Trot. Jazz-Band. F. Canaro.

LA SEMANA PROXIMA APA-
RECERAN LOS SEIS PREMIOS
RESTANTES DEL GRAN CONCUR-
SO DEL DISCO DOBLE "NACIONAL"

Segundo Premio:
"PA QUE TE ACORDES", F. Lomuto.
Tercer Premio:
"ORGANITO DE LA TARDE", C. Castillo.
Cuarto Premio:
"CON TODA EL ALMA", J. C. Farini.
Quinto Premio:
"AMIGAZO", J. de Dios Filiberto.
Accésit:
"CAPABLANCA SOLO", E. Delfino.
Accésit:
"EL PUA". A. de Bassi.

LA PUA IDEAL para sus
DISCOS. Caja con 200 $ 1.-
Exija la palabra "CON-
DOR" grabada en cada púa.

VISITE EL PABELLON DEL DISCO DO-
BLE "NACIONAL" EN LA EXPOSICION
DE LA INDUSTRIA ARGENTINA

CREDITOS

CON FACILIDADES
DE PAGO

SOLICITE DETALLES

MAX GLÜCKSMANN

Nuevos Discos Nacional

BUENOS AIRES
CALLAO y R. MITRE
FLORIDA y LAVALLE

ROSARIO
CORDOBA 1048/52
MONTEVIDEO
18 DE JULIO 966

Nuevos Discos Nacional

were added to them so that Carlos Gardel could also record
them. One of the prizewinners,
"Organito de la Tarde" by Cátulo
Castillo, was probably the most
memorable of all, and was made
into a film directed by José A.
Ferreyra, directly based on the
lyrics written for Gardel by the
composer's father, José Gonzalez
Castillo. Max Glücksmann's con-
tests continued to be very popular until 1930, alternating
between the Grand Splendid and
the Palace theaters. Fui the 1927
edition he decided to divide the
contest into two categories:
instrumental tangos and tangos
with lyrics. Francisco Canaro,
who was in charge with his
orchestra of the final round,
decided to present the duo of
Agustín Irusta and Roberto

Francisco Canaro

Fugazot intoning the words of the winning theme, the tango "Noche de
Reyes" by Pedro Maffia and Jorge Curi.

In 1926 Francisco Canaro had tried using the human voice employ-
ing the singer Robert Diaz to, in effect, illustrate part of the words, as if
the voice were another instrument. One of the problems of using singers
was the technical deficiency of the recording system. In 1926 the electrical recording system replaced the acoustic system and the sound quality
of the records got noticeably better. After trying the Irusta-Fugazot duo,
Canaro found a singer at the end of 1927 with whom he would standard-
ize the use of singers of lyrics in tango orchestras; he was called Charlo.
Canaro did a lot of work with him between 1928 and 1932, besides being
his accompanist in his solo work. Charlo also sang choruses with other
orchestras, and between 1931 and 1932 became the first famous artist to
record simultaneously with the two most important recording labels, RCA

Opposite: The announcement of "Sentimiento Gaucho," the top award of the
Max Glücksmann 1924 tango contest that was broadcasted by L.O.W. Radio
Grand Splendid.

and Odeón. Until 1927 tango orchestras had no singers, but the fashion caught on and they soon appeared in the cinemas. As there were no sound amplifying systems, the singers had to use a megaphone to be heard. However, it was not in the cinemas but on the radios that singers would become a fundamental part of the orquesta típica.

It did not take the film industry long to discover the possibilities of radio in terms of publicity. In 1927 L.O.Z. Radio La Nación (launched two years before by the daily paper with the same name) presented a weekly program called Radio Club Metro-Goldwyn-Mayer, with information about the lives of movie stars, Hollywood news and prizes consisting of autographed photographs or tickets to see a movie. Argentine broadcasting reached a milestone on the 25th of May 1927 when, on the occasion of the international exposition of radio, cinema and photography, a transmission from Radio Splendid was heard through the principal radio stations in Berlin, Paris and London. Francisco Canaro was one of the entertainers in the international event.

The Popularity of Carlos Gardel

There are many memorable artists in the history of the recording industry. Among them there are artists who besides having artistic prestige, are special because of their sales; few would ever achieve the same results as Carlos Gardel. Since he started his career with Max Glücksmann, on the 9th of April 1917, until this very day, Gardel has continued to produce earnings for EMI, his recording company.

Gardel was born Charles Romuald Gardes in the city of

Carlos Gardel

Toulouse, France, on the 11th of December 1890 and was brought to Buenos Aires by his mother when he was three years old. His love for singing criollo songs was born before he became Carlos Gardel. His first teacher was Arturo de Nava, possessor of more vocal resources than the rest of the popular singers of his time, resources that were passed along to the young Gardel. As a young man Gardel was also a great fan of opera, and this led him to take lessons with a number of singers, and allowed him to acquire a vocal technique that was completely new for criollo singing. According to Roberto Selles: "This happened in 1917, until then Gardel had exclusively sung country songs, that were captured in his early recordings (Columbia 1912). These recordings and the vocal quartet with Saúl Salinas, Francisco Martino, and José Razzano were left behind when he formed the celebrated duo with Razzano."

Indeed, the Gardel-Razzano duo was the most popular of its time. At first when they started recording, nearly all the records had on one side a song sung by both together and on the other a song by Gardel alone, and as time went by more and more were by Gardel alone, until Razzano finally retired in 1925. By then Gardel was the most important tango singer of all. The key moment was really in 1917, when he recorded his first tango, "Mi Noche Triste," with music by Samuel Castriota and lyrics by Pascual Contursi.

Selles says "The choice was prophetic: it was the first time that the main character of a tango complained that he was abandoned by the woman he loved, compared to the happy lyrics of earlier tangos, where the principal worries were the worship of courage and dancing ability. To this must be added that tangos started to be sung in way that was unknown until then. A surprising conjunction of technique and sensibility is present in Gardel as a tango singer. From then on no tango singer could evade the rules fixed by this immense performer, not even the most modern."

Notwithstanding the popularity of this tango, Gardel continued to sing country songs, with an occasional return to tangos, until he triumphed as a solo tango singer after 1922. As has been said, his influence was enormous.

In that year his friend Francisco Canaro signed a contract with Max Glücksmann to record with his orchestra. Canaro understood from his first moments of popularity that he should record as many records as possible to take advantage of the opportunity, thus he became one of the most prolific recording artists in the world. This example was followed by various colleagues, and also by Gardel, who became the most prolific tango singer, with more than 800 recordings (Charlo had more if you take into account his refrain singing).

With the beginning of their broadcasting activities both Canaro and Gardel discovered a means of communication that was ready to open its doors to them, and until the end of their respective lives they spent long hours in the recording studios increasing their body of work. In terms of popularity, there was never anybody to match Gardel, though, his friends Agustín Magaldi at RCA Victor and Ignacio Corsini at Odeón (whom he had join the Max Glücksmann company, even sharing the numbers of their respective recording series) achieved a well-deserved approval. Together, the three of them set the standard for all tango singers.

Gardel made his movie debut in the film *Flor de Durazno*. The result did not please him, nor did his appearance, so he decided to lose weight until he once again resembled his famous image. In 1922, besides tangos, and without abandoning folk songs, Gardel started to record shimmies and fox trots.

In 1923, with his recording of the tango "La Muchacha de Arrabal," he commenced recording musical themes from local and foreign films, such as *Nerón, El Templo de Venus, Circe* and others.

On the 12th of June 1929, Max Glücksmann started showing sound films in the Grand Splendid Theater with the First National film, distributed by MGM, *La Divina Dama*. A short time later the poet Enrique Cadícamo wrote a Spanish version of the waltz that was the musical theme of the film, and Carlos Gardel recorded it on the 25th of August.

And in this manner the sound movie revolution started.

5

THE FIRST SOUND FILM
EXPERIENCES IN ARGENTINA

The First Exhibitions

As has been said before, between 1907 and 1911 Eugenio Py and Max Glücksmann tried synchronizing films with a recorded sound track. Later, as has also been said, Jose A. Ferreyra tried to synchronize the exhibition of the film *La Muchacha del Arrabal* with records in 1923 at the Esmeralda Cinema, but according to Roberto Firpo, without success. But the possibility of seeing sound movies was speculated upon in the news media over the years, and the different experiences in Europe and the United States were followed regularly.

On the 28th of July 1927, the Argentine public saw a sound movie for the first time. The event was at the Empire Cinema, with a large audience filling the hall. Music, singing and speeches were shown with the De Forest Phonofilm system. As the newspaper *La Prensa* said, "It lacks, from a technical point of view, greater perfection. Still, just as it is, it is an admirable innovation. It comes to add new merit to the movies, and is a formidable competitor for the orchestras."

A short time later Max Glücksmann had a sound film projector installed at the Florida Cinema and started regular exhibitions of De Forest productions, distributed by the Corporación Argentino-Americana de Films, together with silent movies and Roberto Firpo and Adolfo Carabelli orchestras, and the organist Julio Perceval.

The First Argentine Sound Films

The Corporación Argentino-Americana de Films, which had the license to utilize the De Forest sound system, had more ambitious plans than just showing foreign films: on January 1928 the Corporación had brought to Buenos Aires the complete technical equipment to make sound movies, for the first time in South America. The team and the technicians arrived in Buenos Aires on the 19th of January 1928, as *La Vanguardia* announced, wishing the corporation good luck, as its films could give a formidable impulse to the stagnant local film industry. The technical responsibility belonged to Agujeree and Harry Jones, the engineers of the De Forest film company. The pre-production of those films started in those days, as reported by *La Razon* on the 27th of January 1928.

The Corporación Argentino-Americana de Films set up a complete studio in Buenos Aires to shoot sound films, and the actor Francisco P.

Alfredo E. Gobbi

Donadío was made artistic director to produce shorts with local artistic themes. According to *El Diario*, the studio started its activities on the 1st of May 1928.

Around the beginning of June the first Argentine sound movie was shot. Its name was *Entre Mate y Mate*; its director was Francisco P. Donadío and it presented the tango pioneer Alfredo Gobbi (father of a very popular tango orchestra director with the same name), Juan Bons, Juan Faggioli, Alberto Palomero and Gonzalo Palomero. This film was followed immediately by *El ViejoTango* with Gloria Faluggi, Carmelo Mutarelli, and Gonzalo

Palomero, with original music by Samuel Castriota. By around the end of the month of June 24 films were produced. They were all directed by Donadío. According to *El Diario* of the 8th of June 1928 these films were as good as any made outside of the country, and the were using good technology, comparable to that used in the USA.

The Corporación Argentino-Americana de Films decided to have a private session to show the advances in sound films, showing Argentine produced films, together with some others made in different countries. The exhibition took place on the 8th of September 1928 at the Gran Palais Cinema. The Argentine films shown, according to *El Diario* of the same day, were these:

1. *El Sepulturero*, a Mexican song performed by Adriana Delhort.
2. *El Poeta*, a humorous monologue by Marcos Caplán.
3. *Felicia*, a tango by Enrique Saborido, played by the Julio Fava Pollero tango orchestra.
4. *Andate Con la Otra*, tango by Enrique Dizeo and C. V. Geroni Flores, performed by the actress San Martín.
5. *Campera*, folk song performed by Mercedes Simone.
6. *El Número Fatal*, a comical monologue by Guillermo Rico (uncle of the actor of the same name who was popular years later).
7. *Chorra*, a parody of the tango by Enrique S. Discépolo, by Marcos Caplán.
8. A short speech by the Intendente (Mayor) of Buenos Aires.

Despite the participation of Mercedes Simone (probably the best female tango singer of all time and occasionally a film actress) the films did not cause the impact that the corporation wanted. With little technique in what refers to camera movement or editing, they were probably not more than a passing curiosity. A performance by an orquesta típica in a cinema was probably more interesting (they were continually updating their repertoire). Even so, these shorts by De Forest were probably more popular than the Argentine silent movie *La Borrachera del Tango*, released in those same days with disastrous results.

Around the end of September, the corporation signed up Sofía Bozán for a couple of shorts. A witness from the newspaper *La Nación* (present at the shooting of the films *Haragán* and *Que Lindo es Estar Metido*) sustained on the 4th of October 1928 that she was perfect for films:

> Just as not everybody has the virtue of being photogenic, that is to say the photographic capacity to be taken and projected by cinema in all the vital force and

Cariñosamente a las distinguidas amiguitas Lydia y María Teresa Ferrari dedico esta modesta composición

¡Por Ella...
Ten Piedad!

Mabel Gladis
protagonista de la película

Tango Canción

—— DE ——

A. POLITO

Antonio Polito

Cantado con éxito por PILAR DE BODAS en todos los
Cines y en Radio.

Filmado por artistas cinematográficos argentinos

Todos los derechos de reproducción ejecución y transcripción etc. reservado

Dieciocho tangos antiguos recientemente reeditados
Alma de Bohemio - Jueves - Lunes - Amigaso
Sábado Inglés - Ando Pato - El Flete - Morochito
Color de Rosa - Entrada Prohibida - Paysandú - El 13
Emancipación - Independencia - Royal Pigall
Tranco a Tranco - Chacarera - La Catrera

Editorial:
HECTOR N. PIROVANO
PASCO 1440   BUENOS AIRES
ARGENTINA

Tango that was sung in a De Forest Phonofilm short in 1928.

expressive eloquence, not all voices have what could be called "photophonic" qualities, that is to say, the capacity of being picked up by a microphone and being reproduced by loudspeakers without losing their clarity and harmony.

To possess both of these qualities that cannot be acquired because they are natural, in one person, is the terrible dilemma that has just appeared for the illustrious Hollywood stars.

If sound films continue and prevail, it will not be enough to have a vaporous figure, eloquent and subtle in its attitudes, exalted to the highest degree of beauty by the lights, and whose seduction deepens the silence of the screen.

A voice will also be necessary, a voice capable of resisting, without loss of its purity, the process of the lighting, the electricity and the amplification.

A double virtue this, that it will not be easy to find present in the selfsame star.

The wittiest of Argentine tango singers, Sofía Bozán, has the luck

Sofía Bozán at the time of her De Forest Phonofilm shorts.

of possessing both qualities, as could be proved yesterday, during the impression of the talking movies carried out in the labs of the Corporación Argentino-Americana de Films, who have the exclusive rights to the De Forest system since last year, and already have the technicians available to obtain local productions.

The slim and beautiful figure and a vast amount of charm that evolves with the unhurried elasticity of her movements, a face that has the virtue of transmitting without effort the play of eyes and mouth, the intimate emotion and the intention that creates feeling, and an extraordinary naturalness in her performance make our singer into a beautiful film personality.

A quality that is all the more appreciable and legitimate if you take into account that it is the first time that Sofía Bozán poses before a film camera.

And that same naturalness of movement has the corresponding virtues of emission and phonetical richness in her voice that the microphones pick up and the loudspeakers reproduce, without impairing its tone and without altering its charm.

These two natural qualities of the actress make her into one of the Argentine performers with the most capacity for making talking movies, whose real effect on the audience and brilliance makes them necessary as fundamental elements for success.

HERMANO

TANGO CANCION

GRABADO EN DISCO "VICTOR"
Y EN LA PRIMERA PELÍCULA
PARLANTE ARGENTINA "THE
DE FOREST PHONO FILM"

Letra de :-

ENRIQUE DIZEO

Música de :-

Julio F. Pollero

QUEDA HECHO EL DEPOSITO
QUE MARCA LA LEY 7092

Tango that was played by Julio Pollero (in the tango) in De Forest Phonofilm short in 1928.

Sofía Bozán's films would be shown together with a more ambitious project, also carried out by the Corporación Argentino-Americana de Films. On Thursday the 18th of October 1928, the release of the first Argentine sound feature film was announced. A few days before (on the 12th of October), Hipólito Yrigoyen took over as the new president of Argentina and De Forest's cameras and microphones were there to record the event. Although far from perfect, it was praised. The difficulties of this kind of production were forgivable as it was made and on theater screens in only six days.

A complicated lighting installation was necessary inside the Congress building for the scenes showing the president and vice president taking the oath of office, and although the lighting and the sharpness were good when the President was speaking, the synchronization of his voice was imperfect at times, although always understandable. The vice president's voice was recorded better. The public's applause and the shouts of the crowd appeared very clearly at times, as well as the music of the bands, especially the bugles and drums. The work of the Argentine technicians was praised, and, according to all the papers, their achievements were better than the sound films from the United States that were then being shown.

The Consequences

By this time, the communications media started to reflect the sound film revolution that was then starting to take place in the United States, and the two systems that were then competing: Movietone and Vitaphone. No films produced with these systems were presented in Argentina during 1928. However a Movietone camera arrived in Buenos Aires in December 1928, according to *El Diario*, to shoot a series of films for Fox Movietone News, at the moment of the arrival of the American president, Herbert Hoover. The people in charge of the Movietone team were Fernando E. Delgado and Mauricio Langer, who already knew Argentina well enough to select the themes to be shot by the camera and shown all over the world.

But these were not Argentine productions. The sound movie revolution had already started in the USA and by the end of 1928 the Argentine public still did not know what was going to happen a short time after. By the end of the year the attendance at cinemas had gone down.

According to *El Diario* on the 31st of December 1928, the De Forest Phonofilm experiments in Argentina failed not because of technical problems, but for artistic reasons. The scarcity, and lack of diversity in those shorts probably bored the audience, relegating those films to second-rate cinemas. Lack of artistic merit, combined with the technical hurdles involved in sound movie production, resulted in a second-rate product, not comparable to what could be found in live theater performances. The producers of the day were incapable of making long pieces that would satisfy an audience, or of producing the variety shows popular at the time. the result, from a Hollywood eager to expand audiences by pushing the new technology, was a spate of short films, dialogues, and songs, not full-length movies. *El Diario* noted the continuing development of computing technologies, and for the time being reserved judgment on which would produce satisfactory films with sound.

6

THE SOUND MOVIE REVOLUTION

Its Impact

On The 24th of May 1932, in the RCA Victor Studios, the great singer Mercedes Simone recorded the tango by Eduardo Ferri and Juan Manuel Arizaga, "Por Culpa del Cine," accompanied by an orchestra. The words of the song goes as follows:

Es culpa del cine, sonoro y parlante,	*Sound movies are guilty*
no sólo la moda de hablar en inglés.	*Both for the fashion of speaking in English*
También por su culpa, del día a la noche,	*And of suddenly making things change.*
las cosas cambiaron y están al revés.	*Now everything is turned inside out.*
Los que antes pasaban chifoleando un tango	*Those who used to whistle a tango,*
la van de saltitos cantando un fox-trot.	*Go jigging around singing fox trots*
Y el que se encantaba jugando a las bochas	*And those who loved to play bowls*
es hoy partidario de ir al ton toon ball.	*Now tap their toes at the Ton Toon Ball*

The song goes on to lament other changes brought about by the movies; the loss of distinct cultural elements, of traditional modes of behavior and dress, and other changes made to conform to an image conveyed by Hollywood. The song encapsulates this perceived rush towards change with the line "life is a motorcar that won't go into reverse."

Although this tango was recorded in 1932, the consequences of the sound film revolution were still being felt. This revolution started in mid 1929 and ended at the beginning of 1931. In between these dates there was a worldwide economic depression, and Argentina was subject to a coup d'état on the 6th of September 1930.

The Argentine journalist Emilio Delboy wrote what follows from the

USA in *La Prensa* on the 13th of October 1929, when the effects of what was to be the sound movie revolution were just starting to be felt: "Not often in the history of manners had an evolution such as that observed on screen been so fast and decisive. Speaking films were only born a couple of years ago, and nobody imagined before the end of 1928 that they would prevail definitively in the space of a couple of months. They have marched firmly into the very heart of silent films, opening a formidable breach, making the whole of its old psychological structure change. Of course, this conclusion did not happen suddenly. The force of habit is not changed, is not abandoned suddenly. He who hears the characters on screen speak for the first time will be disconcerted; but once the visual and acoustic senses are identified, as the sound and movement are synchronized now in phonetic cinema, the illusion is so perfect that our old habits will disappear, and we will find new interest in what we thought would never satisfy us, because it then clashed with what was habitual in us."

American Films in English

The sound film revolution in Argentina started on the 12th of June 1929. To reach that end, Max Glücksmann had the Grand Splendid Cinema refurbished for the exhibition of both kinds of sound projection: Vitaphone (sound on records) and Movietone (a sound track on the film). A short time after, the principal Argentine cinemas would start to prepare to show films with both systems, while those with less financial possibilities only converted to Vitaphone.

For the first sound film exhibition, MGM presented a First National Pictures film, *The Divine Lady*, (with Corinne Griffith and Victor Varconi in the leading roles, directed by Frank Lloyd) together with some shorts. At the beginning, as they still did not know how to solve the language problem, they chose this film because it was practically silent, although Corinne Griffith sings the waltz that gives the film its name. It was written by Nat Shilkret, and it soon acquired Spanish lyrics (by Enrique Cadícamo), and was recorded by Carlos Gardel for Max Glücksmann.

The next month, July 1929, the newspapers and magazines made it clear that in the USA sound movies had taken over. But nobody knew what to do with the audiences that spoke different languages, and the same publications held that the sound films would prevail only in those places where English was spoken. At the same time, in some European countries they were starting to organize their own sound films.

While the United States were trying to resolve this dilemma, some sound films were distributed in Argentina in silent versions. Some that had been shot as silent and then transformed into sound come out ahead when they were shown in their original versions. But the films that had their sound suppressed almost never had the same fate; among them were some of the first films with the voices of famous artists. The results would be disastrous, and the first film shown was *Interference*, from Paramount. The film was centered on the voices of Clive Brooks, William Powell, Evelyn Brent and Doris Kenyon; without dialogues, the results were very poor.

The first sound films shown in the country were practically still silent, and did not speak. That is to say, there were no dialogues, scarcely any songs, and generally speaking, the first films shown in Argentina were not the first made by each company. But sound films had arrived and they had to be made to prevail. The company that would do more than any other in those times of doubt was Metro-Goldwyn-Mayer.

While it is true that in cinema history MGM was the last company to start to produce sound films, it was the first in Argentina, and the best prepared. Although in some cases they suppressed the dialogues of the films, they took the trouble of shooting additional scenes to fill in the gaps, and on the 29th of August 1929 MGM reached an important milestone when Max Glücksmann showed the sound and speaking film *The Broadway Melody*, the first talking feature film shown in Argentina.

It was not shown in a silent copy that also existed, but in its original sound version in English. How did they solve the language problem? The film introduced what were then called "explanation captions" in the lower potion of the screen. They were later known as subtitles. The idea of including subtitles was probably more Max Glücksman's initiative than MGM's, though they would adopt it a short time later. The first subtitles for foreign films were done at the Cinematográfica Valle labs, the work of Antonio Merayo (later a cinematographer) and Arnoldo Etchebehere.

The use of Spanish subtitles made *La Melodía de Broadway* into one of the most successful films of 1929. With this method, a spectator who did not know the original language could follow, by means of these captions, all the script, even understanding the most dramatic parts of the plot. The foreign language was no longer a difficulty in perceiving what was happening on screen, and what is more, made the whole production more valuable.

A few months later Universal announced the release, which took place on the 21st of November 1929, of the film *Noches de Broadway (Broadway)* as the first film spoken in Spanish. Directed by Paul Fejos, the leading actors were Evelyn Brent, Glenn Tryon, Merna Kennedy, Otis Harlan, and Robert Ellis. However, this film was one of the most absolute disasters recorded. The Spanish synchronization was bad, and the audience protested loudly all through its projection.

The actors did not speak in Spanish, it was their "dubbers"; that is to say, a group of Spanish-speaking actors who replaced the original ones at the microphones. This system for showing films in Spanish was known in the beginning as "vocal reproduction in Spanish," and was later known as "dubbing." The showing of dubbed films was never successful in Argentina, although several companies tried it. Some good films failed when they were shown dubbed, and today these versions are only used for child audiences and television channels.

However the public wanted to see films in Spanish, and the Hollywood studios decided to give it a try. So, on the 22nd of February 1930, Max Glücksmann premiered the MGM film called *Ladrones*, totally spoken in Spanish, in the city of Mar del Plata. Produced by Hal Roach (whose name still did not appear in Argentine advertising) it was the first talking film that the Argentine audience saw by the comedians Stan Laurel and Oliver Hardy. After a series of silent shorts, the actors, who were known among Argentines as "el Gordo y el Flaco" (Fatty and Skinny) reached with this film what was possibly the most sensational popularity that film stars could then achieve. It would be confirmed with a handful of later films in Spanish that alternated with others in English. The interesting thing about the film was that they both had to learn Spanish for it. Of course their accent was clearly Anglo-Saxon, but, instead of being a defect, it only added a special charm to the whole.

Before *Ladrones* Sono-Art Productions shot the movie *Sombras de Gloria*, released on the 12th of May 1930 in Buenos Aires. It was the first of a whole series of films made simultaneously in English and Spanish in Hollywood. The actors and technicians from one version were usually replaced by others for the alternative version. The Spanish versions of many films were almost always the ones shown in Argentina, although they were later removed from distribution. The main character of *Sombras de Gloria* was played by Argentine artist José Böhr (according to some sources he was Chilean, although he was born in Germany). Böhr is better known as a composer of some memorable tangos, and he also cut some records as a tango orchestra leader at Victor, in 1926, and as a singer with the Francisco Canaro Orchestra in those years. *La Prensa* said about *Sombras de Gloria*, which was called *Blaze O'Glory* in its English version, that you have to acknowledge that it has "estimable values and defects easy to correct in the future…. Good synchronization, and we should not ask more from the first film in Spanish. Others will come with less intricate plots and better actors. *Sombras de Gloria* will continue to be an estimable work because it is the original impulse, imposed on the mountain of difficulties ensuing from the moment."

The films in Spanish made in Hollywood make up a period worth being dealt with exclusively, and shall be discussed in the next pages.

Sound movies would prevail definitively in the 1930 film season. Although there were still some silent movies being shown, they were specially prepared versions of sound films, because silent films were no longer produced in the USA, and some distributors were starting to distribute the first European talking films with subtitles in Spanish. In Argentina, the big film companies would adapt to the public's demands in the course of the year.

After MGM, Paramount also started exhibiting sound films, but the few shown were shown in English and without subtitles, while the great majority were shown in silent versions. Starting with *The Love Parade* their films were shown in English with Spanish subtitles.

The then new film company, RKO, achieved one of its biggest failures with the release of the feature *Río Rita*, on the 9th of May 1930. Its principal defect was that it was a version dubbed in Spanish, except for the songs. The idea of having other voices replacing those of the actors was always badly received and rejected by the Argentine public.

This film was distributed in Argentina through the Sociedad General Cinematográfica, by Julián Ajuria, who also distributed Columbia and Warner Bros. films. This was the last year in which the producer of *Una Nueva y Gloriosa Nación* was to work in the film marketplace. The big Hollywood studios decided to stop working with Argentine distributors, taking over the distribution themselves. The pioneers stopped working, and only Max Glücksmann was to continue a few more years as the exclusive distributor for RKO.

Sound films turned Warner Bros., which was a small company, into one of the most important, as it was one of the first to invest in the new technique. However this did not happen in Argentina: a part of its production was distributed by Julián Ajuria and another (the First National label, which it bought in 1928) through MGM. *The Divine Lady*, distributed by MGM, was the first sound film that the studio premiered in Argentina, only a few months after its release in the USA. *The Jazz Singer*, from 1927 and considered to be the film that started the sound revolution, was only seen three years later, through the Sociedad Argentina Cinematográfica, after Argentina had already seen several better and newer productions. What is more, Warner presented failure after failure when they showed their films in silent form, without their dialogues.

The first spoken Warner film, shown on the 15th of May 1930 (before starting their own local distribution) was *Sally*. Even though it was a film totally spoken in English, with Spanish subtitles, this film starring Marylin

Miller was very popular. When it was shown in its original version, without converting it into a silent film, and without dubbing it with Mexican or Spanish voices, it managed to be well received by all. Those who knew English could enjoy it. Those who did not could also do so, thanks to the subtitles, which were understandable, fast, and did not interrupt the action.

After bombing with *Noches de Broadway*, Universal adopted Spanish subtitles, and on Tuesday, 13th of August 1930, presented *All Quiet on the Western Front*. According to the daily *La Nación* it was a masterpiece, and a masterly example of all the requisites achieved by sound movies.

The Fox Company's relationship with Argentina is very long. It started at the end of the second decade of the century, when Fox it was the first studio to establish its own local distributor. During all the silent period it had musicians under contract (Emilio Iribarne, Mario Valdez, José Tinelli) who wrote melodies, occasionally tangos, as themes for these films, and that reached some popularity in their time. Fox was one of the first studios to experiment with sound films, starting in 1927.

But they did not take advantage of the experiences. All their first sound films were shown in silent versions, and they only decided to distribute sound material in 1929, after other companies, in the form of newsreels, Fox Movietone News, and the feature *Four Devils* directed by F. W. Murnau. As the silent film era came to a close, they decided to continue showing their films without dialogues, and they attained failure after failure until the end of 1931. They also held on longest to the idea of showing films dubbed in Spanish, without ever being successful. They very slowly started using subtitles, and even decided to re-release a lot of films in their original versions.

Although American films spoken in Spanish will be analyzed further on, it can be said that with the premier, on the 14th of August 1930, of *El Precio de un Beso*, which was spoken in Spanish (and simultaneously shot in English), Fox started a whole series of films shot in Spanish with Latin-American and Spanish actors that was to continue for five years. With *El Precio de un Beso*, the company's first talking film premiered in our country, the Mexican tenor José Mojica and the Argentine actress Mona Maris (who would always have problems with her Spanish pronunciation, but this was not taken into account by Argentine audiences) were firmly established. Notwithstanding this first effort, American producers and actors still had to learn the best way of making sound films in Spanish.

While sound and talking films had arrived from the USA since 1929, they started coming from Europe at the end of the following year in versions subtitled in Spanish. The films sometimes had been done in one version in one language with a certain cast, and an alternative in another language with some of the same actors (or changing all). In general, in our country, only one version was presented except when the film became very popular, and then the alternative version was also released.

Between these films *Veneno en los Labios* (*The Flame of Love*) was shown; shot in English and in German by the British International Pictures and the Richard Eichberg Film GMBH. The English version was released in Buenos Aires on the 5th of November 1930, with Anna May Wong (also present in the German version), George Shell, John London and Moyna Goya in the leading roles. In the film Anna May Wong plays to great effect, a woman in Tsarist Russia who sacrifices her life to save the man she loves.

One of the first French sound films shown in our country was *Les Trois Masques*, produced by Nathan Productions and directed by Hugon. Its actors were Jean Tulot, Françoise Rozet, Renée Heribel and Marcel Vivert. Based on a play by Charles Meré, the results were very good.

While subtitles in Spanish allowed one to see films in their original language, it took American producers at least a full year to find it out. So, many of the first talking movies were seen in silent versions that failed one after another. The release on November 8th 1930 of *Noches de Nueva York* (*New York Nights*), from United Artists, should have been Norma Talnadge's first talking film in Argentina, but was not, and the outcome was mediocre.

Another example of a spoken sound film shown without sound, and even less known, was the film *Mexicali Rose* (*Enigma de la Rosa*) starring Barbara Stanwyck and Sam Hardy for Columbia. Its premier, on the 16th on November 1930, was a disaster: In order to make it into a silent movie a lot of scenes were suppressed, and the ending was incomprehensible.

The first Paramount film to present a sound track without dialogues was *The Wedding March* (*La marcha nupcial*) directed by Erich von Stroheim, which premiered on the 28th of July 1929. This film is only the first part of the story that von Stroheim had originally conceived. Paramount re-edited the film, cutting it in two. The second part, *Honeymoon* (*Luna de miel*) was released on the 31st of December 1930 and was one of the last silent films released by a Hollywood studio. According to the reviews at the time, the first was the best part of von Stroheim's work; the plot of the first film continued in the second, although the results were notably inferior, though Zasu Pitts did an excellent job. *Luna de Miel* included cruel deaths, and was slow and affected, even though it included many of the director's virtues.

The transition from silent to sound films was a difficult period for actors, directors, producers and the public in general. Much has been written about the problems that actors, producers and directors had to face. Many of the first talking films were based on dialogues and lacked action. The audience slowly started to tire of these films and started to protest loudly. Consequently, the premiere of the film *High Heels*, with William Powell, Helen Kane, Fay Wray, Richard Gallagher, Phillips Holmes, Eugene Pallete and Adviene Dorée was the worst failure in the history of Paramount, the company that produced it. During its first viewing there were loud protests from the audience, and although part of the audience left during the projection, there were disturbances inside the cinema, and the police had to intervene to calm people down. According to *La Nación*, "The agencies that represent the producers in our country should be more careful in choosing the films meant for our public, and their managers should worry more about getting to know the characteristics of the Argentine spectator. The case of *Tacones de Punta* can serve as an example, and also as an indicator of what the public is capable of doing in the future."

The United Artists Company presented *City Lights* by Charlie Chaplin on the 21st of May 1931, and achieved an important success with a silent film while sound films were trying to take over the market. This film inspired a tango called "Luces de la Ciudad" by Francisco Oréfice and Osvaldo Sosa Cordero. *La Prensa* had this to say about its premier:

> In *City Lights* Chaplin leaves us a superior film, one of his best. The spectator laughs with his gags and is distressed with his sorrows. Perhaps he repeats himself in the comic effects, as if he were no longer charmed by them. There are weak episodes, like the millionaire's attempted suicide and the "cabaret" scenes. But most of it produces a spontaneous, unexpected, reaction of mirth. His criticisms of the empty, hollow speeches when they inaugurate a public monument, and of talking films, when he replaces the orator's voice with a saxophone are sharp and appropriate. Another funny detail, that of the hero swallowing a whistle and producing ventriloquistic whistles, has been utilized in an original manner. He has not had to use talking innovations to construct his film. It has been enough for him to synchronize the silent original film with some very well chosen musical fragments, adapted by him with good musical taste. He said, and he is right: "I express myself better on screen if I don't talk. Talking can be the expression of one individual, but it cannot be a symbol, and silence is." Nothing is fairer. The silences of the epilogue of *City Lights*, full of uncontainable emotion are worth the whole film.

By the middle of 1931 the problems of the talking films coincided with a fall in the number of spectators who went to the cinemas. Max Glücksmann maintained that this situation was determined, in the first place, by the increase of the cost of films, which had forced the rise in prices of the cinema tickets. "The cinema must be essentially a popular show, with

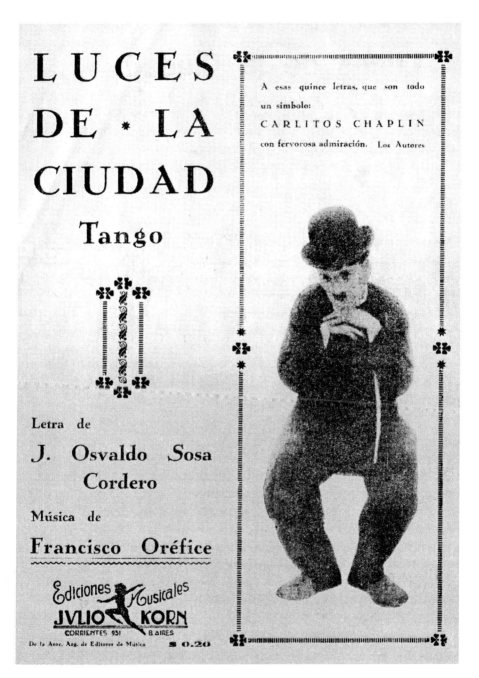

"Luces de la Ciudad," a tango dedicated to Charlie Chaplin after the release of his film of the same name (*City Lights*).

reduced prices, and it is not possible with the current cost of the productions. Films are, above all, action shows, and the producers must agree that the successes will not be, except exceptionally, films that are 100 percent spoken, but those that have at least 80 percent of pure action. What can be done to ward off this evil? Lower film prices, to allow lower ticket prices, and a faster film distribution; and films with more elements of success, than can be only given by words, is what the cinema needs. As can be seen, the remedy is always in the hands of the producers."

In those difficult days, European producers started to distribute talking films in Argentina. Although sometimes a second version of a film was made in another language, generally what arrived in Argentina was the film in the original language with Spanish subtitles. In many cases the other version was also exhibited later, or at the same time, always with subtitles.

By the middle of 1931 silent films were no longer being made; that does not mean that they were no longer shown, although their days were coming to an end. With the release of *Taboo* by F. W. Murnau on the 15th of October 1931, the silent film era practically came to an end. This film consisted of a romance between a couple of natives who were persecuted because the woman had been chosen by the Gods, and its ending was tragic. Adequate music was added to the silent actions.

Some studios decided to add sound tracks to some of the silent successes of the past and release them again. On the 25th of December 1931, MGM released *Ben Hur* for the second time. It was originally released in Buenos Aires in 1927. The sound additions gave its development more vigor and intensity, above all in the spectacular scenes, although they really did not add much more.

The chances of seeing silent movies were getting smaller. Among those still to be seen was the Russian film *El Cadáver Viviente* (*The Live Corpse*), released on the 4th of July 1932, based on a story by Leo Tolstoy, and directed by Sedor Oxep and Vsevolod Pudovkin. Apparently it was a sound film whose dialogues had been cut out.

Another silent film that arrived at Buenos Aires in March 1932 was the last film made by Fritz Lang in Germany, *Un Viaje a la Luna* (*A Trip to the Moon*). Its plot was poor, and its actors were not outstanding. The silent cinema was becoming history. On the 18th of October 1932 Erich von Stroheim's *Queen Kelly* was released, starring Gloria Swanson, just before the arrival of sound films. This film was the subject of the following commentary in *El Diario* one day before its release:

Four years after that filmed piece of art, which was essentially mimed, and which many people yearn for as a lost treasure, and dream of a hope for its return, the announcement of the news of its release will be received, without doubt, with an excited curiosity, because of what it means nowdays, when that kind of film was considered irretrievably lost.

To speak of a silent release today, with the presence of Gloria Swanson and with the contribution of Erich von Stroheim, as the director, is like imagining something impossible, because it is so far away from today's cinema.

However, is it not true that a pleasant sensation flows from that truth, provoked by the suggestion of an affinity with the glorious past that awakens so many memories and moves our sensitivity so much? Who would dare to deny the charm of the contents of *Queen Kelly*, if, through its silent action, the film asks each spectator the question: will silent films return?

A whole world of presumed digressions will be formed, and a suspicion of a return to old times will appear in each brain.

The presence of a silent film that arrives at this moment showing such a prestigious origin, has the strength of a beautiful experiment, because, we will be able to know what amount of sympathy and interest exists for the old kind of cinema in the audience now. And don't doubt it, this will be an extraordinarily interesting event, and it is only fair to start preparing to feel the emotions that our recollection will spin, facing the spectacular process of a silent film, without missing any details, where a pair of lovers will display their elegant forms: Gloria Swanson and Walter Byron.

Nothing of what was planned worked. This film suffered from a series of problems that held up its release for years. Ignoring its other troubles, *Queen Kelly* was not successful as a work of art. Its story was weak, and it could not be saved by its producers or actors, although Seena Owen's performance was memorable. The entire industry made a landmark decision in 1933—from then on, all the big film companies would abandon the sound system based on records and adopt the sound track.

The sound system with records known as Vitaphone had economic advantages, and for that reason it had lasted since 1929, especially in second-rate movie theaters and in other theaters throughout Argentina. It was only necessary to add a record player to the silent film equipment. But the records were fragile, and they broke very frequently. Besides, a simple alteration of the spiral groove was enough to deflect the needle, ruining the synchronization between image and sound, and making it intolerable to the audience. These problems caused protests in the audience during the years that this method was in use, and it was only replaced with films with a sound track on one side of the frames in 1933, when the great majority of worldwide cinemas invested in the necessary technology.

The last silent film released with added sound was *The Big Parade*. The release of this 1925 film was on the 14th of January 1933. The music, songs and appropriate noises added little.

From then on silent films disappeared from the principal film theaters. These films would be relegated to film clubs, film archives, and later, occasionally, to television series and a few re-editions on videotape. From that point forward, the history of films has already been published in many books. However, in Argentina there were some films that took a long time to be released, and some that were never shown. There were many that were censored. However, most would be shown sooner or later in the right circumstances.

Except for films made for children, movies would be shown in their original versions, and with Spanish subtitles. *La Prensa* published the following article on the 17th of September 1933:

> When talking films appeared they had so many defects that a lot of people doubted that the invention would ever be successful, especially those who thought that the screen had to continue to be silent, as it had been until then, to continue to be called an "Art." But when they started to "talk," and better and better each time, with the improvements in its technique, nearly everybody thought that the universality that it had enjoyed during its long silent infancy was dead. But this time the majority was wrong. Even though they are more and more deplorably loquacious, films are regaining their old internationality day by day, thanks to the development of the new literary form that the "subtitles," with whose help films spoken in foreign languages are shown, have demanded.
>
> This new literary form offers enormous difficulties, of which the audience is not aware. What is more, the better the subtitles are, the less the audience perceives the enormous difficulties that the author has had to overcome, since the public ends up by having the illusion that it almost understands what the actors are saying. That is why the wish to go unnoticed, together with the capacity to manage it, are the two indispensable qualities that mark the good "subtitle writer," that the new "screen international," with their hardly suitable titles, tend to demean.
>
> Above all, the "subtitle writer" must know how to transmit emotions constantly, that is to say that he must be an artist; an artist that, in order to enable a film be successful in different languages, is at least as important as the actors, the director, the photographer, and the author of the original dialogue, and it is possible to affirm that he is still more important than him, since the good "subtitle writer" is obliged to transmit with all due emotion, every comical or dramatic idea in the dialogue, with a twentieth of the words used by the author himself.
>
> What is more, when the good "subtitle writer" has to translate a dialogue that would go against good taste, or the taste of a particular audience, he has to appeal to his own creativity to ensure the success of films that not were always successful in their own countries.

Argentine Sound Films

Ten years before the sound film revolution, many Argentine movies could compete on equal terms with those that came from foreign lands.

But as time went by, the local industry lost financing, quality and the public. Besides, when sound films arrived, films were in a critical position, because very few people wanted to see an Argentine film, all the more so if it was silent. For example, the year 1929 ended with the premier of the film *La Ley Sublime*; there is little information about this film, other than the fact that it was released on the 24th of December, and that the actress Carlota Rossi played its leading role.

According to *El Diario* of the 10th of January 1930, Max Glücksmann was studying the possibility of producing sound films for our country in the USA with actors and musicians well known in Argentina taking part, especially Francisco Canaro. But none of this happened. The company that had made the De Forest Phonofilm short sound films, the Corporación Argentino-Americana de Films, no longer existed, and all the material produced ended up in the hands of Julián Ajuria's Sociedad General Cinematográfica, which would also disappear a short time after.

There were no technical or financial capacities to produce Argentine sound films, so silent films would go on being produced for some time. On the 9th of February 1930 La *Leyenda del Mojón* from the Filmadora Prince Company was released, starring Estela Bertana and Armando Dix. Based on a poem by Juan Pedro López, it was the story of a gaucho who discovers that his wife is unfaithful. The results were not good.

When sound films started, the American film companies had the necessary means to exploit the new technology all over the world. However this situation was not true for the European producers that still had many silent films waiting to be released. To overcome this problem, Genaro Ciavarra and Alfredo Murúa started the Sociedad Impresora de Discos Electrofónicos, S.I.D.E., that was to make Vitaphone records with synchronized music for foreign films. S.I.D.E. would also add music to practically all the last silent films (or the earlier films that were re-released) made in Argentina. The man responsible for the music at the company was Eleuterio Irribarren (who recorded jazz for Max Glücksmann); he was later replaced by José Vázquez Vigo. In addition, this company set up a sound film studio, which after some trials, would be let out to several local producers.

The first Argentine film to have a sound track was *Adiós Argentina*, written and directed by Mario Parpagnoli for Cinematográfica Valle and finished in December 1929. Its leading actors were, besides Parpagnoli, Libertad Lamarque, Pierina Dealessi, Carmen Valdez, Ada Cornaro, Ana Fábregas and Silvio Romano. The technical and photographic responsibility was borne by Alberto Etchebehere and Tulio Chiarini; and for the occasion the celebrated author of the tango "La Cumparsita," Gerardo

The S.I.D.E. Studios

Matos Rodríguez, composed a tango with the same name as the film, which Libertad Lamarque (in her film debut) sang in the sound track that was added to the silent original.

Adiós Argentina released on the 13th of March 1930, turned out to be an absolute failure, and the film had to be taken out of distribution three days after its premier. The poor story, with practically no plot, consisted of a gaucho, played by Parpagnoli himself, who makes love to a woman and then leaves her, to go to Europe on a liner. But the worst defect of the film was the appearance of a caricature of a gaucho, much worse than the model that was so criticized in Hollywood films. After taking it out of circulation, its producer, Federico Valle had *Adiós Argentina* re-edited, introducing a series of changes in its structure, removing details that had no effectiveness, and releasing it again on the 16th of July 1930. The outcome this time was average.

A few days before, the first Argentine sound and talking film was to be released called *Corazón Sin Ley*. Originally released successfully as a silent film several months before, the S.A.C.H.A. Manzanera Company had sound added at S.I.D.E.

In its sound version, *Corazón Ante la Ley* presented some scenes with dialogues. But they were not shot again; the voices were dubbed in, without achieving a good recording, and the words did not correspond to the number of words pronounced by the actors in the original version. It starred Nelo Cosimi, Olga Casares Pearson, Florentino (Floren) Delbene, Victoria Real, Edith de Rosa, Alvaro Escobar, Miguel Gómez Bao and Ricardo Passano. The director, Nelo Cosimi, was able to shoot a new scene for the sound version, and the actor Miguel Gómez Bao became the first actor to sing a tango in an Argentine feature film. The tango was "Chinita," and its authors were Eleuterio Irribarren and Enrique Carrera Sotelo. This addition marked the success of the film at its premier on the 11th of June 1930.

A week later, the Asociación Cinematográfica Argentina held a festival at the Paramount Theater, to show the first two sound films made in the country, two years after the experiments with the De Forest Phonofilm system had led to the production of a whole series of sound shorts. On the 17th of June 1930, some of the first sound film experiences made at the S.I.D.E. studios by various film companies were shown. Among the films shown was a short from the Ariel Company called *Variedades sonoras Ariel nro. 1: Mosaico Criollo*, directed by Roberto Guidi (retired since 1924, but invited to take charge of it), the film that Domingo Di Nubila wrongly thought to be the first sound film shot in Argentina. Taking part in this film were the singer Joaquina Carreras, singing "Triste está mi rancho," the dancers Giménez and Suarez, doing a malambo, a piano solo by the organist Julio Perceval, and the singer Anita Palmero, singing the tango "Botarate" by Alberto Acuña and José de Cicco. Eleuterio Irribarren was responsible for the music.

The same day they exhibited *Variedades sonoras Ariel nro. 2*, in which Lina and Carmen Castiglioni sang the chacarera "Bajo el

Corazon Ante la Ley

Alero—Doña Rosario" by Guillermo Barbieri and José Rial. This short also included a brief sketch written by Enrique Maroni called *El Adiós del Unitario* (also known as *Sketch Federal*) performed by Nedda Francy and Miguel Faust Rocha. This sketch starts with a caption that says "first talking production in Argentine cinema" and was directed by Edmo Cominetti.

Other films shown on this occasion were a reel from the feature *Defiende tu Honor* from the Sociedad Cinematográfica Argentina (which was released later), It was directed by Nelo Cosimi, with musical direction by Heriberto Fiocco, and a speech by the actress Orfilia Rico, who was already retired because of an illness. She invited the audience to see the coming premier of the sound version of *Nobleza Gaucha*, in which she had taken part fifteen years before.

A month later Federico Valle started to produce his newsreel *Film Revista Valle* with sound, and called it *Actualidades Sonoras Valle*. It was the first Argentine sound film in the Movietone system, with the soundtrack in the film itself. It showed some horse races at the Hipódromo Argentino racetrack on the 6th of July 1930. According to *La Prensa*, "It is an experimentation that shows that the domestic film industry has good operators and efficient complementary elements, to which they have now added the adoption of the Movietone sound system. Two Actualidades Sonoras Valle will be released each month in Buenos Aires."

At this point, it is necessary to look over some Argentine history.

On the 12th of August 1928, Hipólito Yrigoyen became President for the second time with enormous popular support, but two years later, the worldwide depression was also felt in Argentina. The Yrigoyen administration was incapable of cutting down unnecessary spending, of executing a policy of austerity and obtaining better financial counsel. All this produced unease in the population and in the armed forces.

The situation reached a climax on the 4th of September 1930 with bloody episodes in the Plaza de Mayo, and the police violently put down a student demonstration calling for Yrigoyen's resignation. With the country in an uproar, the government declared martial law and Yrigoyen turned over the presidency to the vice-president, Enrique Martínez.

It all ended on the afternoon of Saturday, the 6th of September 1930. The Army marched into the Government House, while a crowd, notwithstanding the police violence, gathered in the Plaza de Mayo. At 5 P.M. General José Félix Uriburu obliged Enrique Martínez to resign and took over the government. A few hours later, ex-President Yrigoyen's home was plundered, as were the offices of the newspaper *La Epoca*, which had supported Yrigoyen, and those of his party, the Unión Cívica Radical. Something worse happened opposite the National Congress: a crowd of sympathizers of the deposed government was attacked by the police, producing twenty dead and more than two hundred wounded. As night arrived the situation started to calm down and the new President of what was called the Provisional Government dissolved Congress, announcing that new elections would be called once the country was in order. The Provisional Government was really a military dictatorship.

This series of events was known as the 30s Revolution. Today it is considered to be the first of a series of military coups that would change Argentine history forever.

Many of the events related here were recorded by the cameras of the film companies that produced newsreels. According to Roberto Di Chiara, Federico Valle personally shot many of these events, and later edited all that he and his collaborators had been able of putting on film.

A few days later, on the 11th of September 1930, Federico Valle and Max Glücksmann premiered their respective productions, which showed the most interesting aspects of the revolution that had been filmed, and also the inauguration of the new government. According to *La Prensa* "they are two interesting historical documents; in both we must point out the courage the camera operators, who insisted in recording the reality of the most dangerous episodes, even risking their lives. These two newsreels offer a welcome synthesis of the singular events that preceded and followed the toppling of the Yrigoyen government."

Finally, a short time later, the newsreel called *Hombres de la Revolución* was released, shot in the Movietone system. It included the president's speeches and others who had taken part in the coup d'état.

Meanwhile, on the 2nd of October 1930, the San Martín Film Company presented the first Argentine film (shot at S.I.D.E.) that arrived at the cinemas shot exclusively in a sound version: *El Cantar de mi Ciudad*. With it, José A. Ferreyra reappeared in the local films industry, directing the actors María Turgenova, Felipe Farah, Lina Montiel, Esther Calvo, Antonio Ber Ciani (then called Antonio Ber), and Alvaro Escobar. Its plot was the story of a young composer who protects a girl who sings tangos at a café owned by a villain, who he ends up killing. The movie included a musical revue and a military parade, and the first all–Argentine sound film to include talking, singing, and sound effects was well received by audiences.

As in many countries all over the world, in Argentina there were amateur film lovers who tried to make their own films. The one who went farthest was Luis Saslavsky, who made a silent movie on 16-mm format film; it had its premier on the 11th of October 1930, and was compared to the most important productions made in the country.

Poster announcing *El Cantar de mi ciudad* (San Martin Film, 1930).

Saslavsky conceived a complicated plot. It was the story of an impossible love affair, between a society girl whose financial situation is collapsing, and a penniless engineer. When he goes to Europe to work, her mother intercepts his letters, trying to marry her off to another man as the solution to her monetary problems. The engineer's silence and her friends' gossip end up convincing the girl that her mother was right. And when, two years later, the traveler returns for his bride, he is undone by the sight of the happy home that she has formed, and knows that he must give up his dreams. The stars of the film were Isabel Villamil and Jorge Weil. The rest of the cast included Raquel Iturralde, Juana Obarrio, Dalila Saslavsky, Susana Villamil, Marcelo Vázquez Mansilla, Benjamín Murillo and Ernesto Vergara.

On the 30th of May the film *Los Ojos del Diablo* was finished. Its name was changed to *Defiende tu Honor*. This film, from the Sociedad Cinematográfica Argentina, directed by Nelo Cosimi, was to be the first completely talking Argentine film, shot at S.I.D.E. Its leading roles were played by Cosimi, Chita Floras, Florentino (Floren) Delbene, Carmen Duval, Jorge Mir and Juan Ballestrini.

Nelo Cosimi and the musical director Heriberto Fiocco synchronized the image and sound, and showed the first act of the film before its release with excellent results on the 17th of June. But the final result, unhappily, seems not to have been that expected. The film finally had its premier on the 26th of October, without sound, and was removed the next day. The action of the film, which took place among fishermen in the south of the country, was about a woman who was seduced by a villain, and her brother, who rescued her.

The second sound production directed by José A. Ferreyra was *La Canción del Gaucho*, produced by Maipo Film at S.I.D.E. and featured María Turgenova, Arturo Forte, Luis Capri and Alvaro Escobar. This film, released on November 1930, was also a failure, and it was retired from distribution.

The story, a melodrama about a peasant who falls in love with a city girl who arrives at the *estancia* where he works, had many emotional situations. The film had serious faults, especially in the indoor scenes, as the country home looked like a lavish Buenos Aires apartment, and the characters did not remove their formal clothes; the men wore tuxedos, and the women party dresses.

The last film released in 1930 was *La Argentina para el mundo: Buenos Aires*, on the 27th of December. It was a silent documentary made by the S.A.C.H.A. Manzanera, directed by Héctor Bates, and photographed by Francisco J. Boeninger. Without being a novelty, it showed wide panoramas of the city. During 1930 other Argentine silent films were also released, about which not much can be said. *El Hijo de una Virgen*, produced by the Cinedram Film Company, premiered on the 21st of April. *La Vanguardia* announced its release: "It is described by its producers as a sociological romance and we only hope that to have earned that description, it is a better production than most domestic films." According to Roberto Di Chiara, it was directed by Nicolás Ercolani and the leading parts were played by Ercolani himself, Lina Ragusa and Belomo Ricciardi. It seems that it was not successful. The Buenos Aires Film movie *Torbellino de Buenos Aires* was not successful either. It was directed by Julio Irigoyen and starred Margarita Blanco and Rodolfo Vismara, and premiered on the 20th of August.

There were also others that apparently never got released. *La Pulpera de Santa Lucía* was an adaptation of a waltz by Enrique Maciel that was very popular thanks to the extraordinary record that Ignacio Corsini cut for Max Glücksmann on the 22nd of April 1929. *La Prensa* announced on the 2nd of June 1930 that the film would be produced soon, and that it would be directed by J. Vitale de Stefano.

El Drama del Collar was a sound and talking production by Federico Valle, based on a story by Arturo S. Mom. The star was Nedda Francy, and the directors were Mom and José Bustamante Ballivián. The first scenes were shot, according to *La Prensa*, at the end of June 1930; but there are no more details about this film, so it must be supposed that its production was abandoned.

The premier of the film *El Amanecer de una Raza*, directed by Edmo Cominetti and with Alberto Biassotti's photography, took place in Mar del Plata on the 23rd of February 1931. It was the first sound feature film from Ariel Film, shot at S.I.D.E., and its Buenos Aires premier took place on the 18th of June. The leading actors were Nora Mármol, Eva Bettoni, Jorge de Val, Diego Medina, Antonio Ber Ciani, Augusto Zama and Juan Farías. It told the story of an old *criollo*, who was opposed to everything foreign until his daughter marries the son of a foreigner, at which point the old man realizes and accepts that he is living in a melting pot. Although the theme was interesting, it was presented by the filmmakers almost as an accessory as they showed more interest in presenting secondary scenes of the countryside and folk dances, thereby cutting interesting situations short and making the end result slower and more monotonous.

The next Argentine film released in 1931 was *Dios y la Patria* on the 5th of April, from the Sociedad Cinematográfica Argentina, directed by Nelo Cosimi, with the collaboration of the Argentine Navy. Its central characters were played by Cosimi, Chita Floras, Florentino (Floren) Delbene, Miguel Gómez Bao, Jorge Mir and Esteban Berría. It was an unsuccessful silent film, and its failure was the end for the company, which was later taken over by S.A.C.H.A. Manzanera, who released it again in a sound version on the 3rd of September. That version, which included the national anthem in its sound track for the first time, was an average success.

In *Dios y la Patria*, Cosimi would walk the same path he had developed in *Corazón Ante la Ley*. In this case he had the collaboration of the Argentine Navy in presenting the story of an orphan girl, who having been raised by a sailor, falls in love with an officer. In the end, both the man who had raised her and the man she loves die, and she decides to go and live with the nuns that had educated her.

We have already mentioned that Hollywood producers had, taking advantage of the sound film revolution, presented old silent films with sound tracks that included sounds and music, without dialogues. In Argentina some local producers decided to do the same. The first of these reruns, released on the 27th of April 1931, was a sound version of *Destinos* originally released two years before.

La Prensa reported on the 1st of May 1931 that Carlos Gardel would sing his tango "Yira Yira" in a short production by Cinematografica Valle. It was to be he first in a series focusing on Argentina artists. As everything else produced then by these studios, it was shot in the Movietone sound system.

The producer Federico Valle engaged Carlos Gardel to make a series of shorts that were shot between October and November 1930. These were very short and were made with the idea of including them, one at a time, in the Actualidades Sonoras Valle. The veteran producer was starting to feel the beginning of the economic crisis and his activities were reaching an end. Production of his newsreels stopped a short time after.

Valle delegated the responsibility of making these films to the persons that had made his newsreels until then: Eduardo Morera was the director, Rodolfo Schmidt was in charge of the camera, and Ricardo Raffo the sound.

From a technical point of view, these shorts were limited to showing Gardel singing some of his most popular songs, accompanied by his guitar players. Neither the image nor the sound was very good, but today these films are valuable documents. In some cases Gardel is shown speaking briefly to Arturo de Nava, Celedonio Flores and Enrique Santos Discépolo before singing his song. In the case of *Rosas de Otoño*, the accompaniment was provided by Francisco Canaro and his tango orchestra, who also appeared before the song.

According to Eduardo Morera around fifteen shorts were filmed, although some were discarded for technical reasons. Ten of them are left today; they were combined, with not much intelligence, into a feature called *Encuadre de Canciones*. An eleventh short, called *El Quinielero* was rescued in 1995.

Of all these shorts made by Gardel, the most important one is *Viejo Smoking*, which dramatizes the tango by Celedonio Flores and Guillermo Barbieri. The scene is well set up by Eduardo Morera, and Gardel acts in it, together with Inés Murray and César Fiaschi, in a couple of scenes that come before his performance of the song, for which he is accompanied by the Francisco Canaro Orchestra.

In 1929, the film *Aventuras de Pancho Talero* had been a success. Its creator, Arturo Lanteri, decided to repeat the experience the next year, making *Pancho Talero en la Prehistoria*. This film, silent like the one that preceded it, was saved by Roberto Di Chiara, but apparently it was never released in Buenos Aires. Finally, on the 12th of July 1931 Lanteri presented *Pancho Talero en Hollywood* as a sound and talking film, made at the S.I.D.E. Studios. Although there is no data about cast, Pepito Petray and Carlos Dux may have repeated their roles. The film criticized the American producer's view of Argentina: Pancho Talero's daughter wins a beauty contest, and as the prize is a trip to Hollywood, she is chosen there for a film about "the lives of the gauchos of the Pampas next to the Amazon...." The results of this production were not as good as the 1929 film, as Lanteri did not know how to take advantage of the possibilities offered by sound film.

On the 7th of August, Patagonia Film presented the sound and talking film *Muñequitas Porteñas* directed by José A. Ferreyra, at the S.I.D.E. studios, starring Mario Soffici in his film debut, Florentino (Floren) Delbene, María Turgenova, and Lina Montiel. As in most of this director's films, the tango was prominent: María Esther, following the story of "Milonguita," leaves the home of her fiancé, a humble composer, his sister and his drunken father to go and live with a lover who makes her a singer in a cabaret. Even though he had few resources to make this film, Ferreyra achieved good results, and the film was well received by audiences and critics of the time.

The most avidly awaited film event in 1931 was *Peludópolis*. Quirino Cristiani was to make another worldwide landmark film, as he had before with the 1917 premier of *El Apóstol*, the first feature cartoon film. *Peludópolis* was the first feature sound and talking cartoon in the world. The film was a parody of the events that produced the coup d'état on the 6th of September 1930, and it included caricatures of all the personalities that took part in those incidents. It also included documental scenes of the making of the cartoons. Cristiani produced the film in his own film labs, and the sound was recorded at S.I.D.E. José Vázquez Vigo was in charge of the music and the songs. The premier took place on the 18th of September 1931, and was a box office success. Cristiani's cartoon film was more than an hour long, with songs and references to the recent political events. Audiences enjoyed the humorous references to important persons, references accom-

Poster announcing *Peludólis* (Christiani, 1931)

panied by funny music and captions. The cartoon characters did show a lack of mobility, but overall the film was successful. The film showed documentary shots of how it had been made.

On the 9th of October *Nobleza Gaucha* was shown again. The 1915 classic returned to the cinemas in a sound version; the film was basically the same. The additions were some inserted musical scenes performed by the Gedeón Trio, the singers Patrocinio Díaz and Marta Swanson, the Lanas sisters and Alfredo Gobbi. The most important additions were spoken parts by of Orfilia Rico, the star of the film, who had already retired because of health problems.

Until this point Argentine sound movies were not entirely sound productions. There were always silent parts. That would change on the 20th of October 1931 with the release of the film *La Vía de Oro*. Produced by the San Martín Company at the S.I.D.E. Studios, it was the first feature production with sound throughout made in Argentina. Arturo S. Mom produced and wrote the story, and it was directed by Edmo Cominetti. Alberto Biassotti was responsible for the camera and Genaro Civarra and Alfredo Murúa took care of the sound. Its leading actors were Nedda Francy, Alfredo Lliri, Carlos Nahuel, Damián Méndez, Alejandro Corvalán, Felipe Farah, Carlos Dux, Clara Milani and Lidia Arce. Alberto De Caro composed the tango that was sung at a certain moment during the film, *La Hija de los Taitas*. The story was about a police raid against a silk

Alfredo Lliri and Nedda Francy filming *La Vía de Oro* (1931), at the S.I.D.E. Studios.

smuggler, and the love affair between a tango singer, the adopted daughter of the smuggler, and one of the police officers on the expedition. The film had many failings; the acting was average, and the dialogue was difficult to understand. While the standard photography were good, the film's action was slow. There were interesting scenes shot in the Paraná River delta, including a motor boat chase. Reviews of the film were mixed, but it was generally well received by audiences.

The last film to be shown in 1931, on the 30th of October, was *Por una Argentina Grande, Civilizada y Justa*. It was the first local feature with the Movietone sound track included in the film. Federico Valle directed and produced this 51-minute documentary showing the political leaders Lisandro de la Torre, Mario Bravo, and Julio Noble. The film was done as political propaganda for the Democratic-Socialist Alliance, proclaiming Lisandro de la Torre as presidential candidate. He was to lose against the government candidate Agustín P. Justo, ending the provisional government installed the year before.

While in 1931 Argentine films were successful with the viewers, they were not successful financially. During 1932, nearly all the producers closed down, and there were only two local releases.

The first Argentine film released in 1932 was, ironically, not a new release, but a rerun. It was the sound version of the film *Perdón Viejita*, the film that José A. Ferreyra had made in 1927 with María Turgenova and Alvaro Escobar, and whose release had gone practically unnoticed. This new version, premiered in the month of May, had a sound track recorded by the Alpidio Fernández tango orchestra. Fernández also composed nearly all the music in the film. The exception, of course, was the tango by Osvaldo Fresedo and José Antonio Saldías that had inspired the film.

The first new release in 1932 was *La Barra de Taponazo*, directed by Alejandro del Conte. As it was practically the only new Argentine film that year, its premier created great expectations with the viewers. It was not successful, and it was the end for its producer, S.A.C.H.A. Manzanera. Its leading actor was Vicente Padula, an actor who had achieved a certain success in Hollywood, appearing there in a number of films shot in Spanish. He was the only one who managed to stand out in *La Barra de Taponazo*. Instead of a plot, the film was loosely based on the tango "Taponazo," a tango dedicated to the soccer star Bernarbé Ferreyra, who appeared in the film. The movie was a disjointed collection of scenes, including a horse race, a soccer match and some musical routines. Julio De Caro and his orchestra appear in the film playing the musical theme; they also recorded it as one of his last records for Brunswick, but it did as poorly as the film.

The second, and last, new film released in 1932 was premiered on the

22nd of December. Roque Funes shot *En el Infierno del Chaco*, a documentary on the war that was then raging between Paraguay and Bolivia in the Chaco region, and it showed the attack and capture of a fort by Paraguayan troops. Its premier was a benefit for the Paraguayan Red Cross. There were also several films shot in 1932 that were never released. *La Prensa* announced the shooting of a film by José A. Ferreyra called *Corazones Gauchos*, with María Turgenova. Perhaps this film is the one known as *Rapsodia Gaucha*, with Ignacio Corsini together with Irma Córdoba and Miguel Gómez Bao. Apparently the dialogues and the songs were unintelligible, and consequently the film, shot in the Movietone process, was never shown. In the opinion of some people, the shorts that still exist with Ignacio Corsini singing, respectively, the tango "Dolor Gaucho," the waltz "Mi Azucena" and the triste campero "Soltando Mis Penas" belong to this unreleased feature film.

Another film that was to have been released in 1932 was *La Canción de Fuego*, directed by Nelo Cosimi, and photographed by Francis J. Boeniger for S.A.C.H.A. Manzanera. It was abandoned because the company shut down. The leading roles were played by Cosimi, Chita Foras, and Rosita Contreras. *El Diario* in its edition of the 23rd of October 1931, picked up some details from the shooting of this production, noting that Nelo Cosimi "has new and modern elements that will allow him, surely, to surpass the productions that he has already given to the local cinema." The paper observed some of Cosimi's work on the movie, and commented upon his efforts to produce lively scenes, his energy and his enthusiasm, and his involvement with even the smallest details of the production.

The high point of the film was supposed to be the fire in a theater, and for this film, Cosimi had the collaboration of the of the city of Buenos Aires Fire Corps.

And so Argentine cinema left the silent period of its history definitely behind. If the outlook of the Argentine film industry in that period looked bleak and terminal, there were, however, two events at the end of 1932 that would change things for ever after: The writer Enrique Larreta achieved success with his play *El Linyera*, and decided to make a film version, and the Argentine radio pioneers, Enrique Susini, César Guerrico and Luis Romero Carranza, after planning it for four years, decided to set up a film studio, establishing the Sociedad Radio Cinematográfica Lumiton.

The Cinema and Tango Musicians' Crisis

From the end of 1924 on, some of the most popular cinemas in the city of Buenos Aires fought over the most popular tango orchestras, to have them playing on their stage while the films were showing, sharing the stage with other musicians that played jazz. Fortunately, the most popular of those orchestras recorded their versions of the themes that they played in the cinemas for various recording companies of those times.

After August 1929, with the release of the first sound and talking film the decision to remove the orchestras from the cinemas started a great crisis. This process lasted until about the middle of 1931, creating terrible unemployment in the middle of the depression, and the first great tango crisis. The films shown, which came from the USA, had music of that origin, sung in English. The record industry, as the sale of the recordings by those same artists went up, started to fire the Argentine tango musicians, and some popular orchestras that managed to survive started to record the popular music that appeared in those films in Spanish.

Francisco Canaro, Roberto Firpo, and Francisco Lomuto were some of those who managed to survive the slump thanks to the popularity of their records, and because they had already been recording foreign songs for years, even including jazz musicians in their groups. In addition, seeing what was happening, they increased the number of musicians in their respective orchestras.

The effects of the depression were being felt soon after the appearance of the first sound films. Many professionals were left without a job, and as orchestras were replaced with sound equipment, the already serious problem was becoming severe.

At the end of 1929, the Argentine public stopped considering talking films a curiosity, and started to think of them as something agreeable, and the cinemas gradually started to adopt the necessary machinery for sound films. And so, all the cinemas started to get rid of the orchestras. Radios were a source of employment for many, but they could never house all the musicians. Many groups then retreated to the outskirts, and to the provinces. The recording companies failed to renew the contracts of many tango artists, due to the advance of records made in the U.S.A.

Sound films were definitely asserting themselves. By May 1930 it was calculated that fifty orchestras with an average of six players each were without work, for a total of three hundred musicians without jobs. The popular pianist Enrique Delfino had this to say: "Sound films are a business like any other, and it seems ridiculous to me, to try to restrain it. The cinema owners have decided to make more money, and that seems fine to me. What frightens me a bit is that sound movies allow records sung by Chevalier, Novarro, etc., in this or that sound film, are starting to put the local record industry in danger.... All will pass. Once people sang 'La Copa del Olvido' ... but no longer. They are spells of luck."

Francisco Canaro, on the other hand, believed that sound movies opened other horizons for Argentine composers: "The day will come when the peoples of Central and South America will demand films spoken and sung in Spanish, and the day will also come when those same films, with all our folk lore, will be an artistic success for the European and American public. Only then will our music be prized. I, personally, have already received offers to head a tango orchestra and record films with tango songs, rancheras, cielitos, gatos, pericones, etc."

But a change of habits concerning record use came about with the popularity of sound films. When these films started being shown, the sale of tango records in Buenos Aires fell by 20 percent, although this did not happen in the rest of the country, where silent films were still being shown. On the other hand, the sale of recordings by film performers or with film music increased by 100 percent. The records from *La Divina Dama*, for example, were sold out quickly after the exhibition of the film.

By the end of the year there were almost no cinemas left showing silent films. However, one cinema, the Metropol, presented Osvaldo Fresedo's típica orchestra, from the 1st of October 1930 on, sharing the bill with Heriberto Fiocco's jazz group and the singer Roberto Díaz. Julio De Caro continued to perform successfully at the Real Cine.

But the end was near: on the 27th of November 1930, the Real Cine started using a sound projection system. It became more and more difficult for musicians. The pianist Adolfo R. Avilés started his activity as a popular folk musician and tango composer, but his real success came when he started to play jazz. When the orchestras were forced out of the cinemas, he became a popular film critic and had his own radio program. He was an exception.

Many of the orchestras under contract to RCA Victor were fired. Some of the musicians, however, managed to get hired as company musicians and took part in the recordings of the Orquesta Típica Victor, and as occasional members of other groups, or accompanied singers.

The saddest case was probably the fiddler Cayetano Puglisi, whose excellent orchestra left 32 recordings at Victor. But as he did not have popular success, although he had critical approval, the group was soon disbanded due to the company's lack of interest. After failing in his attempts to form a new group, he took part in different groups, until in 1940 he started as first violin in the Juan D'Arienzo orchestra, playing a type of tango that did not agree with his personal tastes until the end of his life. There were surely many more cases, and it also happened with other kinds of music. Cayetano Puglisi died largely forgotten.

The recording company that had done most to spread Argentine music was Disco Nacional-Odeón. But Max Glücksmann, its owner, was going through a crisis. The sale of records made by Argentine artists had shrunk markedly and he could not sustain the minimum quantity of sales set by the Gramophone Company. This company, during 1931, had merged with the Columbia Gramophone, creating a new conglomerate of record labels: EMI or Electrical and Musical Industries. After the launching of EMI, Glücksmann began to lose control over his own record company, and at the same time stopped taking part in the management of Radio Splendid. Regarding films, his newsreel stopped being produced, and he was never to produce a film again.

From an artistic point of view, Glücksmann received another hard blow. He had already lost Azucena Maizani and Osvaldo Fresedo, who went over to Brunswick (Maizani in 1929 and Fresedo in 1930). But the hardest blow was the loss of Francisco Lomuto, the most popular artist of the time, who immediately started a new series of records for RCA Victor, in August 1931. Although he still had valuable artists, such as Carlos Gardel, Francisco Canaro and Roberto Firpo, the empire that he had started to build years before was crumbling.

Alfredo Améndola had founded the Atlanta label in 1913 and Telephone in 1917, which in 1923 made room for the Electra label. Some of the big orchestras in those years recorded for this company until it shut down in 1929. A new company appeared then that was to take prestigious artists from both Victor and Odeón; it was called Brunswick. But at the end of 1932, Brunswick also closed, as did Columbia in March. This label had licensed the Cinema and Music Company in 1930, but as this company became a part of the EMI conglomerate, the contracts were not renewed.

With the closing of these companies, a lot of musicians, singers and very good orchestras lost all chances of recording. Only very few managed to record again.

After the carnival dances of 1931, practically all the cinema orchestras disappeared. The last orchestra to give way to sound movies was, according to Luis Adolfo Sierra, the tango orchestra that performed at the Metropol Cinema, under the lead of the fiddler Elvino Vardaro and the pianist Osvaldo Pugliese. The other members of the group were Alfredo Gobbi (violin), Miguel Jurado, Ciriaco Ortiz, Aníbal Troilo (bandoneons), and Luis Adesso. In the future, these would be some of the most important musicians in tango history.

Without silent films, cinemas occasionally presented a live show with pianists, singers or orchestras. But they were an extra, an extension to the films shown. The end came for the cinema orchestras on the 6th of August 1931, when, after a European tour, Julio De Caro performed again at the

Elvino Vardaro and Osvaldo Pugliese, conductors of the last of the silent film orchestras.

Real Cine, which was by then showing sound films. A way of experiencing films had passed.

Two reminders are left from the cinema orchestra time, both born from ideas by Max Glücksmann. The first is a recording of the tango "Tu Disfraz" by the Osvaldo Fresedo orchestra, with a refrain sung by Ernesto Famá, recorded at the Grand Splendid Theater on the 12th of March 1928. The other is a series of ten records recorded by Julio Perceval on the 5th of July 1930 on the Wurlitzer organ belonging to the Gran Cine Florida. Perceval recorded tangos and some theme songs from the sound movies shown then. Glücksmann started selling them a short time later, and they were well received by both the critics and the public.

And so, the musicians left the cinemas to go to (or to return to) the cafés, dance halls and radio stations. Some of them, however, were to find jobs in the Argentine film business, which was preparing to leave many years of frustration behind and become, once and for all, an industry.

7

ARGENTINE CINEMA BECOMES AN INDUSTRY AND HOLLYWOOD MAKES FILMS IN SPANISH

Planning Comes to Argentine Film Production

After many years of frustration, Argentine cinema, between 1933 and 1934, would achieve a level; at which the films produced in the country could compete as equals with films imported from foreign lands. While it would never stop improvising, the film industry, which until then had practically been just a dream, started to grow with strength and vigor. New people and veterans of the industry managed to bring the industry out of its stupor, and great actors and good directors would emerge.

Of all the films released in that short period three would especially influence the development of the industry: *Los Tres Berretines*, *El Linyera*, and *Riachuelo*. The first of these films was produced by the Lumiton Company. This company was formed by the same men who had been the pioneers of Argentine radio in 1920: Enrique Susini, Miguel Mujica, César Guerrico, and Luis Romero Carranza. They had reached the conclusion during the sound film revolution that Argentina could very well be a Spanish film production center, and, after several years of thinking about it, they opened a film studio with all the necessary imported equipment, and a technical staff able to develop local workers.

Before Lumiton offered its first film, another new company, Argentina Sono Film, presented its first production on the 27th of April 1933, *Tango*. Considered by many the first Argentine sound film. It was the first local feature film with its sound track on the film, as the use of records to reproduce sound had been abandoned. Its producer, Angel Mentasti, had decided to establish an enduring production company. For this first production he hired important actors from the Argentine stage and song, with the idea of achieving a great success. Included were Libertad Lamarque, Tita Merello, Alberto Gómez, Pepe Arias, Luis Sandrini, Juan Sarcione, Alicia Vignoli, Azucena Maizani, Meneca Talhade, Mercedes Simone, as well as the Juan de Dios Filiberto, Pedro Maffia, Osvaldo Fresedo, Edgardo Donato y Ernesto Ponzio–Juan Carlos Bazán tango orchestras. The script was written by journalist and poet Carlos de la Púa, and its director was J. Moglia Barth. Not having his own studios, Mentasti produced it at the studios belonging to Federico Valle, who was nearing at the end of his long professional activity.

In the film a young girl's lover and a criminal who also courts her face each other in a duel. The hero defeats his rival, but cannot evade justice. He goes to jail, and after several years of imprisonment, returns to his neighborhood, searching for the girl. Despite all his efforts, he does not find her, and decides to go to Paris, counseled by a friend who says that he will find her there. He loses hope of finding her in the French capital, so he returns to Buenos Aires, engaged to a tango singer. But that relation ends when he discovers his first love, and they both decide to never separate again.

A lot has been written about *Tango*. What is not frequently said is that the film was a huge failure. Other than the plot, the only interesting things that the film offers are the tangos played by the orquesta típicas and the singers. But even these are spoiled by the terrible quality of both the sound and the cinematography. No actor manages to stand out, and the worst portrayal is that of the central character played by: Alberto Gómez. Gomez was a great tango singer, not an actor, and in *Tango* he does not sing very often.

Most of the critics did not like the film, especially the anonymous critic from *La Vanguardia*: "Frankly, the only word that we can find to better condense the accumulation of ridiculous situations and badly done things is this: rubbish. Because however much good will we show, our conscious cannot remain silent considering such an assault against this local industry, that needs effort and good intentions from everybody, in order to reach a degree, if not of perfection, at least of what is acceptable. And these efforts and good intentions do not exist in *Tango*. It is a film that never should have left the experimental camera, and a lot would have been gained, especially concerning the reputation of its actors, and in the concept of our popular song."

The next release of an Argentine film, on the 2nd of June 1933, was

Los Tres Berretines, the first film from Lumiton, and it marked the beginning of a new era for the industry. The film, based on a play by Arnaldo Malfatti and Nicolás de las Llanderas, made the leading actor Luis Arata, and even more so Luis Sandrini, into the first real local film stars. It is thought that the film was directed by Enrique Susini, but as there are no credits for the director or for the technical collaboration, it is quite possible that someone else from Lumiton played a part in the final result, possibly the cinematographer John Alton.

Seen onscreen, the theatrical action became more lively and agile. *Los Tres Berretines* proved that films worthy of being shown not only in the best cinemas in Buenos Aires, but also abroad, could be made in Argentina. Luis Arata was revealed as a great character actor, and Luis Sandrini, playing the same character that he had played onstage, introduced a pleasant comic sense.

Adolfo R. Avilés, who had distinguished himself formerly as a folk tune and tango composer and as the leader, from the piano, of a jazz group, was by then a popular film critic, and he wrote the following review in *El Diario*: "It can be said, and justly so, that the Argentine film that we were all waiting for, has been made at last. It is a light comedy where the fun

Luis Sandrini in *Los Tres Berretines* (Lumiton, 1933).

and high spirited wit of our local characters and commonplace acts of our background predominate. We must celebrate, and it is important to say so, that as the first example of films to be seen in the future, it offers a pleasant movie, that with honest means produces a healthy happiness, instead of the underworld tragedy seen so often onscreen, in other local productions. Making *Los Tres Berretines*, Lumiton has shown what can be done: Photography, sound and camera effects are impeccable."

After years of working with Federico Valle, the cinematographer Roberto Schmidt and the sound technician Ricardo Raffo (who together with Eduardo Morera had made the Carlos Gardel shorts), set up their own independent company: Magnus Film. This company reached an important landmark for Argentine films, because for the first time a Hollywood studio distributed an Argentine film. The studio was Universal, and the film was *Los Caballeros del Cemento*, written and directed by Ricardo Hicken, with Luis Arata, José Otal, Mecha Delgado, Olimpio Bobbio, Francisco Plastino, Arturo Bamio, Carlos Betoldi, Eduardo González, Pascual Pelicciota and Florindo Ferrario. The photography was by César Sforza. The music was played by Augusto P. Berto's tango orchestra, which accompanied the actress Blanca Ríos in the scene where she sings the tango "¿Para Qué?" by Rodolfo Sciamarella, specially written for this production. This comedy was released on the 1st of June 1933, although it was shot at the beginning of the year before. The story was about a group of criminals who take over a property, and pass themselves off as its owners, until the real owners turn up. Although there also was a romantic situation between a delinquent girl and one of the victims, the director emphasized comedy over romance, and the acting was skillful. *Los Caballeros del Cemento* was not the success that its producers had dreamed of, but, it gave them the chance to make a new film which would be the first really successful Argentine sound film, both with the critics and the audience. The playwright Enrique Larreta, who had achieved a great theatrical success with his play called *El Linyera*, decided to join forces with Magnus Film to make a film version. It was shot mostly at an *estancia* (ranch) owned by Larreta himself, between December and February 1933.

About his film, Larreta himself said: "If you put great passion into the making of each facet, the cinematographic art is so rich, so magical, that it sometimes gives you back much more than what you give it. In effect, there is great torment in all the progressive steps in the making of a film, because of the innumerable quantity of things that you have to take into account. But after having worked like a laborer who loves his occupation, and joins it all together and orders it into a real concert, with a well studied orchestra, one surprises oneself with all that he has achieved."

Released on the 11th of September 1933, *El Linyera* had a great impact, and was favorably received both by the critics and by the audience, making its leading actor Mario Soffici one of the most important persons in Argentine cinema. The fact that it was distributed by a Hollywood company, Universal, also allowed it to be shown abroad. The film opposed a gaucho and a tramp against a primitive background. The film was mostly shot in natural settings, and managed to show the environment faithfully, with excellent photography and good sound quality. Besides the excellent work of Mario Soffici, Nedda Francy, Domingo Sapelli and Julio Renato performed well. The rest of the cast were not actors, but people from the shooting location.

John Alton was a Hungarian cinematographer who had carried out his career in the U.S.A. before passing through Europe, and ending up as head of cinematography at Paramount's Joinville studios. It was there where he was hired as head of cinematography by Lumiton Studios, with the idea of taking part in two films. After arriving in Argentina in 1932, he was responsible for the images of *Los Tres Berretines*.

After this film, Alton left Lumiton and formed his own company, Altonfilm, and decided to direct his first film, *El Hijo de Papá*, filmed in the province of Córdoba. Trying to repeat the success of *Los Tres Berretines*, Alton cast Luis Sandrini in the leading role; his character was called

Poster announcing *El Linyera* (Universal 1933).

Berretin, no less. The film also had the actors Rosa Rosen, A. Sandrini, Enrique Duca and A. Priano. The film was a comedy, and took place in the town of Calamuchita, in the province of Córdoba. Its plot was about a competition to solve the economic crisis that had paralyzed all local activity; the prize was a ticket to Buenos Aires.

El Hijo de Papá did not turn out to be the success that Alton had dreamed of. Released at the Paramount Cinema on the 23rd of October 1933, it was retired from circulation only two days later. The final results were so poor that the audience reportedly protested loudly all through its projection. A few years after, Luis Sandrini bought the negatives from John Alton and together they proceeded to destroy them. Except perhaps for a few stills, inaccessible to the public today, nothing remains of this film. John Alton, who would never direct again, later took part in some productions as a cinematographer, went to Argentina Sono Film in 1935 as head of cinematography, and in 1940 went to work in film studios in the U.S.A. Alton obtained a modest but notable achievement in Argentina that he would never repeat in Hollywood: his name appeared in the advertisements of the films that he had shot personally.

According to Domingo Di Núbila, when Argentina Sono Film was created in 1933, it tried to deal with the commercialization of Argentine films seriously: "Until then, the directors and producers, who had put every cent they had in the production of a film, were completely helpless facing the exhibitors, and had no choice but to accept the ten or twenty pesos per show that they were offered. Some other films that were produced without so much financial pressure, but independently, could not find a proper commercialization." The idea was to form a company on the basis of three films, and not release the first until the second had begun shooting, and the third announced. This gave the impression of people working in an organized manner; for the first time films were negotiated en bloc.

The company's first film, *Tango*, was an absolute artistic and business failure. The second *Dancing*, based on a play by Alejandro Berruti, released on the 9th of November 1933, was a better production but a worse failure. The saddest thing was that many actors that would later reach real success and standing would have their first appearance on screen in this film, especially Tito Lusiardo, who was one of the few to do well in the film.

Based on a play by Alejandro Berruti, *Dancing* had no plot. It was a series of loose episodes, never losing its theatrical characteristics, with a total lack of cinematographic action. Still, it had good comic moments, and some attractive variety numbers; among them the work by Roberto Firpo's tango orchestra and René Cóspito's jazz band, both good additions to the action. Rosa Catá, Alicia Vignoli, Alicia Barrié, and Amanda Ledesma were among the actresses, and actors Arturo García Buhr, Severo Fernández, Héctor Quintanilla, Tito Lusiardo and Héctor Calcaño played the male lead roles in the film. The first film released in 1934, on the 16th of March, was *Calles de Buenos Aires*, directed by José A. Ferreyra and produced by Federico Valle. This film told the well-worn story of a girl from the country drawn by the glamour of the city, who leaves her mother behind and trades her boyfriend for a rich suitor. in spite of its oft-told plot, the film achieved a modest success because it was done with simplicity, with capable actors, and with technical and material resources of the highest standard. Nelly Ayllón, Guillermos Casali, Miguel Gómez Bao (in a comic role), Enrique Mazza, Leonor Mazza, Guillermo Verding and Mario Soffici were the stars.

After *Los Tres Berretines* the Lumiton Company tried another kind of film, releasing *Ayer y Hoy* on the 25th of May 1935. It did not achieve the same success as Lumiton's first film, but it was outstanding for its sound and photography, on the same level as many foreign films. The name of its director did not appear, although Enrique Susini was almost certainly responsible. Before its premiere, one of the copies that was ready to be shown spontaneously combusted, as they were still using cellulose nitrate–based films, and this delayed the release a few days.

The film was based on a story by Ricardo Gutierrez, adapted for the screen by its author and José B. Cairola, and told two stories. The first took place in 1840, and was about a young girl, who, despite loving an officer, is obliged to marry another man for money. Her life is sheer martyrdom, only lightened by her son, and the knowledge that when the officer died, he would die still loving her. The other story is set in 1934, and is quite like the former, although it differs in that it has a happy ending. Its makers did not manage to bind together the two episodes of the film, which also lacked emotion in its more dramatic moments. Its leading actors were Alicia Vignoli, and Miguel Faust Rocha. Also appearing in the film were Mario Danesi, Victoria Garbato and Iván Caseros.

While that Lumiton did not know how to take advantage of the success of *Los Tres Berretines*, another company did. After two failures, and not in a position to allow themselves another, Argentina Sono Film, with its producer Angel Mentasti and the director L. J. Moglia Barth, released the film *Riachuelo* on the 4th of July 1934. It became their first big success as a team.

They had taken advantage of all previous experiences, both theirs and others, in order to make a good film. The leading actor from *Los Tres Berretines*, Luis Sandrini, had the leading role, playing the same character.

He had been unsuccessful in *El Hijo de Papá*, but *Riachuelo* made him a film star, the first on the domestic screen.

The film was a very simple comedy about two good petty delinquent lads who are regenerated thanks to the love of their humble fiancées. The comic scenes, though a bit naïve, were effective, and Luis Sandrini became popular. Maruja Pibernat and Margarita Sola, making their debut in front of the cameras, turned out to be very expressive, as did María Esther Gamas, Alfredo Camiña, and Héctor Calcaño. J. Pérez Bilbao and Juan Sarcione ably played the villains. The music was provided by Edgardo Donato's tango orchestra.

Although it was still a short time away, it can be said that after *Riachuelo*, Argentina had a film industry able to making films capable of reaping artistic and commercial successes to be compared with those of the films brought in from abroad.

While it is true that Argentine cinema was marching towards a prosperous future, this does not mean that makeshift films, or those that had little to offer, would disappear. On the 12th of September 1934 *Galería de Esperanzas* was released, a Cabildo Company production, with a script by Enrique Cadícamo and Enrique Rosas, and directed by Carlos de la Púa. Both Cadícamo and de la Púa were great writers and poets, but their film activity would never be memorable. The film was a failure, with poor production and an unoriginal plot. It told of an aspiring singer who falls asleep and sees himself triumphant, flattered first in Buenos Aires, and then in Paris, only to suddenly wake up to his harsh reality. The songs, by Luis Díaz, were the only good things that the film offered. The rest of the film displayed bad set design, bad photography, and undistinguished acting by Luis Díaz, and the actresses Tulia Ciampoli and Nelly Quel. After the success of *El Linyera*, the people from Magnus Film joined up with tango musician Francisco Canaro to form the Río de la Plata Film Company. Canaro was to personally produce all the company's films. The first was called *Idolos de la Radio*, and it was the first time that several radio artists were used in films. It was a very popular film, and was the first Argentine film to be released at the Monumental Cinema, which would become the first important cinema to present Argentine films almost exclusively. The most outstanding performance in *Idolos de la Radio* were by Olinda Bozán and Tito Lusiardo, both destined to have long and popular careers in Argentine movies.

The theme of the movie, based on an original script by Nicolás de las Llanderas and Arnaldo Malfatti, was lost among a set of performances by artists from the radio, which made the movie boring at times. When the action and the comedy returned, the film was more satisfactory, although the sentimental scenes did not work because of the paucity of the dialogue and the poor acting of Ada Falcón and Ignacio Corsini, who were better singers than actors.

At the end of 1934 Alonso Film released *El Hombre Bestia*, written and directed by C. Z. Soprano, based on his novel called *Las Aventuras del Capitán Richard*. According to Roberto Di Chiara (who owns a copy), this film was shot in the city of Rosario, and was originally presented there in 1932, which would make it the first fictional Argentine film with a Movietone sound track. It is about a pilot who, after crashing in hostile territory, is converted into a beast, only to fall into the hands of a scientist who experiments on him with a drug that makes him chase women. Unhappily, there are no reports about its reception in Buenos Aires. The film featured Carmen Quiroga, Saverio Yaquinto, Raúl D'Angeli, Lito Bayardo and Elvira Ratti.

José A. Ferreyra had to face many financial and technical problems in order to be able to make his films in the days of silent movies. In the sound era, after years of experience, he managed to make films that were liked by the public, never abandoning his favorite tango themes. *Mañana es Domingo* was released on the 8th of November 1934, and it was well received by both the public and critics. The plot concerns a group of employees of a large commercial enterprise. An employee's brother stole money from the store, driven by his gambling debts, and her boyfriend, the cashier, decides to assume the blame. When the girl is ready to satisfy the amorous requirements of the manager to free her boyfriend from blame, the brother repents and confesses the truth. Then the manager, in a sudden and conventional turn, gives up his requirements, to allow the happiness of the leading couple. The film had some comic scenes between a bellhop and another employee, a small episode about another employee's engagement and some background sketches well accomplished by Ferreyra. Maruja Gil Quesada and Roberto Salinas performed well in the leading roles, but most outstanding was José Gola, in his first part. The comic performances of Miguel Gómez Bao and Anita Jordán were effective, and Héctor Calcaño, José Mazilli and Margarita Burke were also good in their parts.

The last release in 1934 took place on the 26th of November. It was a documentary about the Eucharistic Congress that took place that year. As *La Prensa* printed a few days before, "all the great ceremonies of the Congress, from the reception for Cardinal Pacelli up to the closing procession of the Congress, including the night-time ceremony and communion at the Plaza de Mayo, have been filmed clearly: the Pope's words, Cardinal Pacelli's speech, the other orators' words, the cheers of the crowd, the words of the announcer. In addition, Monsignor Dionisio R. Napal has commentated the scenes of the film, so the historic film is even more valuable."

La Prensa also reported that the President of the Executive Committee of the Congress, Monsignor Daniel Figueroa, said that "This is the only official film of the great ceremonies of the Congress, and apart from that, it is the only one that gives an idea of the grandness of the ceremonies that were celebrated, because all the rest are just short newsreels that do not make up a comprehensive film."

This film was produced and directed by Federico Valle, and was practically the last of his film career. According to Roberto Di Chiara, Valle continued to occasionally produce newsreels in other cities of Argentina up to at least 1939, when he decided to retire.

By the end of 1939, the Argentine film industry was starting, after so many years, to leave behind the problems that had held back its growth for so long. What is more, films had changed in twenty years. Many pioneers were no longer working, although others were still administrating cinemas. Max Glücksmann had been the distributor and exhibitor of the great Hollywood studios for years, until, ten years before, these companies had started to distribute their productions themselves. From 1933 on Glücksmann distributed the films of the only American studio that still did not have an Argentine subsidiary, RKO Radio Pictures. Glücksmann reflected on the changes he had witnessed:

> I have directed and managed 50 cinemas in Argentina. Today I have only 16 in our country and 40 in Uruguay. Times have changed a lot. Before, and I am proud to have been one of the crusaders, you had to persuade, convince the owners of the buildings that it was good business to build places dedicated to film shows; you had to give them guarantees, assure them of a high profit, and I did it. I built cinemas on my own; promoted the building of others, hiring them beforehand. Today it is the opposite. My personal initiative is no longer necessary; there are many private initiatives.... The conditions for the existence of the exhibitors are not as stimulating as they should be. In Rosario de Santa Fe, where I manage 8 cinemas, and am, therefore, the third most important taxpayer of the city, they have established a municipal tax on new films, that the exhibitor must pay, added to the many that already exist. Think about what would happen to us if the process became general, it would mean the establishment of municipal customs.... On the other hand, and returning to the management of theaters by my company, the fact of the reduction of our activity is important. It does not seem fair, doing what I do, which is distributing RKO films, to have to go out and compete with the distributors on unequal terms. The times have changed a lot, and I must repeat, what was necessary before is now detrimental.

The reason for Glücksmann's sad assertion was another problem. A month later, EMI, on the 18th of March 1934, announced that from that date on, they would distribute themselves the records that he had been producing successfully for so many years. And so, from then on, the Nacíonal-Odeón records were to be called "Criollo-Odeón," and after 1936, simply "Odeón."

While it was true that no artist or office employee lost his job (Mauricio Godard continued to be the artistic director of the EMI Odeón Company almost to the end of his life), Glücksmann's saying goodbye to his own company was a sad end: he had built the record company from nothing. Besides, the loss of his record company started rumors that he could also lose his cinemas. It did not happen. He continued to control them all, and to manage the activity of some of the most prestigious cinemas in Buenos Aires, continuing to show his ability in doing it.

Glücksmann had called his company for distributing RKO Radio Pictures films Radiolux. In 1936, RKO ended its association with Glücksmann, and became the last big studio to establish its own affiliate in Argentina.

From then on Radiolux distributed European films, and those from small American companies. What was more important was the decision made by him to distribute and show Argentine films. As an exhibitor he opened his cinemas to local productions, and as a distributor, he took care to take many Argentine films to areas that were considered less commercial.

Max Glücksmann, film recording and radio pioneer in Argentina, the person who presented the great artist Carlos Gardel to the world, died on the 20th of October 1946.

North American Films in Spanish

One of the problems that always hurt the development of the Argentine film business was the lack of money for productions. Hollywood silent movies could satisfy the moviegoers' demand of films, since dialogue was not required. After the introduction of sound films, the situation changed. While subtitles in Spanish were soon adopted for the exhibition of foreign films, the public wanted to see films spoken in their own language. The Argentine film industry did not have enough resources to satisfy the demand, and only managed to do so after 1935. Until then, Hollywood studios made a series of films to be shown in different parts of the world in several languages. Those that reached Argentina were mostly spoken in Spanish, although some in other languages were also shown.

In their book *Cita en Hollywood* edited by Ediciones Mensajero (Bilbao) in 1990, Juan B. Heinink and Robert G. Dickson tried, quite successfully, to compile these films in Spanish produced by American studios. The difficulties of showing films in a language other than English effectively postponed the sound film revolution. Spanish subtitles were immediately adopted in Argentina for films done in English. On the other hand, Hollywood studios used dubbing, in which the actor's voice was replaced by another in a different language.

One of the problems that Hollywood producers always had, both in films shot in Spanish or those shot in another language and dubbed, was the actor's accent. Although the grammar is basically the same, the Spanish spoken in Mexico is not the same as that spoken in Argentina, Colombia, Chile, Spain, or elsewhere. Each country has its own characteristic accent. Consequently, the Spanish Latin American Film Bureau drew up the following resolution for all the producers who planned to shoot films in Spanish, that also applied when the time came to dub films made in other languages, originally published in Argentina in *El Diario* on the 27th of January 1930,

The time has come for producers to think seriously and learn the truth about the so controversial accents and dialects used in Spain, Central America, and in the rest of the Spanish speaking countries.

There is a marked tendency in the producers to shoot films in Spanish using actors that have, or use, exclusively, the accent from the provinces of Castille. Castille is a part of Spain, and Spain is one of the few, if not the only Spanish speaking country, in which there are provinces that have, and use, their own dialects, For example: Catalonians, Basques, etc. The idea that dialects are used in Mexico, Central and South America and the rest of the countries is completely erroneous. All these countries speak Spanish, but use their own idioms, or as they say in the U.S.A., "slang."

If some of these countries use words or phrases incorrectly, that have another meaning elsewhere, that does not mean that the Spanish from one country will not be understood in another. Besides, schools teach correct and pure Spanish, just as in the United States, even though Americans use their own slang, (idioms) in their daily conversations, schools teach a correct and pure English, which is used in commerce, social relations, literature, etc.

As a consumer market, the South American and Spanish speaking one, taken as a whole, occupies the second place in the North American film business. It would therefore be unfair, and un-commercial to provide that market with films in which the actors use the Castilian accent exclusively. This attitude, taken by the producers, would affect the interests of the American industry in these markets, just like giving the American audiences films where the actors only used a British accent. This is not the case, naturally, unless the film has a regional background, and it takes place in a certain country.

Besides, no accent, if it is strong, comes out well in sound pictures: the Castilian "c" and "z" produce a lisping effect, the Argentine "y" and double "l" are pronounced like an English "j." The Chileans drop the last letters of a word, and so do the Cubans, etc.

We are against all synchronization, because we firmly believe that our countries have the right to demand films made in their own language.

WHAT MEASURES MUST BE TAKEN?
1. Make versions (if the film is foreign) in a correct and pure Spanish.
2. Search for actors that speak without strong accents and with a clear diction.
3. Demand that these actors say their parts just as they are written. You will then have a talking film in Spanish that will be successful, commercially speaking.

A Spanish for talking films must be created, just as after much experimentation, the Americans have created an English for talking films that has been accepted and approved by all the English-speaking peoples.

This resolution contained a serious mistake: there is no correct or pure Spanish. Nor is there a neutral accent. Besides, one can guess the origin of the dubber from the expressions used: in the United States these versions are usually from Mexico, and the viewer can tell.

So, right from the beginning, dubbing was rejected by most of the audience and the critics. Not much time passed before Hollywood decided to adopt subtitles to show their films in Argentina. Today dubbing is only used by some television channels and in films for children, because it is difficult for a child to read the subtitles.

But in 1930, whether the films were shown in their original language or not, people wanted to see films spoken in Spanish.

The first film shot in Spanish and shown in Argentina was *Ladrones*, with Stan Laurel and Oliver Hardy. They did not speak Spanish, and had to do so using phonetics. But they used the difficulty as a comic resource, and a series of films with Laurel and Hardy had an impressive popularity.

If *Ladrones* was a great success, the following film was an even bigger one. When *Vida Nocturna* was released at the end of May 1930, it was greeted with more enthusiasm than any recent comic release. After showing for several weeks, *Vida Nocturna* proved much more successful than other more "important" productions.

The Laurel and Hardy films in Spanish were "sister" versions of those spoken in English. They were shot simultaneously in both languages, or, they were shot in English and later in Spanish. This procedure was introduced with the film *Sombras de Gloria* (also shot in English with another cast) mentioned earlier, with José Böhr in the leading role. This film was not made by one of the big Hollywood companies, but by one of the many small enterprises trying to take advantage of the Spanish sound film novelty. The next film by Böhr for this company, together with Lola Vendrell and Lelia Magana, was called *Así es la Vida*. The outcome was bad, and the film was a failure; it looked like something improvised with the only purpose of quickly exploiting the Latin-American markets.

Not counting Laurel and Hardy, the first successful film in Spanish was *El Cuerpo del Delito*, the first in Spanish produced by Paramount. Released on the 27th of May 1930, with María Alba, Antonio Moreno, and Ramón Pereda heading the cast, it was one of the few good productions in Spanish to be seen in those days. Based on a novel by S. S. Van Dine, the results were fairly good, as it had action and the Spanish spoken was to the audience's liking.

The big studios could have put any of the great actors that they had under contract to speak Spanish in a film in 1930, but they were only do it with those with Hispanic origins. The one exception was Buster Keaton at MGM, who followed Laurel and Hardy's example when the time came for him to speak in Spanish. His first film was *Estrellados* a sister version of *Free and Easy*, although it included some scenes dubbed in Spanish. The premier of this first Buster Keaton talking film was on the 21st of June in Buenos Aires. Like Laurel and Hardy, Keaton took advantage of his ignorance of Spanish, using it to comic effect.

¡Concurra Vd. al carnaval de la risa!

BUSTER KEATON
habla castellano en

ESTRELLADOS
LA SENSACION COMICA DEL AÑO
con Raquel Torres & Don Alvarado

ESTRELLADOS
se exhibe diariamente en los cines
PALACE THEATRE -- GRAND SPLENDID THEATRE

METRO-GOLDWYN-MAYER

Poster announcing *Estrellados* with Buster Keaton (MGM, 1930).

The reputation of the big Hollywood studios that tried to make their films in Spanish with the highest quality possible was tarnished by the small companies that tried to capture the market. *Charros, Gauchos y Manolas*, made by the Hollywood Spanish Pictures Company and the musician Xavier Cougat, was an absolute disaster. This production was done in complete ignorance of what Argentina was like, with a total lack of artistic sensibility, to the point that it was much worse than the local silent films. The foreign producers of movies in Spanish should have put more effort and thought into their films; their efforts were quickly to become discredited.

The film *Cascarrabias* released on the 17th of April by Paramount, and with Ernesto Vilches (who was of Spanish origins but already a favorite of the Buenos Aires stage) as the hero, was the first chance for a really popular Spanish speaking artist to appear in an American film. The results were satisfactory, although critics faulted the acting of Carmen Guerrero and Barry Norton.

The presence of Adolphe Menjou in the Paramount film called *Amor Audaz*, together with the Argentine actor Barry Norton and the Mexican actress Rosita Moreno in her movie debut, was the only incidence of a real North American film star talking (or trying to talk) Spanish on screen. The outcome was bad: Adolphe Menjou's Spanish was strained, he had an American accent, and the good actors in the film found themselves saddled with a naïve, false and uninteresting plot.

During the shooting of this film in Hollywood, Paramount had a studio built at Joinville, on the outskirts of Paris, France, with the purpose of making films in different languages, starting with alternative versions of those spoken in English. The Chilean Adelqui Millar, formerly an actor and now a film director, was responsible for Paramount's Spanish-language films that would begin showing in 1931. *Olimpia*, released on the 18th of November 1930, was produced by MGM. Its leading actors, María Alba, Elvira Morla, José Crespo, Juan Aristi and Luis Llaneza were not stars. Still, the film was of outstanding quality. It was based on a play by Miguel de Zárraga, and stuck closely to the original.

The Fox Film Corporation started its sound film activity in Argentina with *El Precio de un Beso*, already mentioned a few pages back. With that film, they found in José Mojica an artist who was popular all over the Continent, and who recorded his songs at RCA Victor. Having such a star, Fox made a series of films with other actors in the leading roles, some of whom would achieve a modest stardom in Argentina.

The Argentine actress Mona Maris, who took part in *El Precio de un Beso*, made the company's second film, *Del Mismo Barro*, about which there is little information apart from that given by Robert G. Dickson and Juan B. Heinink in *Cita en Hollywood*.

The third Fox film in Spanish, called *El Ultimo de los Vargas*, was a western that established its three leading actors in Latin America: Jorge (or George) Lewis, Luana Alcañiz and the Argentine actor Vicente Padula. Based on a Western novel by Zane Grey, the film was the story of a son who avenges his father's death, at the hands of bandits, and frees the heroine from the clutches of the villain.

By the end of 1930, the only films in Spanish of any quality were those by Stan Laurel and Oliver Hardy. The Spanish versions were longer than their "sisters" in English, with oddities and comic routines that were not known in the U.S.A. When these films were shown the English versions were not distributed in Argentina; their success allowed others, produced only in English, to be shown successfully, along with their last silent films. As *La Prensa* reported on the 1st of January 1931, "the case of Stan Laurel and Oliver Hardy cannot be compared to anything in films. They are now the outstanding comedians. Only a year of continuous work has elevated them to the most comfortable of popularities. Their films, that are short, already have a steady audience. The fact is that the silly thin man and the immense fat man display great sympathy and naïve tenderness. Laurel and Hardy have fashioned one of the fastest artistic careers, getting to reap the preference of the crowd. We have celebrated them in *Ladrones*, *Vida Nocturna*, *Los Pibes del Ford*, *Delicias de la Vida Conyugal*, *Noches de Duendes*, *Radiomanía*, *Cama para Dos* and *Tiembla y Titubea*. And as the success of their films continues to grow, the fame of them both has grown so much in the past year that they are the only comedians that this years' spectator can recall."

The producer of the Laurel and Hardy films, Hal Roach, had directed a film for the MGM Studios. The English version was known as *Men of the North*, its Spanish version was released on the 12th of February 1931, as *Monsieur Le Fox*. MGM produced the film in five languages simultaneously, and the intricacy of producing a film with these characteristics produced a change in policy regarding these special versions, according to Robert G. Dickson and Juan B. Heinink. The new technique was to wait until the original version was finished (and if possible released, so as to know how successful it was) and use it as a guide to copy all that was necessary, using substitute personnel, gaining speed and reducing costs.

The next film in Spanish from MGM was *De Frente Marchen*, the second and last Buster Keaton film shot in Spanish in Hollywood. He would make another later on in Mexico, in 1947. This Spanish version of the film *Doughboy*, directed by Edward Sedgwick, was distinguished by the acting of Conchita Montenegro. The results were reportedly good, even when Keaton spoke in Spanish. Although the film was liked in Argentina, the result was not what MGM expected, so that its following productions were in English, with Spanish subtitles (although some were also produced in French).

With *Noches de Broadway*, Universal introduced dubbing in Spanish with disastrous results. Trying to correct that bad impression, the company presented its first production shot in Spanish, *Oriente y Occidente*, with the Mexican actress Lupe Vélez and the Argentine Barry Norton, under the director George Melford. The production, acting, and direction were of a higher quality than that of most earlier efforts.

The next film made in Hollywood in Spanish encouraged new hopes. It was *Presidio*, from MGM, which premiered on the 17th of March 1931. Despite the inexperience of its actors and other obstacles deriving from the production of non–English-language films, the results were excellent. The dialogue was restricted to only a few scenes where it was necessary, giving the film action, speed, and energy. MGM's effort was successful, and *Presidio* was on the billboard of the cinema where it was released for more than a month.

As mentioned earlier Paramount had opened new studios at Joinville, outside Paris, France, meant to make versions in different languages of some of their Hollywood productions, although they would later produce some films exclusively in Spanish or French. One of the first Paramount productions from Joinville released in Argentina was *La Incorregible*, directed by Leo Mittler, with Enriqueta Serrano, and Tony D'Algy. The results were only average.

Among the films spoken in Spanish, there were some that had better luck than their original versions in English. *The Big Trail*, by Raoul Walsh and featuring John Wayne, was the first production shot on 70mm film, although there was also a standard version on 35mm film. This movie was also made in Spanish, French, Italian and German versions. Both the English versions were great box office failures, and it would be several years before John Wayne would become a popular film star. The film did not deserve its poor reception, as its quality has endured quite well. The Spanish version, called *La Gran Jornada*, with Jorge Lewis in the lead was released on the 8th of April 1931 and was a great box office hit, running all year long. The story about a group of settlers crossing rivers, valleys, mountains, and deserts, was done with visions of the spectacular; it was vigorous and colorful, shot almost completely in natural settings. The performances of Jorge Lewis (in the leading role), and Carmen Guerrero, Carlos Villarías, Martín Garralaga, Allan García, and especially Roberto

The musical theme from *La Gran Jornada* (Fox, 1931).

Guzmán, were very good, and the Spanish was adequate. *Dracula*, with Bela Lugosi and directed by Tod Browning, was a box office success in the United States. Universal shot another version in Spanish at the same time, with different actors and another technical staff, that premiered in Argentina on the 17th of April 1931. This second version is generally considered to be better than the production in English. While it is true that the Spanish version is better, the same virtues and defects are found in both. *Dracula* in Spanish was a great box office and critical failure, so Universal stopped making films in Spanish. As this film is one of the few Hollywood productions spoken in Spanish that can still be seen today, the first defect that hits the eye is the mixture of Spanish, Mexican and Argentine accents in the cast. Its unfolding is slow, heavy, and lacking in emotion and attractiveness. The cast, headed by Carlos Villarías in the leading role, produced performances as weak as the script.

The Joinville Paramount studios did not have a success with *La Incorregible*, according to *La Prensa*, *Toda una Vida*, released on the 28th of May 1931 (directed by Adelqui Millar and with Carmen Larrabeiti and Tony D'Algy in the main roles) did not manage to make an impact on the audience either:

> We have already said all there was to say about the Spanish language films produced by the French studios at Joinville when they released *La Incorregible*. They lack directors and actors. As long as they do not definitely transform the way they work, nothing good will come out of those studios. We saw it again last night; *Toda una Vida*, a film spoken in Spanish, coming from there, though better than *La Incorregible*, shows the same faults: the absence of a heedful director and the presence of stage actors, absolutely divorced from the cinema.
>
> Can't a decent film in Spanish be made at Joinville? It is really difficult to believe. Those who have seen those phenomenal studios praise their organization, and their discipline. The success of films made in French, German, and English is well known. Each film is made in several different languages, in certain cases up to eight. They are all satisfactory, except those in Spanish. What hidden resources, what complicated maneuvers do these producers ignore? Men capable of directing versions in different languages fail miserably when they try Spanish. They have not chosen a single capable artist. They have not sought a single consultant with a significant capacity. And these are only two of the unsolvable problems. We trust that the sad fate of the Spanish films released so far will make them understand their error.

Laurel and Hardy reappeared on the 11th of June 1931, produced by Hal Roach and MGM, speaking in Spanish in *Politiquerías*, and achieving another hit. The original English version of this film, called *Chickens Come Home*, is a short film lasting approximately half an hour. *Politiquerías* lasts

A pair of posters announcing *Politiquerias* with Laurel and Hardy (MGM, 1931).

practically an hour, and included some very funny gags that were not seen in the United States. The story basically consisted of Oliver Hardy's political aspirations being tarnished by a villain, and the vain efforts of Stan Laurel to avoid her and reach Hardy's home. The film was a hit among Argentine audiences.

One of the few films produced by Warner Bros. in Spanish was *La Dama Atrevida*, released on the 27th of June 1931. Ramón Pereda and Luana Alcañiz distinguished themselves in this film directed by William McGann, who could not, however, resolve some naïve situations that harmed the final result.

Columbia Pictures, which was then a young company without much presence in the American film business, opened a subsidiary in Argentina to distribute its films. The first film that this company released in Argentina was called *El Código Penal*, and it was regarded as one of the best films in Spanish to be shown up to that point. Its story was vigorous and well produced; Barry Norton's leading performance was a positive progress for his career; and Carlos Villarías and María Alba also stood out in the film.

MGM presented Stan Laurel and Oliver Hardy in a feature spoken in Spanish which premiered on the 8th of July 1931, *Los Calaveras*. What was not known in Argentina at the time was that this film was composed of Spanish versions of two shorts in English by Laurel and Hardy. The end of the second, the inheritance from Laurel's uncle, was made for this special version, as the original short had another ending. La Nación had the following to say about *Los Calaveras*: "The friends' eternal discussions and fights, the fat man's patience put on trial by the thin man's stupidity and

Poster announcing *La Dama Atrevid* (First National, 1930).

impertinence, the things that always happen, in conclusion, their admirable characteristics, make up this new production, that in a superlative degree is a new comic hit."

Beyond those with Laurel and Hardy, no film in Spanish by Hollywood studios had managed to hit upon a film star to be compared with those appearing in English-language films. But history would change on the 22nd of September 1931 when Paramount Pictures released a production shot in the Joinville Studios called *Luces de Buenos Aires*. It was directed by Adelqui Miller, assisted by Manuel Romero, with a script by Romero and Luis Bayón Herrera, and this film made its hero Carlos Gardel into a great movie star.

It differed from previous films from the Joinville studios because it was not a version of some other film in English, but an original work, with an Argentine background, an Argentine accent, and some of the most popular actors from the Buenos Aires stage. The same can be said of the authors

Carlos Gardel, Sofía Bozán, Gloria Guzmán, Adelqui Miller, Manuel Romero, and others during the filming at the Joinville Studios of *Las Luces de Buenos Aires* (Paramount, 1931).

of the music: Gerardo Matos Rodríguez (the composer of "La Cumparsita"), Enrique Delfino, Gardel himself, and Julio De Caro, who also took part onscreen with his orchestra. Up to that point the Argentine film industry had not yet managed to produce a sound film of such stature, and its release roused considerable expectations. On the occasion of its release, Paramount organized a Hollywood-style premier, unseen until then among Argentines, with the presence of all the artists that took part in the film: Gardel, Gloria Guzmán, Sofía Bozán, Pedro Quartucci, and Vicente Padula.

Las Luces de Buenos Aires was Paramount's most important success in Argentina in 1931. The songs of Carlos Gardel and the performance of Gloria Guzmán were the most notable aspects of the film. However, the film displayed emotions and aspects of Argentina that were deformed and exaggerated: the owner of the *estancia* never takes off his poncho or his boots in his Buenos Aires hotel room, and the gauchos that accompany him to the city are dressed as if for a Carnival party. The most absurd thing is the climax, when these gauchos kidnap the star of a play from the theater in the middle of the performance as if they were lassoing cattle.

Despite these defects the results were very good. Carlos Gardel, who until then had was only a great singer, proved to be a good actor too. Audiences received him with applause, celebrating each of his appearances in the film. On the 23rd of October 1931, *Presidiarios* was released, with Stan Laurel and Oliver Hardy. Its English version, called *Pardon Us* was the first full-length feature film by the popular pair, although they had already done other films as long as this one in Spanish, that were only shown outside America. *Presidiarios*, besides being a parody of the film *Presidio* (and its English version, *The Big House*), turned out to be a better film in Spanish than in English, as it included several scenes that were not seen in the U.S.A.

Presidiarios was the last film that Laurel and Hardy made in Spanish. MGM, distributor of these Hal Roach productions, stopped producing films in Spanish and asked Roach to do the same. Laurel and Hardy's popularity was such that when some of their films made only in English were shown in Argentina, they received the same warm acceptance from the public. This allowed Laurel and Hardy to continue acting exclusively in English. Even so, a few years later, in 1937, they again said some words in Spanish in the film *Pick a Star*, almost surely as a way of greeting an audience that was as faithful as the Latin American public.

The film industry therefore lost the only long-lasting American stars who made films in Spanish. The few stars that still made films in Spanish were all of Mexican or Spanish origins, although they had had more success in the past.

Antonio Moreno made some Spanish-language films, although the most important part of his career was in silent films. The same can be said of Ramón Novarro, who had a hit as a singer and actor with the film *Sevilla de Mis Amores*. But as he was still popular in the U.S.A. he continued his career in English at MGM, where he was under contract. At the end of his contract in 1934, seeing that his popularity was waning, he tried his luck as a singer and was hired for a series of shows in Argentina by LR3 Radio Belgrano. He did not manage to overshadow the more popular singers of the time. Gilbert Roland also did several films in Spanish, but was really distinguished as a supporting actor up to the end of his career. The very popular Dolores del Río never shot a film in Spanish in the U.S.A.; she would do so in Mexico many years later. Most of the films shown in Spanish were failures, one after another, and the public came to understand that filmmakers in the United States could not achieve the things that could be achieved in countries like Argentina, Mexico, or Spain, where the artists belonged to the place where the films took place.

By the end of 1931 practically all the Hollywood film companies had decided to end the production of Spanish language films. The results had been disappointing. Arthur Loew, who was in charge of the international distribution of MGM's films, made the following declarations to the United Press news agency in San Juan, Puerto Rico, on the 12th of February 1932, after a tour of practically all Latin American countries: "I have observed that the newspapers in Latin American countries have come out against films spoken in Spanish, and in general prefer those in English, because the audiences do not like to hear Spanish spoken with a different accent than that used in each particular place. That is the reason why the studio that I represent has decided to not make any more sound films in Spanish."

The two big studios that continued, Fox Film Corporation and Paramount Pictures, were forced to show capacity and talent in their productions, but they did not always manage.

A very sad year for Spanish-language films was 1932. With only one Argentine fictional film and one documentary released, the North Americans could have captured the Spanish film audience. They tried but they did not succeed.

The first new release in 1932 took place on the first day of the year. It was the film called *Media Hora* (in the United States and in Spain it was known as *El Secreto del Doctor*), directed by Adelqui Millar for Paramount, with Eugenia Zuffoli, Félix de Pomes and Tony D'Algy in the leading roles. This film was based on a play by James Barrie; the play was meant to last half an hour, yet the movie was an hour and a half long, without adding anything new. Not surprisingly, it was a failure.

Each of the Paramount releases from Joinville produced a similar commentary: they were weak films, boring, and uninteresting. There were some distinguished films, beyond those by Gardel, including *¿Conoces a Tu Mujer?* with Carmen Larrabeiti and Rafael Eribelles. Released on the 15th of January 1932, the film was only meant to make the audience laugh, and it succeeded. The most important news concerning the Spanish-language cinema came from Spain: Paramount presented *Las Luces de Buenos Aires* at the Rialito Cinema in Madrid, obtaining an unprecedented success, comparable or perhaps even bigger than the one obtained previously in Buenos Aires. When Gardel sang the tango "Tomo y Obligo" the show had to be interrupted as the audience demanded that the scene be repeated. The tango was then shown again. Nevertheless, Paramount decided to close its Joinville studios. The public was rejecting most of the films coming out of them. Therefore the number of films in Spanish produced by Hollywood companies was reduced drastically. *Hombres de Mi Vida* was one of the few films in Spanish produced by Columbia Pictures, with

Ramón Pereda, Lupe Vélez, and Gilbert Roland in the leading roles. Based on a novel by Warner Fabian, the film was only moderately successful.

The studio that produced most films in Spanish, Fox Films, presented *Eran Trece* on the 23rd of July 1932. This film was a Spanish version of *Charlie Chan Carries On* with Warner Oland as the Chinese detective. The original film, also released in Argentina, achieved some modest success, but this version in Spanish did not. Manuel Arbó, in the role of the Oriental detective, passed the time trying to imitate Oland's performance with unfavorable results.

The successful release of the film in French *París, Te Amo*, directed Louis Mercaton, on the 9th of October 1932 (with Henry Garat in the leading role), which Paramount produced at its Joinville studios, made people think that this company had definitively abandoned the production of films in Spanish.

The end of 1932 coincided with the end of the Paramount experience at their Joinville studios. Before the release of the Gardel films made that year in those studios, Buenos Aires got to know *¿Cuándo te Suicidas* on January 1933. This film was released on the 24th of December 1931. Together with the previous film *La Pura Verdad*, it was the beginning of Manuel Romero's career as a film director. Romero had contributed to the making of *Las Luces de Buenos Aires* and Paramount assigned him the responsibility of directing two films at Joinville. The results were not memorable, above all because he was obliged to remake in Spanish films originally produced by someone else in English. However, it was a useful precedent that would open the doors of Argentine cinema a short time later.

Paramount's bad luck with its films in Spanish continued when they released, on the 25th of February 1933, *El Hombre que Asesinó*. It was shot in England, according to Robert G. Dickson and Juan B. Heinink, who also state that its director, Dimitri Buchovetzki, had shot it two years before in English at the same time as in Spanish. Rosita Moreno was the heroine in both versions. *La Prensa* savaged the film in its review, saying that the director "shows very little ability," and comparing his work to "primitive, exclusively superficial, theater," while describing the leading actors as having "no merit."

Fox Film presented a new feature with José Mojica, who was joined by Mona Maris, three years after *El Precio de un Beso*. This film, called *El Caballero de la Noche* and directed by James Tinling, had a fair success when it was released on the 15th of March 1933. *La Prensa* said:

> The Renacimiento Cinema renewed its program with the release of the film *El Caballero de la Noche*, a musical comedy spoken and sung in Spanish based on the adventure novel *Dick Turpin*.

It is well produced, with good details in the settings and the costumes. The photography is sharp, with several good angles. All this contributes to the good impression made by this film. The dialogues in Spanish are often witty and are correct and restrained generally speaking.

José Mojica plays the principal role correctly; he has managed to correct the pompousness and mannerisms that spoiled his earlier work. He acts naturally, in a contained way and he gives his character the liveliness it needs. He sings several songs, generally pleasant and catchy, that the artist performs with his usual correctness. Mona Maris in the leading female role, shows some progress; she has softened her former hardness a bit, although she has not managed to give her voice the right inflection according to the phrase that she has to speak. Andrés de Segurola, Romualdo Tirado, Manuel París, and Lita Santos complete the cast.

By the end of March, 1933, the Paramount offices in Buenos Aires announced that they had received the copies of the films that Gardel had made at Joinville· *Espérame*, the short *La Casa es Seria*, and *Melodía de Arrabal*. After studying them, Paramount decided to postpone the release of *Espérame* and *La Casa es Seria* as *Melodía de Arrabal* was a superior film, with which they expected to repeat the impressive success of *Las Luces de Buenos Aires*.

Espérame with a script and direction by Louis Gasnier (who did not speak or understand Spanish) was released on the 6th of October 1933. Produced with the exclusive purpose of allowing Gardel to shine, his songs, together with other musical numbers, were the only memorable things. The film was a too-weak melodrama, and the final results showed serious problems that must have arisen during the shooting. The most obvious of its errors was that the story developed in Spain, but the film showed Spanish peasants dressed as Argentine gauchos.

The short *La Casa es Seria* was released on the 19th of May 1933, along with the Maurice Chevalier and Jeannette MacDonald film *Love Me Tonight* directed by Rouben Mamoulian. Unfortunately, this film that Gardel made with Imperio Argentina, directed by Jaquelux and based on a story by Alfredo Le Pera, has been lost. Roberto Di Chiara was able to recover its complete sound track, from which it is possible to guess the contents of the film, which is a comedy: Carmen Rivera (Imperio Argentina) goes to a café in the Buenos Aires downtown unsuccessfully trying to escape from Juan Carlos Romero (Gardel), a famous tango singer. After singing, Romero tells Carmen that he loves her and wants to see her again. Bored by him, she tells him to come to her house at a certain time at night, and whistle, and she will throw him the entrance keys. Once there, the singer whistles and a lot of keys fall at his feet; so he understands what kind of a place it is, and that he has fallen in love with a prostitute. *La Casa es*

Seria was not considered important by the journals of the time, as opposed to the other films that Gardel had made. But at least one of the songs, the tango "Recuerdo Malevo," was considered to be good enough for Gardel to record for the Max Glücksmann Company, as he did with all the songs from his movies.

Melodía de Arrabal, released on the 5th of April 1933, was the biggest success that Paramount had in Argentina that year. Louis Gasnier directed the film, based on an original script by Alfredo Le Pera. Its leading actors, apart from Carlos Gardel, were Vicente Padula and Imperio Argentina. Argentina after a whole series of films in Spain and Joinville became a favorite of the Argentine public with this movie. She later starred in films in Europe and Buenos Aires.

The film shows Gardel as a gambler, who, for the love of a teacher, decides to abandon his way of life and make a living singing. But his past catches up with him, and he is obliged to kill a criminal, generating some very well done scenes. The Argentine background that Harry Stradling's photography reproduced in the French studios was quite authentic. Gardel's voice, and his songs, one with Imperio Argentina, and his natural charm compensated for his limitations as an actor. Imperio Argentina proved an effective and pleasing actress, as well as a very good singer. Vicente Padula, Jaime Devesa, Helena D'Algy, Felipe Sassone, and Manuel Paris all collaborated very well. Since sound films started and Hollywood productions in Spanish were first tried, no company ever managed to have a success of the same magnitude as this film. A week after the release of *Melodía de Arrabal El Diario*, reported the following:

> Something strange happened last Sunday at the Porteño Cinema.
>
>   They were showing Carlos Gardel's *Melodía de Arrabal*, and when he was singing the tangos "Silencio" and "Melodía de Arrabal," the audience interrupted the film with its applause and demanded that they repeat the parts in which you can hear and see Gardel sing those tangos, as only he can do it.
>
>   As we see it, it was the first time that an "encore" was done in the middle of a film, and the fact is, that our tango encloses so much emotion on screen, that it provokes the public's enthusiasm, and even more so when the music is sung by the great Carlos Gardel.

Gardel had already received the honor of having his songs repeated with *Las Luces de Buenos Aires. Melodía de Arrabal* started this trend in Argentina, and it would be repeated with all his films for many years.

Fox Film did not have a star of the same magnitude as Gardel, but they tried to make their own contribution to Spanish language films with the release of *El Ultimo Varón Sobre la Tierra*. It starred the Brazilian actor and singer Raul Roulien and was directed by James Tinling. The film was released on the 25th of April 1933, without replicating the success obtained by the popular Gardel. But Roulien managed to express his spontaneity and naturalness, in contrast to the rest of the cast headed by Rosita Moreno.

Roulien returned shortly after, obtaining a modest success, together with Catalina Bárcena and Antonio Moreno, in *Primavera en Otoño* presented by Fox Film on 11th of May 1933. Based on a play by Gregorio Martínez Sierra, who adapted the script, the film was ably put on screen by the director Eugene Forde. Catalina Bárcena distinguished herself in the leading role. Antonio Moreno, Luana Alcañiz, Roulien, and Mimí Aguila also performed well.

Catalina Bárcena once again distinguished herself with the release of *Una Viuda Romántica*, based on the play *Sueño de Una Noche de Agosto* by Gregorio Martínez Sierra playing a role that she had played on stage, the actress achieved a new success for the Fox Studios, well backed up by Gilbert Roland, Mona Maris, and Romualdo Tirado, in a film directed by Louis King.

At the beginning of 1934 everything showed that films in Spanish made in Hollywood were losing their audience. Argentine films were finally filling the public's desire to see films spoken in their own language and dealing with their own stories. Argentine film producers were about to take advantage of Gardel's success, and the two Hollywood studios that still produced films in Spanish, Paramount and Fox, did not want to lose a star of this magnitude, the only real film star to work in these films. While Fox did not have Gardel, their films in Spanish were making money, and they were practically the only important Hollywood film company producing movies in Spanish.

On the 22nd of February 1934, Fox presented *No Dejes la Puerta Abierta* with Raúl Roulien, in Buenos Aires; this is *La Prensa*'s review:

> The Renacimiento Cinema renewed its program with the release of a pleasant film called *No Dejes la Puerta Abierta* produced by Fox Film spoken and sung in Spanish.
>
> This happy, amusing, amiable, and elegant film is added to the good productions that the same company presented last year in our language, and it is gives us excellent hopes for its future activities. The great market that the Spanish speaking countries are for North American producers has made them understand the need of offering them productions that are more accessible to the public at large, and repeated experiences have convinced them that the failure of earlier productions in Spanish were not due to this fact, but only to all kind of deficiencies that they had. And so, as their quality got better so did their success and acceptance. The very favorable reception that the public of the Renacimiento gave to *No Dejes la Puerta Abierta* demonstrates what we are saying.

A production such as we have seen very few times before in films in Spanish, a variety of settings, very good photography and sound, together with a fast and agile rhythm and the happy spirit that floats all over the production, leave the audience with the best possible impression.
Lew Seiller's direction in *No Dejes la Puerta Abierta* is very good.

Fox presented another successful film on the 9th of June 1934, *La Ciudad de Cartón*, directed by Louis King with a script by Gregorio Martínez Sierra (the first that he wrote expressly for the screen). According to *La Prensa*:

The fairly original plot has interesting situations, and shows well achieved scenes. The sober dialogue is attractive, and as the settings could not be better, the film leaves a satisfactory impression. The secrets of life in Hollywood, secrets already revealed for the most part but always interesting to the public, about the making of films, and the short appearance of well known stars and other pleasant details make *La Ciudad de Cartón*, an effective film.
Catalina Bárcena who is more and more sure of herself facing the camera and the microphone, plays her role very well, adjusting her character dedicatedly, and understanding it ably. Antonio Moreno is correct in his work. Luis Alberini is funny though a bit exaggerated. José Crespo, Andrés de Segurola, and the rest of the cast help in achieving success.

After these two good results, Fox Film had a flop, according to *La Prensa*, when they released *Un Capitán de Cosacos* on the 29th of August 1934 with José Mojica in the leading role. The reviewer lamented the fact that American producers were "reverting to their old sins" of sloppiness, that the film "shows a lack of direction, to the point of giving the impression that each one of the actors does as he likes." José Mojica's singing was praised, but his acting was not. Tito Coral was "unconvincing" as the villain, with "a fair voice but little talent as an actor." John Reinhart directed the film. With respect to popularity, Carlos Gardel was about to take José Mojica's place and even surpass him as the only real star in Spanish-language American films, and Paramount Pictures was about to release Gardel's first film shot in the United States.

Carlos Gardel as a Film Star and His Tragic Death

Few in Argentina would dispute the assertion that the most important Argentine singer of all time is Carlos Gardel. As a singing artist, he was a true professional, and knew very well which songs and what things he should sing or do.
Carlos Gardel always made his wishes prevail when he had to cut a

record, and he obtained success after success for Max Glücksmann. He could record a song several times, until he had the best possible version, in his opinion, to put on sale. He decided to reject his first recording with the orchestra of his great friend Francisco Canaro, because of its technical defects. He also did not want his guitar players to shine too much. He was the star.

Once the acoustic system of recording was abandoned in favor of the electrical system, Gardel's first recordings were not released because the technicians were still not familiar with the new technique, and he briefly returned to the old system. Gardel used the new technology to the hilt, once they had overcome the technological obstacles; he had many of his old acoustic recordings changed for those recorded electrically.

Knowing how important the circulation of his records was for him, Gardel was allowed, through the Gramophone Company, to go on recording while he was on tour, in studios in Paris or Barcelona. He always did his best while recording. In contrast to his dapper image, Gardel would record dressed only in his underclothes at the Max Glücksmann studios on really hot days. He also knew how to get the most out of each of his records, recording dialogues and jokes with his guitarists (these are sometimes difficult to understand by those that are not familiar with the artist). He also recorded some records in a duo with himself, becoming the first person to record in this manner.

When Gardel started to work on the radio, he also got the best out of this medium. Analyzing his discography (including the rejected recordings), one gets the impression that Gardel lived practically inside a recording studio. The same could be said about the way that he took advantage of his radio appearances.

Gardel had not yet managed to get control of his films. By 1933, the Argentine film industry was already definitely getting organized, and that same year it had shown that Argentine films could approach the quality of Hollywood films in Spanish. But the industry was not quite there so Gardel went to France at the beginning of November to negotiate a new contract with Paramount at Joinville. Nobody knew it then, but it was the last occasion in which Argentina would enjoy the presence of its greatest artist.

In France, Paramount suggested that Gardel should go to New York to negotiate the continuation of his contract in the United States. Once in New York, while negotiating his new contract, Gardel did a series of singularly successful radio shows for NBC. As he did not speak English, he had to use phonetics. However, on the 5th of March 1934 he did a special radio transmission in Spanish, for Argentina; Gardel sang from the NBC

Studios, while his guitarists accompanied him from Buenos Aires (all the artists were provided with earphones) from the LS5 Radio Rivadavia Studios, and going on the air linked to LR4 Radio Splendid. It was the first of a series of transmissions that he would make from New York, the last being on the 17th of March 1935.

While he was re-negotiating his contract with Paramount, after December 1933, Gardel received an offer to make films in Spanish with the Fox Film Corporation in March of the following year. But Paramount was not about to lose such an important artist, and on the 10th of April 1934, Gardel signed a new contract for a series of films to be distributed by that company all over the world.

His contract was unprecedented because he had managed to get a certain autonomy. The films would be produced by his own company, Exito Productions, also known as Exito Spanish Productions, at the Paramount Studios at Astoria. With the exception of such stars as Charles Chaplin or Douglas Fairbanks, no star in the United States in 1934 would have control over his films. The films were to be in Spanish, with scripts by Alfredo Le Pera and music and orchestrations by Alberto Castellanos (later replaced by Terig Tucci).

Gardel also signed a contract with RCA Victor to record the songs of all his films. However his contract with Disco Nacíonal-Odeon had not expired; it was probably due to his loyalty to Max Glücksmann, who had been removed from his own company by EMI, that Gardel decided to work with its rival company. This situation produced a difficult lawsuit between RCA and EMI that was cleared up by Francisco Canaro in Buenos Aires, whom Gardel knew that he could trust (and whose orchestra would record all the themes written by him in the United States). So developed the unprecedented scenario in which both companies would share all the recorded music and commercialize it separately. As compensation, EMI gave RCA a series of Gardel's old master disks with the purpose of re-editing several songs that had proven successful with the Victor label (this would happen after 1960).

A few days after signing with Paramount, production began on *Cuesta Abajo*. It was released in Buenos Aires on the 5th of September 1934, and was a new triumph for the studio. It was the best film made until then by foreign producers on an Argentine theme. The plot is about a lad who is in love with the daughter of the owner of a café, but is also deeply attracted to a bad woman, played by Mona Maris. He abandons everything to follow her, but after countless humiliations and frustrations he discovers the bad woman's disloyalty and leaves her to return to the good girl. Gardel's songs were the highlight of the film, and made the film better than the aver-

Poster announcing *Cuesta Abajo* (Paramount, 1934).

age productions shown at the time. Although Mona Maris appeared in more than 50 films with such stars as Buster Keaton, Humphrey Bogart, Cary Grant, Victor McLaglen, Jeannette MacDonald, George Sanders, José Mojica, Mary Pickford, Rita Hayworth, Bela Lugosi, Victor Mature, Adolphe Menjou, Basil Rathbone and others, the public will always remember her with Gardel in *Cuesta Abajo*, a film that she always considered to be her favorite. She never had an Argentine accent, as she herself explained, due to her leaving the country when she was four years old to go and live with a grandmother in France. She had practically lost her native language until Hollywood started to produce films in Spanish, when she managed to regain it speaking with Mexicans. She said about Gardel that he was "charming and very handsome. Gardel had reached great intellectual maturity and refined habits but none of these attributes made him lose spontaneity, and the natural strength of his personality. At work he was very helpful to his companions, especially those that were just starting. Besides he was completely honest, something not very frequent in people that famous. He knew that he had many problems as an actor and confessed it without shame. He did not know what to do with his hands, but he was very dedicated and I was sure that he would have got to be a good actor, as Bing Crosby or Frank Sinatra were, both of whom got to the cinema as singers and were excellent actors." She also said that Gardel was not a myth, but "he was a reality and still is. He sang the music of his people like nobody else and they are still appreciative."

In the United States some film companies, seeing Gardel's success, considered the possibility of producing new films in Spanish, but the public was unconvinced. Fox, however, would be the only one to still produce a series of films in Spanish. They also decided to finally give up distributing films dubbed in Spanish in Argentina. This change of policy was confirmed on the 22nd of January 1935 when they re-released *The Yellow Ticket* with Elisa Landi, Lionel Barrymore, Laurence Olivier, Walter Byron, Sarah Padden, Mischa Auer, Arnold Korff, Boris Karloff and Rita Le Roy, directed by Raoul Walsh. This film had been shown already two years before, dubbed in Spanish, and had suffered the consequences. If it had been shown as it was in 1935, the commercial results would have been much better.

Although Fox would no longer present versions dubbed in Spanish (except, just as any other film company, if the film was meant for an audience of children), their films that were shot in Spanish would not have the success of Gardel's. This was demonstrated, according to *La Prensa*, on the 7th of March 1935, when *Nada Más que Una Mujer* with Berta Singerman was released. While the photography and set design were good, Harry Lachman's direction was unexceptional, and the script was weak and conventional.

While the films in Spanish from Fox were not working, those by Gardel were. Paramount had a new success when it released *El Tango en Broadway* on the 12th of March 1935. It was not as successful as *Cuesta Abajo*, and the film suffered from the same problems as other films produced by Hollywood in Spanish, although the songs by Gardel assured its success. The script was a poor and common comedy, and seemed done with the only purpose of exploiting the talents of its actors. It told the story of an Argentine living in New York who is the owner of a theatrical agency. Facing the sudden arrival of an uncle, he passes off his lover as his secretary, and his real secretary as his fiancée. He ends up falling in love with his pseudo fiancée, and the uncle ends up marrying the ex-lover.

Beyond its faults, Gardel's acting was adequate, and audiences applauded each of his songs.

After the film with Gardel, Fox presented a new film with José Mojica called *Las Fronteras del Amor* on the 30th of April 1935. It was the last film he would make in the United States. The results were good, and Frank Strayer's direction provided abundant and agile action. The songs by Mojica added to the quality of the film. Rosita Moreno appeared in the film, displaying her talent as a dancer.

With the end of the series of José Mojica's films, Hollywood lost a star who was popular in Spanish-speaking countries. Shortly after the release of this film, the Fox Film Corporation became 20th Century Fox, and one of the first things that the new company decided to do was to definitively abandon making films spoken in Spanish, releasing the last few that Fox film had produced.

The star of American Spanish-language films was now Gardel, who had already finished three films that would be released later, *El Día que me Quieras*, *Tango Bar* and *The Big Broadcast of 1936*. Paramount had decided to make use of Gardel's success in films in English, although he was ambivalent about having to sing in English. Gardel would take part in a film that was a musical revue with such artists as Jack Oakie, Ray Noble and his orchestra, Richard Tauber, the Vienna Boys' Choir, Bing Crosby, George Burns, Ethel Merman and others. Two versions were prepared for release: one in English, and the other with Gardel's scenes in Spanish meant for distribution in our countries.

Although Gardel's films were shot in France and in the U.S.A., they must be considered as a part of the history of Argentine films, and they made a most valuable contribution at the moment that the industry was taking shape after many years of frustrations. Although some have underestimated their worth, to value them properly it is necessary to compare them to what was being produced then.

Miguel Angel Morena, in his book *Historia artística de Carlos Gardel* (Ediciones Corregidor, Buenos Aires, 1998, 4th edition) invites the reader to consider some aspects of the production of those movies: the speed with which the participants worked, both in preparing the scripts and in rehearsing; the few good actors that they could count on to work with the singer; and all kind of problems that occurred with the directors, who, as they were foreigners, knew no Spanish and even less about Argentine habits. Even though Gardel had a certain control over his films, Paramount, being the producer, always had the last word.

Morena quotes some letters in which Gardel talked about with the problem. The following was sent by the singer to his agent, Armando

Defino on the 19th of June 1934: "...I would like them to give me some time between the second film and the other two, to prepare it properly. You cannot imagine the number of problems that we have had to overcome to finish these films. We have had to kick up a fuss every day and we still have to do it. The tremendous difficulty is with the actors. It is impossible to establish a good cast and to get the two or three Argentine central actors necessary to give the film a Buenos Aires feeling. In *Cuesta Abajo* we have come out decently, but the cost has been terrible rages. In the second film the thing is more serious. They turned down Gloria Guzmán and they are now getting desperate looking for women that are worthwhile...." In another letter to Defino on the 16th of October 1934 he says "...think I will be much better working with artists. You cannot imagine how terrible it is to work next to beginners that end up by making you feel small, when what I need is someone to make me bigger.... When you see *El Tango en Broadway* you will realize how difficult it is to make honorable films without raw material."

Alfredo Le Pera, the author of Gardel's scripts and lyrics for his songs, wrote what follows in a letter on the 24th of March 1935: "As you well know the films that we are making here do not satisfy us at all, and we have almost reached the conclusion that there is nothing that can be done to make them better. In the one that we have just finished [he is referring to *Tango Bar*] we had an excellent cast: Carlos, better each time as an actor and unsurpassable as a singer, Rosita Moreno, Tito Lusiardo, and Enrique De Rosas. I wrote the script where we took advantage of the qualities of each one. It would sound like an incredible story if I told you how each thing was ruined by a series of obstacles that put us in a situation of overwhelming inertia and complete demoralization. *El Día que me Quieras* is, or was, the best film made by us ... well, after the script was approved by Paramount the usual things started, the clash with the director who does not understand, changing the situations, dehumanizing and clowning them. After struggling hard we managed at last to give the film an interesting unity despite the director. Then the inevitable happened: the editing massacre. That is where Argentine films die. Amputated dialogues, entire scenes disappearing. I can imagine Tito Lusiardo's bitterness when he sees himself in the film and notices that almost all his work has disappeared...."

In a letter sent to Adolfo R. Avilés on the 19th of April 1935 Le Pera said: "I wish Carlos, who I love a lot, and in whom I firmly believe, only one thing: to never again shoot a film in Spanish outside of Argentina...."

Gardel was supposed to shoot two more films for Paramount in English, and then he was to return to Argentina, where he would have joined his film career together with that of Francisco Canaro, who had opened his own studios in Buenos Aires.

But these things were not to be.

On the 28th of March 1935, Gardel went on tour in several Latin American countries. For this tour Gardel was reunited with his faithful guitar players after two years apart and, a short time before leaving the United States, they recorded the last song that the singer would ever record: "Guitarra Mía," a song from the film *El Día que me Quieras* on the 20th of March 1935. Five days later Gardel cut his last record: an advertisement for RCA Victor announcing his tour. The tour would be very successful, and Gardel would personally verify his popularity in all the countries on the continent. The tour was never completed.

The following is the United Press cable dated the 24th of June 1935 from Medellín, Colombia:

> Nineteen lives, including that of Carlos Gardel, the celebrated Argentine singer and actor, were lost today as a consequence of a collision between an airplane belonging to the Saco Company and a three motored machine called *Manizales* belonging to the Scadta Company.
>
> According to eye witnesses there the Saco machine, that carried Gardel and his committee, was starting its take off when a violent gust of wind threw it against the *Manizales* with the result that a strong explosion was heard and in a few seconds both planes were in flames. Two hours were necessary to extinguish the fire, and meanwhile both machines and the bodies of the victims were burnt, with only three of the occupants escaping with serious injuries.
>
> The body of the idol of Latin America women presented a terrible appearance, having been reduced to a carbonized mass with its face contracted by fear and pain. It was identified by its teeth and a ring on its left hand.
>
> Other victims have been identified as Sr. Henry Swartz, manager of Universal Films of Colombia, and Alfredo Le Pera, Argentine author of the songs of Gardel's films. One of the bodies is that of a young girl.
>
> Hundreds of weeping women were among the multitude that invaded the field, which was heavily guarded by troops.

The following is a list of the victims of the Medellín tragedy. Passengers and crew of the F31 belonging to the Cía Saco: Carlos Gardel, Guillermo Barbieri (guitarist), Alfredo Le Pera (literary collaborator), Celedonio Palacios (Chilean businessman), Ernesto Samper Mendoza (pilot), Henry Swartz (theatrical impresario), Jose Corpas Moreno (Gardel's secretary), Willis Foster (radio operator), Angel Riverol (guitarist, who died 48 hours later), Alfonso Azzaf, Gardel's agent, who died a few hours later). Passengers and crew of the *Manizales*: Hans Ulrich Thom (German pilot), W. Fuerts (copilot), Hernando Castillo (waiter), Estanislao Zulueta Ferrer (Colombian

The scene of Carlos Gardel's death.

banker), Guillermo Escobar Velez (Colombian writer), Lester Strauss (Universal's agent). The survivors were: Jose Maria Aguilar (guitarist), Jose Plaja (Gardel's English teacher), Grant Flynn (Sacco's traffic manager).

Gardel's death was mourned all over the continent. In Argentina there were moments of silence in his memory, and no tangos were played that day. With his death, the most popular singer in the history of the country was gone. No one managed to enjoy the admiration and love of the people as Gardel had. His success with records, radio, and the movies left a void that was never to be filled.

In the United States, Gardel's death was a terrible blow for Paramount; he was one of its principal stars, and his death was a major loss. The founder and chairman of the Company, Adolph Zukor himself, made the following statement: "The stage and radio have lost a beloved artist with the untimely death of Carlos Gardel, the highest exponent of *criollo* singing. Gardel was an artist with exceptional popularity all over the world, because, above all, what mattered were the artist and the human being. He never lost contact with the people, and even when he had risen to great heights in the consideration of tens of millions of his admirers, he was unassuming in all his things."

The film director and producer Ernst Lubistch, who was then the production manager at Paramount, also made a statement: "The loss of Carlos Gardel deprives us of a great artist, internationally known, at the peak of his career. His absence will be deeply felt in the professional world, and by the millions of persons who enjoyed moments of happiness with his songs and his music."

Theodore Reed, who had directed Gardel in *The Big Broadcast of 1936*, said "I am astounded and saddened by Gardel's death, when I worked with him in *The Big Broadcast of 1936*, I discovered that he was an excellent actor, a superb artist, and a great friend. I wish to let all Latin America know of my sincere sorrow for this irreparable loss."

The co-director of *Cazadores de Estrellas*, Norman Taurog said "The irreparable loss of Carlos Gardel has been a terrible blow for all the artists and executives that worked with him in the great super-production *The Big Broadcast of 1936*. We are deeply sorry about the loss of a great artist."

Even Charles Chaplin made a statement:

> I met the great singer at Nice... in March 1931. A friend introduced us when I was at the Mediterranean Palace... He had the superior gift of his voice and his figure, and an enormous personal sympathy that immediately gained him everybody's affection. The sympathy that he inspired in me was so enormous that I remember perfectly well that we reached the dawn after a night of fun that will now never be repeated... I predicted his unqualified triumph, and I advised him to work in films... When he came to the United States he came to visit, and was my guest, and he certainly gave me the chance to hear his beloved songs again... He already spoke good English, and he told me that he was going on tour to Central America, an idea that I applauded. Tell the public that I lose in Gardel one of my most enjoyable friends, and let the South American countries know that they had no better representative among us. As for the film arts, they have lost a top performer, who can never be replaced.

Facing this situation, Paramount decided to release the films that Gardel had made before going on tour earlier than planned. *El Día que me Quieras* was released on the 16th of July 1935. Gardel himself had written some reflections to his agent Armando Defino five days before his death:

> I saw the film here in Bogotá, in private, and Paramount is in love with the film. I will just say that they are going to launch it at five cinemas at the same time in a city with only fifteen movie theaters!... The film produced a wonderful impression on me, and I still think that it is my best work in films, and that we have topped everything with its songs. I think that these songs will be hits, and that *Cuesta Abajo* will be forgotten. I believe the same about the records.

Gardel was not wrong; *El Día que me Quieras* is one of the most important hits in the history of Argentine cinema, and its songs, above all the one that gives its title to the film, are still popular with many contemporary singers. It is also, surely, the best film in Spanish made by Hollywood studios. When he sang the tango "Sus Ojos Se Cerraron," in a situation that could very easily have fallen into elementary melodrama, he did it with a notable dramatic emotion that was the best measure of his qualities, both as an actor and as a singer.

The plot of the film was simple but interesting. The son of an entrepreneur, an amateur singer whose father wants him to marry the daughter of a financier, prefers to live as an artist. He is disinherited and marries a dancer, played by Rosita Moreno. When the girl, in love with a rich boy, is about to suffer the same humiliations that he had gone through, he manages to make all their problems disappear. Tito Lusiardo was outstanding in his part as Gardel's friend. Rosita Moreno (in a double role) and the rest of the cast contributed to the success of the production, which was well directed by John Reinhardt. Some weeks later, on the 22nd of August 1935, Paramount presented the next to last (or the last, if you take the production dates into account) film by Gardel, called *Tango Bar*. Although it was not as good a film as the one before, it was still a success.

Directed by John Reinhardt, the story is about a singer, played by Gardel, who leaves Buenos Aires by ship, searching for better luck overseas. Attracted by a woman, played by Rosita Moreno, he discovers on board that she is a gambler's accomplice. After saving her from a difficult situation, he reprimands her for the lies in her existence. The end is logical, with the heroes getting together. Besides the good acting and singing by Gardel, Tito Lusiardo's performance was applauded, and Rosita Moreno was also good. Enrique de Rosas as the villain, did not manage to get rid of his theatrical effects.

Gardel's funeral rites took place on the 5th and 6th of February 1936, and were certainly among the most important that ever took place in Argentina.

Paramount presented *The Big Broadcast of 1936* or *Cazadores de Estrellas* on the 13th of April 1936, advertising it as Gardel's last film, although some of its scenes were shot in December 1934, before *El Día que me Quieras* and *Tango Bar*. It was the story of two owners of a bankrupt radio station who obtain a special television device that allows them to receive anything that is happening anywhere in the world. The film included the presence of very popular international artists, although the result was a bit tiring. Besides Gardel, the film presented musical numbers by Bing Crosby, Bill Robinson, Ethel Merman and Richard Tauber, among others.

There are no scenes with Gardel in the copies known today, and probably some other scenes are missing too. However, this film was constantly

Carlos Gardel's funeral in Buenos Aires on February 1936.

shown in Argentina (as were all the others by the singer) in second-rate cinemas until the end of the sixties, so it is quite possible that there is a copy, without any cuts, in some film archive in Argentina. The part that Gardel played in this film can only be known from the recordings of two songs that don't appear in edited version's of the film. In 1983 RCA Victor edited, for the first time, the version of the tango "Amargura," with its refrain in English called "Cheating Muchachita," almost certainly the one that he sang in the version seen in the United States. The other song that he sang in English is lost. On the 5th of April 1936 *La Prensa* published what would be its last review of a record by Gardel (in this case from that film) because by that time his earlier recordings were already being re-edited:

> The quantity of the new records by Gardel that appear continually, make the myth that Gardel is still alive seem true. There is almost no Sunday in which we do not have to review a posthumous recording by Gardel with his unmistakable voice and unmatchable style.
>
> The last record in which we hear Gardel sing has the tango "Amargura," a pleasant song from the film *The Big Broadcast of 1936*, that Gardel sings in his own special way, together with the ox driver's song called "Apure, Delantero Buey," a

melody that evokes scenes from the countryside. The music is pretty and the listener will probably miss the arrangements "made in Hollywood."

What nobody missed by then were the Hollywood films in Spanish. Without Gardel the few films from the United States spoken in Spanish were shown as fillers, without the importance of the great releases from those years. Paramount tried to repeat both Gardel's and José Mojica's success with Tito Guizar. But the results were not comparable.

By that time Argentine films were been accepted by the audience and it was no longer necessary for Americans to make films that could as easily be made in Argentina. Thanks to Gardel's success, great commercial possibilities were starting for local producers, and they would take advantage of them. About the only films that can still be seen today, of all the Hollywood films in Spanish, are those with Carlos Gardel. Some are better than others, but they all are considered classics.

Opposite: Poster announcing *Cazadores de Estrellas* (Paramount, 1936).

8

ARGENTINE FILMS AT THE BEGINNING OF THE GOLDEN AGE

The First Real Triumphs on Argentine Screens and the Appearance of Local Film Stars

By the end of 1934, Argentine cinema was on the way to being consolidated, and much was expected from the local film industry. The producer Angel Mentasti's production plan was getting results. This plan said that a film company should be supported by not one, but three films: the first was to be released, while the second was announced and the third was in production.

They learned the hard way: the two first films from this company, *Tango* and *Dancing* were failures and put the future of the company in danger. *Riachuelo* was a turning point in the history of Argentine film: from then on, unlike in the past, many films made in local studios would be very well received by the public. In a similar fashion a lot of artists would become real films stars, following the path opened by Luis Sandrini.

The conditions for the success of Argentine films were ideal. Between 1930 and 1934, most of the films spoken in Spanish were produced by Hollywood studios. By 1932, these films had fallen out of favor because they did not managed to achieve the success that the film companies wanted. Argentine producers, until then, did not have enough financing, and after the successful experience of *Los Tres Berretines* and *El Linyera* in 1933 and above all *Riachuelo* in 1934, everything indicated that Argentine films could prevail over, and replace, American productions spoken in Spanish.

Many of the most popular artists of the local stage passed successfully to the screen, and so did some radio artists. Their images would appear on the journals dedicated both to the radio and to the cinema, even including advertising.

Carlos Gardel's films were an important influence. Their success in all of the Spanish-speaking countries produced an enthusiasm for Argentine films. His death was a hard blow for both the cinema and the tango as businesses. However, his achievements would be the starting point for the final consolidation of the Argentine film industry, while the tango managed to regain popularity without even trying to fill the space left by Gardel. In 1935, an important cinema in downtown Buenos Aires decided to begin showing Argentine films exclusively; this was the Monumental Cinema, and many Argentine films would be released there.

The year 1935 started with the release of the film *El Alma del Bandoneón*, which Argentina Sono Film presented on the 27th of February at the Monumental. The cinema did not expect it to be successful; a week later, it stopped showing the film to leave room for Francisco Canaro and his orchestra and the carnival dances that they had organized. The film was released before the beginning of the film season during a heat wave, when people did not go to the movies.

Despite the poor expectations, *El Alma del Bandoneón* was a great box office and critical success. Its director, Mario Soffici, had been prominent as an actor in some films, especially in *El Linyera*. Without technical training, he learned how to make films (according to his own statement) next to José A. Ferreyra in *Muñequitas Porteñas* and *Calles de Buenos Aires*, where he even directed some scenes. *El Alma del Bandoneón* made him celebrated as a film director; most of the actors who took part in the film received acclaim too. This melodrama was about the son of an *estancia* owner, who preferred to devote himself to music, overcoming any obstacles that appeared in his way. Libertad Lamarque and Santiago Arrieta played the leading couple, backed up by Dora Davis, Domingo Sapelli, Héctor Calcaño, and Enrique Serrano, as well as the singers Ernesto Famá and Charlo. The music of the film was composed by Enrique Santos Discépolo. Outstanding among his songs were the tango "Cambalache," and the title song of the film, sung by Libertad Lamarque accompanied by an orchestra with one hundred bandoneons.

While *El Alma del Bandoneón* was a great success, the next Argentine film to be released was a step backwards. It was a film called *Virgencita de Pompeya*, based on an original story by Enrique P. Maroni who played in the leading role, and directed by the writer and poet Enrique Cadícamo. The script was melodramatic, superficial and uninteresting. The acting of Maroni and Luis Díaz was deemed mediocre, while that of Silvio Spaventa and Inés Murray was viewed as fair.

While *Idolos de la Radio* was the first domestic film to feature an artist who worked on the radio, *Bajo la Santa Federación*, was the first occasion in which a radio soap opera was done as a movie. It was a series, about Rosas' tyranny between 1834 and 1853, written by Carlos Max Viale Paz and Héctor Pedro Blomberg, which was on the air during 1933 on LR3 Radio Naciónal (afterwards Radio Belgrano). The film's script was prepared by Viale Paz (who died before completing it), Blomberg, Manuel Lema Sánchez, and Daniel Tinayre. The music was by Enrique Maciel, Blomberg's usual collaborator in songs and tangos. The songs' themes were similar to themes in the film and were all recorded by Ignacio Corsini. Twenty-five-year-old Daniel Tinayre directed the film at the beginning of his very long and distinguish career on the Argentine screen. *Bajo la Santa Federación* was released successfully on the 21st of March 1935. Its cast included Tulia Ciámpoli, Arturo García Buhr, Domingo Sapelli, Josefina Muñoz, María Esther Gamas, and the singer Domingo Conte.

After two years in existence, the Lumiton Company presented its third production, *Noches de Buenos Aires*, on the 27th of March 1935. This film was the start of Manuel Romero's career in Argentina (after passing through the Paramount studios in Joinville) although it was not a great box office success. He wrote the script together with Luis Bayón Herrera, trying to duplicate the success that both had obtained with Las Luces de Buenos Aires four years earlier. The film featured some very popular actors who, in some cases, would have long careers onscreen. The story was about theatrical life, and not very well developed, the film's comic moments were somewhat successful. Irma Córdoba's acting was adequate, and Tita Merello sang some of the songs that had made her famous. Fernando Ochoa reportedly performed well, as did Enrique Serrano as the villain, while Héctor Calcaño and Guillermo Pedemonte collaborated well.

Argentina Sono Film was getting ready to repeat and even exceed the success of *El Alma del Bandoneón* by presenting *Monte Criollo* with a script and direction by Arturo S. Mom, with Nedda Francy in the leading role; she was by then a veteran of the Argentine screen. Mom had been a film critic for *Atlantida* magazine and had a column of film information in the newspaper *La Nación*. He had already taken part in Argentine films, in the making of *La Vía de Oro* by Edmo Commineti in 1931. While shooting *Monte Criollo* at the S.I.D.E. studios Mom declared in *La Razon*, on the 29th of January 1935, that "The public has been asking for Argentine films for four years. Since sound film started, movies have stopped interesting the great masses of public. The ignorance of the language in which the dialogues of the film are made is an insurmountable barrier to understanding the essence of a film. We should have started making our own films then. There were some names, very well placed in our film industry, which should have given an impulse to our industry. They have not done so, they have missed out on a good business and they have delayed the success of our productions. But I now firmly believe that our Argentine film industry will triumph."

Monte Criollo was shown very successfully on the 22nd of May 1935. The music was by Francisco Pracánico. The singer Azucena Maizani took part in the song that gave the film its title. It was specially written by Pracánico and Homero Manzi and Maizani also recorded it for EMI. The celebrated Agustín Magaldi–Pedro Noda duo also appeared in the film singing the *cueca* "Sanjuanina de Mi Amor." The song was written by A. Pelaia, V. Greco and F. Martino who, strangely enough, did not record it, although they were under contract to RCA Victor. This film made the actor Francisco Petrone a star and made Marcelo Ruggero (in his first sound film) a popular character actor. The story was about the dispute between two men over a crime committed for the love of a woman. Nedda Francy played the female lead, opposite Francisco Petrone. Florencio Ferrario, Marcelo Ruggero, Domingo Sapelli, Olga Mom and Oscar Villa rounded out the film's cast.

Picaflor, by L. J. Moglia Barth was released on the 25th of June, one day after Carlos Gardel's death. This comedy from E.C.A. had Severo Fernández, Margarita Solá, Guillermo Casali, and Juan Carlos Cohare in the principal roles. Not surprisingly, the thoughts of the Argentine people were elsewhere.

After *El Alma del Bandoneón*, Mario Soffici directed *La Barra Mendocina*, also for Argentina Sono Film, released on the 2nd of August 1935. In this effort the leading actors were José Gola, Elsa O´Connor, Marcelo Ruggero, Alberto Anchart, Anita Jordán, Pilar Gómez and Oscar Villa. But the result was not as good as the earlier film. The story is not very different from those of American films about those who go to Hollywood and do not achieve the success that they expected. In this case four boys arrive at Buenos Aires from Mendoza seeking fame and fortune. Two of them become drug dealers, ending up in jail, and the other two become popular comic singers. The first scenes promised more than the rest of the film delivered, and the actors' performances were unremarkable.

A new film by José A. Ferreyra called *Puente Alsina* was released unsuccessfully on the 6th of August 1935. The inconsistent, arbitrary, and conventional plot of this film from P.A.C., shot at the S.I.D.E. studios, told the story of a worker who saves his boss' daughter and earns her love. José Gola, Belia Durruty, Miguel Gómez Bao and Pierina Dealessi were the heroes of the film. While Ferreyra's photography was good, the actors were poorly make up and the dialogue was poorly written.

On the 15th of August 1935 Lumiton released a film that was an important artistic and commercial success, *El Caballo del Pueblo*, written and directed by Manuel Romero.

Manuel Romero's artistic career was very long, starting in journalism in 1913. Little by little he was won over by the theater, abandoning the press, to become first an actor and then a director. Romero managed to enhance a relatively minor type of theater, the review. As he also loved tangos, he wrote a long series of memorable songs to be included in his plays that soon gained the audiences' preferences by themselves. In 1919 he started to write plays with Ivo Pelay, with *Teatro Breve*, the first of nearly a hundred and eighty plays (some written in a very short time). His first successful tango was "El Taita del Arrabal," with music by José Padilla. His best known play, *El Bailarín de Cabaret*, is from 1922. Ignacio Corsini became famous singing "Patotero Sentimental," which Romero had written together with Manuel Jovés.

Around 1931, together with Luis Bayón Herrera, he went on an unsuccessful theatrical tour of Madrid and Paris. In Paris he met Carlos Gardel,

Manuel Romero

and they had the idea of making the film *Las Luces de Buenos Aires*. Adelqui Millar directed the movie which included songs with lyrics by Romero. It was filmed at the Joinville Paramount studios.

The success of this film allowed Romero to start his career as a film director at Joinville, although his first two films for Paramount were unimportant. However, according to Nestor Pinzón, the influence of Hollywood was essential: "He shot quickly, rather carelessly, with the sole purpose of finishing and achieving quick results. However, Romero created a style that was much appreciated by simple audiences that were only eager to see the artists that they heard on the radio, or read about in magazines. Today seen from a distance they represent, in fact, they are, testimonials of an age; without pretending to the exactness of a document, he gives us a painting, a watercolor of the different sectors of our society in the thirties and forties, besides leaving us a full-length accurate document, concerning the actors, singers, actresses and female singers that can be appreciated there, and not only through records." In all Romero made 53 films and all of them can be compared to what was normally produced in the United States, adapting American popular themes to Argentine backgrounds. He had the musical help of tango musicians such as Alberto Soifer (the piano player of the memorable Carlos Marcucci orchestra from the silent film days), Enrique Delfino, Francisco Lomuto and others.

El Caballo del Pueblo made Romero popular, and he would be a successful director for many years, the envy of Argentine producers. He did most of his work at the Lumiton studios, helping to consolidate their commercial base.

Several authors have written that Manuel Romero wrote *El Caballo del Pueblo* with Carlos Gardel in mind for the leading role (they co-wrote many tangos, "Tomo y Obligo" among them, that was recorded by Gardel) and that the tragedy at Medellín cut off the project. This is not so. The film was shot around January 1935, while Gardel was shooting *El Día que me Quieras*, that is to say before Gardel's death and when his contracts did not allow him to work in Argentina. This does not mean that the filmmaker was not inspired by Gardel and his passion for horseracing when he thought of the leading character, played by Juan Carlos Thorry (until them a jazz and tango singer and from then on a very popular actor in films, the theater, radio, and then television).

The script of *El Caballo del Pueblo* had plenty of lively action and was well performed by the cast. The story was about horse racing, and climaxed with a well-staged race, won by the hero's horse. The hero was a tango singer who earned the heroine's love. Irma Córdoba's acting was expressive and restrained. Juan Carlos Thorry turned out to be a good actor with an agreeable voice. Olinda Bozán and Pedro Quartucci appeared in a series of comic situations. Enrique Serrano was, once more, an excellent villain.

After this great success came a failure: *Crimen a las Tres*, released on the 24th of August 1935, directed by Luis Saslavsky (who had started his activity in films five years earlier with *Sombras*. The film had a weak plot: to protect a woman he loves, a man takes the blame for a crime he didn't commit. At his trial the guilty party appears and the truth is revealed. Héctor Cattaruzza, María Nils, and Blanca de Castejón play the principal roles.

The next Argentine film to be released was also a failure: *Internado* released on the 25th of September 1935. Its directors were Héctor Basso and Carlos Muñoz. Carlos Muñoz was a journalist and writer who used the penname Carlos de la Púa; he was never acclaimed for his work in films. *Internado* is the story of a medical student who leaves the woman that he was engaged to, seeking a theatrical career. The girl falls in love with the main character's brother, and the student's parents stop him from giving up his studies.

The movie left much to be desired. The production was very bad, the sound was badly synchronized with the action, and on more than one occasion the camera shows the microphones. The performances of Tulia Ciámpoli, Irma Córdoba, Florindo Ferrario and Roberto Páez did not measure up to their work in other films. The next film released was *Escala en la Ciudad* on the 30th of October. The differences of opinion between one paper and another regarding a film today are not so surprising if compared to reviews of this SIFAL production. It received a bad notice from *La Vanguardia*:

> This second production from the SIFAL Company is an assault on our local cinema. It is the work of a group of snobs that, not having anything better to do, and nothing better on which to spend their money, have had a good time playing at "making a movie," all with the greatest inconsistency and an absolute ignorance of what film art is all about. It is impossible to imagine the point that can be reached in making bad films without having seen this, which starting with its plot, dialogues, direction and acting is the opposite of what a film should be.
>
> Among all these valueless things there are only some well-done photographs worth mentioning, that can do nothing to improve the value of the film when opposed to such a large dead weight of blunders. Of them we shall say nothing and will try to forget them soon. It is painful to remember them....

La Prensa's critic had a completely different view:

> The Argentine SIFAL film company presented its second film at the Renacimiento Cinema called *Escala en la Ciudad*, a production spoken in Spanish with a script and direction by Alberto de Zabalía and dialogues by J. Elizalde.

Seen in the totality of Argentine films this one offers as its outstanding point the will to do better, that while it is true that it is not totally achieved due to beginner's faults, the director's and the leading actresses', especially, it deserves encouragement and support.

The first acts of the film, and even its title are a faithful copy of the production's central idea, and impress very well. It confirms the attempt to keep away from what is always done on screen, a logical attempt, because we must expect new artists, in a budding art, once that it finds its voice, to express something, and at least try something new.

In spite of these positive comments, *La Prensa* went on to criticize the film's often pointless plot developments, its extremely poor dialogue, its "lack of inventiveness," and a "false simplicity that is really pretentiousness."

La Prensa praised the acting of Ester Vani, while noting that she needed better direction. It also complimented the work of Cecilia Lazard, Eduardo Berri, and Matilde Mor. Hector Cataruza's performance was described as "restrained, at times too much so."

On the 1st of November 1935 Francisco Canaro presented his second film production, *Por Buen Camino*. On this occasion he tried to repeat the experience of his earlier film *Idolos de la Radio*, but showing popular sports personalities this time. The outcome was fairly good, although not as good as in his earlier film.

The story presented two brothers, one dedicated to sports, and the other who lived by night. The love of a girl causes the second brother to settle down. Audiences reacted most favorably to the comic scenes that were added to the abundant sport scenes, which featured several of the most celebrated sportsmen of the times. Everything in the film, directed by Eduardo Morera, was banished to the background by the presentation of the sports scenes. José Gola, Armando de Vicente, Blanca de Castejón, and Ana Lang performed well, but the comic scenes, in the care of Olinda Bozán, Paquito Busto, and Marcos Caplán were the highlight of the film.

The last local release in 1935 was the Argentine-Brazilian production called *Noches Cariocas* in Spanish and *Noites Cariocas* in Portuguese, on the 23rd of December. Jardel Jercolis, María Luisa Palomero, Carlos Perelli, Carlos Viván, Eduardo Arouça, Manoel Vieira, Ana María Machado and other Argentine and Brazilian artists took part in this film. Directed by the poet and writer Enrique Cadícamo, who was also the author of the script together with Luis Iglesias and Jardel Jercolis, it was based on a story by F. Gianetti. The results were disastrous , and, from then on, Cadícamo was to restrict his film activity.

The first Argentine film from 1936, released on the 6th of April, was

La Muchachada de Abordo, written and directed by Manuel Romero, based on his own play. The main actor of this comedy was Luis Sandrini, who returned to work at Lumiton with this film, renewing the partnership that had produced *Los Tres Berretines*. The film was a great box office success, but was not as popular with the critics.

The next Argentine release took place a week later. Argentina Sono Film presented *Puerto Nuevo* achieving a similar success to *El Alma del Bandoneón* a year before. This film presented the singer Charlo and the theatrical comedian Pepe Arias, who had both already performed onscreen, and made Arias, who was then a very popular actor in theatrical revues, a valuable film actor. Among those that took part in making the music for the film were Hans Diernhammer, Luis Rubistein and Francisco Canaro, who decided not to work only for his own company, but also took part as an actor or as a musician (sometimes only in name, due to the use of one of his tunes) in other producers' films. The directors were Mario Soffici and Luis César Amadori, who until then worked in the theater and as a tango lyricist.

The story was about a rich girl who discovers a singer in a shantytown, and has him make his debut in a theater. After a series of adventures, including comic moments, the singer and the girl fall in love. The film, while not great, was well produced. Pepe Arias was able to repeat on film the effectiveness that had made him a star onstage. Charlo, even though he was very photogenic, was no actor, and only distinguished himself by the songs that he sang, especially the tango "Yo También Soñë," by Amadori and Canaro. Sofía Bozán, a sound film pioneer, started a series of film appearances with this movie that allowed her to show her talent as an actress and songstress.

The less successful *Sombras Porteñas* was released on the 25th of February 1936; it was directed by Daniel Tinayre. The music for this film was by Pedro Maffia and Sebastián Piana and the lyrics were written by Homero Manzi.

The songs that Mercedes Simone sings and the music of the film were its highlights. A criminal, after committing a murder, takes refuge in a remote town on the shores of the Nahuel Huapi Lake, taking his lover with him and obliging her to work as a singer. The girl falls in love with an honest lad. At the film's conclusion, the lad and the villain meet in a long and tiring fight, in which the hero never suffers a scratch despite all the blows he receives. At the end the girl kills the villain, and feeling that she is an obstacle in the life of the man she loves, she abandons him and returns to Buenos Aires. Maruja Gil Quesada, Francisco Petrone and Pedro Laxalt also appeared in the film.

The next release was on the 11th of March 1935. It was the film *Vértigo*, and it was more documentary than fiction. Directed by Napy Duclout, its plot, about a racing car driver who quarrels with his father because of his profession, was barely an excuse to show an international automobile race that had taken place recently. The documentary scenes were very well produced, while the dramatic ones were not.

According to the chronicles of the time, the public would have preferred that the dramatic scenes performed by Jorge Soler, Venancio Muñoz, Emilia Harold, Lucía Montalvo, Delia Martínez and Juan Vítola had been left out. Consequently, three days after its release, the producer decided to remove all the accessory scenes, leaving it only as a documentary about the international car race.

The next film release was *Canillita*. Premiered on the 26th of March 1936 it was a minor film which, oddly, did not give the identity of the child actor whose character gave the film its title. Written and directed by Lisandro de la Tea and Manuel Roneima, it was an unassuming film about a coachman whose daughter leaves him after he tries to make her marry a man that she does not love and obliges her young son to sell newspapers. The film was fairly successful, with good performances by Gregorio Ciacarelli, Héctor Calcaño, Robert Páez, "Lopecito," Victoria Olmos, Benita Puértolas and Adolfo Alsina.

Directed by Gerardo Huttula and with John Alton's cinematography, *Compañeros* was released on the 17th of April 1936. It told the story of an Italian immigrant who falls in love with an aristocratic rich girl, despite the opposition of her parents. Despite many obstacles, he manages, with great effort, to buy an *estancia*. At the end the hero must return to Italy to tend to his ill mother, but he does so with the girl.

Beyond a conventional plot and slightly naïve dialogues, the film had some very well achieved situations. Nuri Montsé, as the heroine, proved to be a capable actress. Emilio Picayo was good as the hero, despite some problems with his delivery. Pedro Quartucci, María Esther Duckse, Héctor Calcaño and Juan Mangiante also appeared in the movie. After his success with *Monte Criollo*, Arturo S. Mom directed *Loco Lindo* for Argentina Sono Film, with Luis Sandrini and Sofía Bozán. The result, released on the 13th of May 1936, was a popular film without the critical acclaim of his earlier production. The music of this film was written by Carlos Di Sarli (the only time he worked for films) who also wrote the theme tango, with lyrics by Ernesto Famá and Conrado Nalé Roxlo. Based on a storyline by José B. Cairola, it was a simple comedy in which a girl is saved from the clutches of a villain. The cast was completed by Ana Jordán, Pedro Fiorito, Miguel Mileo, Tomás Simari and Ernesto Fama.

After years of working as a film studio for different companies, the Sociedad Impresora de Discos Electrofónicos (S.I.D.E.) started to produce its own films. Alfredo Murúa started out as a film producer with a success written and directed by Manuel Romero, with Luis Sandrini in the leading role: *Don Quijote del Altillo*. Its release took place on the 3rd of June 1936, and it was a simple comedy about a boy who falls in love with a neighbor in his lodgings; she prefers the rich landlord, but in the end the hero gets the girl. Despite the simplicity of the plot, the production was good, as well as the music specially composed for it by Alberto Soifer. The cast was completed by Nuri Montsé, Eduardo Sandrini, Mary Parets, Roberto Blanco and Luis Nogueras.

A classical Argentine book reached the screen on the 8th of July 1936, brought by Angel Mentasti and his production company, Argentine Sono Film. For years local film industry had not dared to touch this kind of matter; the film was *Amalia*, based on José Mármol's novel. It had been made into a movie in 1914 by Max Glücksmann, Eugenio Py, and Enrique García Velloso. On this occasion, the director was L. J. Moglia Barth and the cinematography was by John Alton, who became the head of cinematography of the company. Despite the effort, the results did not surpass in quality the other films made then. Its rhythm was languid, and it lingered on details that added little to the story. Herminia Franco made her debut onscreen in the leading role, although Floren Delbene, as the hero, made a better impression. The cast was completed by Ernesto Raquén, Herminia Manzini, Nélida Franco, Delia Codebó, and Miguel Gómez Bao, in a caricature of a part that was given more importance than it really deserved. Francisco P. Donadío, the director of some of the first Argentine sound films, returned to directing after several years with *Poncho Blanco*, based on a story by Ricardo Hicken (who had directed *Los Caballeros de Cemento* earlier). It was released on August 12th, 1936, and had music by Rodolfo Sachs. It was a conventional melodrama in a folk background and was only distinguished by some beautiful shots of the Córdoba hills. The cast included Luisa Vehil, Ida Delmas, Benita Puértolas, José Otal, Juan Bono, César Fiaschi and Héctor Duval.

Libertad Lamarque, after the success of *El Alma del Bandoneón*, wrote a script for her own benefit that would become S.I.D.E.'s second production, *Ayúdame a Vivir*. The veteran José A. Ferreyra, who from then on would make all his films at S.I.D.E., was the director of this film, which would become one of his most famous (the first of three with Lamarque). It was released on the 26th of August 1936.

The movie was not very successful when first released, and it was full of technical defects, but it was the beginning of Libertad Lamarque's pop-

John Alton, L. J. Moglia Barth, and Bruno S. Royal reading a *Sintonia* magazine on the set of *Amalia* (Argentina Sono Film, 1936).

ularity on both American continents. Its plot follows a woman who marries the man she loves; he is unfaithful, and she finds him out, but they are reconciled at the end. Working with a poor script, Floren Delbene, Perla Mary, Atilio Supparo, Santiago Gómez Cou and Delia Durruty collaborated well in their respective parts. Ferreyra's direction stressed the melodramatic character of the film, as if it was the description of a tango lyric. In this sense, the most noteworthy scene of the film consisted of a tragic situation when Libertad Lamarque discovers her husband's infidelity, and the action is interrupted to allow her to sing the corresponding tango. Despite its other shortcomings, the film's songs were good.

The newspaper *La Nación* reported the following in its 12th of June 1936 edition:

A business deal has just been closed between the General Manager of Paramount of Argentina, Mr. John B. Nathan, and the A.I.A. society from La Plata, by which the North American company, which released the films starring Carlos Gardel, will carry out the distribution in the Argentine territory, South America, Central America, Mexico, and Spain of the first production of the new Argentine Film Company that, according to Paramount, will have unlimited funds to "produce films of great quality."

The first film produced by A.I.A. will start shooting next week, with a cast that includes Gloria Guzmán, Alicia Barrié, Carmen Lamas, Olinda Bozán, Sussy Derqui, Benita Puértolas, the Desmond sisters, Marcos Caplán, Alberto Vila, Juan Carlos Thorry, Héctor Quintanilla, Carlos Enríquez, José Ramírez, and Juan Mangiante, which allow us to suppose, even though it is not mentioned, that it will be a musical comedy. Manuel Romero, who also wrote the script, will direct this production, which starts an interesting period of practical experimentation that can have a strong influence on the future of Argentine cinema.

The film was called *Radio Bar*, but the A.I.A. company disappeared immediately, and everything indicates that this was the first time that a Hollywood film company decided to produce an Argentine film with Argentine technicians and actors, something that would rarely happen again. On this occasion, Paramount evidently did not want to lose the market for Carlos Gardel's films and turned to the most popular director in Argentina. Manuel Romero proved his capability once more, and the film (his third and best film for this Hollywood studio) was released only three month after its shooting, on the 10th of September 1936.

The almost movie's nonexistent melodramatic plot was an excuse to bring together many popular artists that were then performing on the radio. The film was a box office success, thanks to the artists' good performances and the music by Alberto Soifer, who had specially composed several songs to the director's lyrics. The participation of the Efraín Cardozo Orchestra, from Colombia; the Almirante Jonás Orchestra, from Brazil; and, above all, the Elvino Vardaro tango orchestra make the film interesting today.

With the release of *Juan Moreira* on the 17th of September 1936, the veteran Nelo Cosimi returned to directing after some years in which several of his projects were unfinished or mere announcements. This new adaptation of the novel by Eduardo Gutiérrez, previously filmed in 1924, was by José González Castillo, who returned to the cinema after many years. His son, the composer, writer and poet, Cátulo Castillo, wrote the music for this film.

The Vaccari and Alonso film production only followed the novel in

Opposite: Poster announcing *Radio Bar* (Paramount, 1936).

its principal episodes, avoiding monotony in its action. The movie was a folk exhibition, with country scenes, songs and dances well placed in its storyline. Domingo Sapelli's performance was very good, and the rest of the cast, including Patrocinio Díaz, Alberto Gomez, Guillermo Casali, Antonio Podestá and Néstor Feria also performed well.

One of the best-known Argentine plays, El Conventillo de la Paloma, arrived as a film on the 24th of September 1936, adapted by its author, Alberto Vacarezza. It was produced by the Julio Joly Company (until then an importer of European films) at the S.I.D.E. studios. Leopoldo Torres Ríos, whose first silent films (some as a director and others as a co-writer of the script and as an assistant to José A. Ferreyra) are practically forgotten and are not to be found today, started his career as a sound film director with this production.

Torres Ríos took El Conventillo de la Paloma to the screen, with considerable faithfulness to the original play, trying not to be restricted by the limits of the stage. Alicia Barrié, in the leading role, acted ably, while Tomás Simari showed comic ability. The cast was completed by Héctor Calcaño, María Esther Duckse, Elena Bozán Guillermo Casali, José Otal, Vicente Forastieri and Oscar Villa.

The last of the series of releases in 1936 by Argentina Sono Film was Goal, released on the 14th of October. It was an unpretentious comedy directed L. J. Moglia Barth. It was the story of a man who must replace an important soccer player who is his exact double. Severo Fernández shone playing both parts, and marking the difference between them well. Pedro Quartucci, Héctor Calcaño, Inés Morrison, Teresa Serrador, and Miguel Gómez Bao rounded out the cast, along with Sofía Bozán, who also sang a tango.

After relying on the popularity radio artists and sport celebrities, Francisco Canaro decided that his third film would show a story that was worthwhile in itself. He decided to produce a comedy called Ya Tiene Comisario el Pueblo; it had been a very popular play written by Claudio Martínez Payva, who directed the film together with Eduardo Morera.

The release of Ya Tiene Comisario el Pueblo took place on the 30th of October 1936, and it was a great success. It was a rural comedy about the romance of boy and a poor girl, who was also wooed by the political boss of the vicinity. The leading role was played by Paquito Busto, repeating the success that he had in the theater with the same character. The cast included Aída Sportelli, Leonor Rinaldi, Héctor Quintanilla, Max Sandler, Antonio Daglio, Froilán Varela, Mary D'Alba, Elsardo Santalla, Atilio Supparo, Alberto Puértolas, José Blanco, and Luis Cicarelli. Agustín Irusta and Roberto Fugazot, who until then, together with the pianist Lucio

Demare, had formed the very popular (in Spain and Latin American countries) Irusta-Fugazot-Demare trio, also took part in the film.

Ya Tiene Comisario el Pueblo was the end for the Irusta-Fugazot-Demare trio (although they were to play together again occasionally). The trio was largely a duet accompanied by Demare on the piano, and sometimes one or the other sang. Irusta-Fugazot-Demare later had a tango orchestra, recording many records in Spain (at Gramophon, including some instrumental versions), and appearing in two Spanish films: *Boliche* (1933) and *Aves sin Rumbo* (1934).

Two important things happened at the Río de la Plata Studios when *Ya Tiene Comisario el Pueblo* was produced: Francisco Canaro shared the musical responsibility of the film with Lucio Demare, who started his career as a film composer in this manner; and Demare's brother Lucas, who until then had been a bandoneon player in the Irusta-Fugazot-Demare orchestra, started to work at the studios behind a camera, exchanging music for films.

The Beginning of the Golden Age of Argentine Cinema

When an Argentine film is released nowadays, it is advertised in a manner that would make it seem a great boxoffice success, as though the industry has reaped a new triumph. However, when the time comes to sum up on purely financial terms, the results are usually discouraging. Neither the advertising nor prizes in international festivals are a guarantee that any film will be a boxoffice success, which is what, in the end, allows the industry to work and to create jobs.

Hollywood films rule over the film market worldwide. Even so, the public appreciates the chance to see work done by Argentine artists, and, for many years, Argentine films and music achieved successes at home that were never attained by foreign artists. Hollywood, after a few more attempts, would abandon the production of Spanish-language films, and Argentine producers finally discovered that they could make very good films themselves.

By 1937, the Argentine film industry had already left behind a past full of frustrations, and was about to enter its period of greatest brilliance. It was the first successful year for Argentine cinema, with many more films released than in any earlier period. There were some very good films among them, others that were no more than average, and of course, some very bad ones. To catalogue all the films made then would mean a very large register, which has already been done well by other authors. The films highlighted in the following pages are some of the most distinguished, together with some others that have not necessarily been well represented in the film history books.

After being unnoticed in the film *Tango*, Pepe Arias, who until then was a popular comedian onstage, became a popular star with *Puerto Nuevo*. His next film, *El Pobre Pérez*, produced by Argentina Sono Film, made both him and the director of the film, Luis César Amadori, famous. Premiering on the 10th of February 1937, this comedy, scripted by Amadori and Antonio Botta, was about the misadventures of a poor soul who helps a dancer who was in love with a rich boy. The film had rhythm and vivacity. Besides Arias' good acting, Alicia Vignoli played the heroine with grace. Orestes Caviglia, José Gola, and Tania, singing a tango by Enrique Santos Discépolo, completed the cast.

March was the beginning of the 1937 movie season; that is to say, the part of the year in which the artistically important films were shown. After having seen some more or less well-done films, the public's desire to see

Charlo and Pepe Arias in *Puerto Nuevo* (Argentina Sono Film, 1936).

Argentine films was high, and people naturally expected the old films to be surpassed. On the 3rd of March, Argentina Sono Film presented a new film directed by Mario Soffici, based on a story by José Antonio Saldías, photographed by John Alton and Antonio Merayo, that was a great success: *Cadetes de San Martín*. This film was Enrique Muiño's and Elías Alippi's debut in sound films, after many successful years in the theater that had made people forget their having taken part in some silent movies at the very start of Argentine films. Both artists, who were great stage actors, were also great in Argentine films.

The story about officer candidates for the army (a subject that appeared for the first time in an Argentine film) had dynamic action and restrained comic interludes, that were controlled and witty. Enrique Muiño proved to be a great film actor, as did Elías Alippi. Angel Magaña had his on-screen, debut playing a cadet. Rosa Contreras, Oscar Villa, Matilde Rivera and Héctor Calcaño completed the cast.

The success of this film was followed by the even greater success of *Los Muchachos de Antes No Usaban Gomina*, that Manuel Romero wrote and directed for Lumiton.

The story of this film starts in 1926 when Manuel Romero gave Francisco Canaro the lyrics of the tango "Tiempos Viejos" to put to music, which he did a short time before going on tour to Paris. The song was a success, thanks to Carlos Gardel, who recorded it on the 8th of May 1926. The tango was the idea around which Romero and Mario Bernard wrote the *sainete* whose title, "Los Muchachos de Antes No Usaban Gomina," was taken directly from the lyrics of "Tiempos Viejos," which was meant to be the most important song in the show. It had its debut on the 21st of October 1926, (the same day as Gardel's recording was put on sale). The play was a great success.

The film was a sensational hit. Among the principal actors Florencio Parravicini, returning to the movies after a great many years. The heroine of the story, the blonde Mireya, was played by Mecha Ortiz, who immediately became a popular star. The tango "Tiempos Viejos" was sung by Hugo del Carril, a singer who was just beginning his career, and who would shortly become an important star, both as a singer and a film actor.

Los Muchachos de Antes no Usaban Gomina was released as a film on the 30th of March 1937. The plot is about a young rich man, who scorns a good girl that he had met in a cabaret and marries a girl that his parents liked. The man is not happy in his marriage, and only remains with his wife for the sake of his children. Finally, after many years, he discovers that the good girl was now a beggar that his son was making fun of.

Manuel Romero achieved with *Los Muchachos de Antes no Usaban*

Gomina one of the real Argentine cinema classics, and it was better as a film than as a play. The reconstruction of Buenos Aires was very good and full of local color. Besides the excellent acting by Mecha Ortiz, Florencio Parravicini proved to be a natural and restrained actor. Santiago Arrieta as the hero of the story played his part well, and Irma Córdoba as his wife was also good. Martín Zabalúa, Roberto Blanco, Juan Pisano, Niní Gambier, Juan Mangiante and Fernando Borel completed a solid cast.

The Argentine film industry had still not shown all that it could do. However, by that time it was beginning to be well received outside of the country. The film that Libertad Lamarque had made for S.I.D.E. the year before, *Ayúdame a Vivir*, had not been a great box office success in Argentina, but it managed to impress Central American audiences.

On the 4th of July 1937, *La Nación* published a long article signed by Manuel Peña Rodríguez about the success of Argentine and Mexican films (which were also starting by then to be organized as an industry and to become popular:

> In Mexico it was believed by some that in Argentina there was nothing less than a systematic obstruction for Mexican films. In Argentina there were people who thought that in Mexico there was nothing less than a barrier for Argentine films. This is a curious fact. With the knowledge of one and the other in the balance, we can assure you that in this question, in which the audience is the supreme judge, both sides are wrong. The discrepancy came from two important facts: bad films and bad distribution. Against bad films, where the question is quality, the remedy is a radical formula: improvement. Against bad distribution, a commercial question that consists of presenting films too late and without enough advertising, the remedy can be found in only one word: organization.
>
> Now the circumstances from both points of view have changed. The films from both countries are getting better. Argentine films are winning markets, and in Cuba and in Central America the cinema managers even await them with a certain anxiety. They are starting to enter Mexico, and we can affirm, judging from a favorable reaction demonstrated by a private showing for people from the industry, of *Ayúdame a Vivir* that had received an avalanche of criticism among us, and was well received there. Mexican films are being shown since quite some time ago, in Central America, in the Pacific nations such as Colombia, Venezuela and some North American circuits, and were shown with favorable results in the provinces of Spain, before war bloodied the land.
>
> Perhaps Argentine films, all together, do not deserve official protection. But we all know that, technically and spiritually, with hard work, with sudden inequalities, they change and get better, and are set on the right path. Even as they are now, with flaws, modest, and often bastardly, they have gained spectators. All they need for their progress is control by the public and the critics, the only dictators, frequently at odds with each other, in the film business.
>
> It is very nice to descend one night to the clean capital of Guatemala, among volcanic tropical mountains, and discover that the name of a comedian who is

applauded in a theater on Corrientes Street in Buenos Aires, is popular among the public there, a privilege that was limited until a short time ago to North American film comedians. It is very nice.

Perhaps it was the situations that this article described that made S.I.D.E. decide to produce *Besos Brujos*. The film was a vehicle for Libertad Lamarque, but, with the intention of improving on the performance of her earlier film, they used a script written by Enrique García Velloso, a pioneer of the Argentine film industry.

José A. Ferreyra directed the movie, which was released on the 30th of June 1937. The film had a series of problems during its production and García Velloso disclaimed the final results. The tale was about a singer who, thinking that her rich boyfriend does not love her, accepts a contract to perform in a remote place in the province of Misiones. Once there she awakens the passions of a rich settler who kidnaps her and takes her to faraway place in the woods, where her boyfriend later turns up to save her.

The results, well photographed by Gumer Barreiros, were not melodramatic, as its makers wanted, but comic. As in *Ayúdame a Vivir*, Ferreyra interrupted some of the dramatic situations to insert a song, notably in the scene in which Libertad Lamarque is about to be raped by the scoundrel, and she moves him away in order to sing the tango that gives the film its name. Other songs allowed the distance between the hero and the heroine to increase or decrease, or let some animals abandon a creek so that she could take a bath. The music for this film was composed by José Vázquez Vigo, and the songs were by Rodolfo Sciammarella and Alfredo Malerba. Carlos Perelli, as the villain, and Floren Delbene, as the hero, stood out in a cast that also included Sara Olmos, Antonio Daglio, the Spanish songstress Santanela, Moreno Chiolo, and Salvador Arcella.

It is certain that the artistic outcome of this film was not what was expected, although *Besos Brujos* turned out to be a popular film; so much so that RCA Victor took back Libertad Lamarque (who had recorded for the company between 1926 and 1933) to make a recording of the themes from the film, as well as those from *Ayúdame a Vivir*.

RCA Victor's relationship with Libertad Lamarque was very fruitful, and not only limited to the songs from her films, as she recorded other themes that were in fashion. The relationship between the recording company and the artist lasted more than sixty years, establishing a record that has never been broken anywhere in the world. By that time, 1937, she was turning into a great film star, and the tango "Besos Brujos" would become her signature song.

Detective movies were among the films in fashion at the time, and were imported from the United States. In our country, Lumiton decided to produce the first Argentine film of the kind, and they confided the job to Manuel Romero, who was already an important person in the industry.

The results were remarkable; after taking part in several films, José Gola became a star in a difficult and disagreeable part. The film was called *Fuera de la Ley*, and was released on the 14th of July 1937. The story had features of a play by Romero, *Los Malandrines*, and was about a policeman's son, who, despite belonging to a good family and having a good education, becomes a dangerous criminal. At the end a police bullet stops the criminal from killing his father.

Luis Arata distinguished himself as the father, above all in the final scenes. Irma Córdoba, Sussy Derqui, Marcos Caplán, Pedro Maratea, Marcelo Ruggero, Roberto Blanco, Esther Buschiazzo, Pedro A. Laxalt, Martín Zabalua and Rayito de Sol made up an effective cast. The photography, sound, and original music by Georges Andreani were first rate. The film was made with the Province of Buenos Aires Police.

Armando Discépolo's play *Mateo* was originally made into a film in 1926, with María Esther Podestá, in a silent version; little is known much about it today, except that it was a failure. Eleven years later, the American company Paramount Pictures, through the short-lived Baires Film, produced a new version that was a great success (possibly influenced by of the former version, with changes made to the original play when adapting it to the screen). It was the second and last film produced by Carlos Gardel's studio. The company must have thought then that it had found a new performer to replace Carlos Gardel and José Mojica in Tito Guizar, but subsequent films were never as popular as *Mateo*, nor did they have the same wide distribution.

Directed by Daniel Tinayre and released on the 22nd of June 1937, the film was an artistic triumph for Luis Arata in the leading role. In his first movie role, Enrique Santos Discépolo, the brother of the author of the original play, excelled at Arata's side. Discepolín (as he was called affectionately, to tell him apart from his elder brother) was already working for the industry composing songs for some films, and he was also responsible for the music of "Mateo."

The tale of an old driver of a horse-drawn cab who is going to be left without work by mechanical progress and who steals and is sent to jail, it is less bitter in the film adaptation (done by the author himself), than in the original. Luis Arata was moving as the cabby, and Enrique Santos Discépolo was excellent as his ominous companion. José Gola, in a supporting role was very good too, as were Paquita Vehil (Marga Montes), Ada Cornaro, Tony D'Algy, Alita Román, and the boxer Oscar Casanovas.

Warner Bros. took a very small and undistinguished part in the production of Spanish-language films once the sound film revolution had started. In January 1937 it took part, together with a local entrepreneur Olegario Ferrando, in the establishment of the local company called Pampa Film. At first it operated at the Lumiton Studios, announcing that Lumiton would distribute its films, although it later it cut itself off from this Argentine company.

Pampa Film produced *Sueño de Una Vida Nueva*, directed by Luis Saslavsky, whose title was changed to *La Fuga* when Warner Bros. presented it to the Argentine public on the 28th of July 1937. The film was a great success, one of the best films of the year. The music was written by César Gola while Juan Carlos Cobián contributed a couple of tangos, "El Campeón" and the famous "Niebla del Riachuelo," with lyrics by Enrique Cadícamo, a year after their success with "Nostalgias."

This film tells the story of a crook, who, escaping from the police and with the help of his accomplices, takes over the job of a rural schoolteacher in a remote place in the north of the country. The new horizons that open up for him, and his love for a good girl, make him change so much that when he is caught, he gives himself up with the hope that he will not have to spend many years in jail. The director, Luis Saslavsky, efficiently added elements from gunfighter films, comic farce, and sentimental comedy with very good results to this story by Alfredo Volpe. Santiago Arrieta as the crook and Francisco Petrone as the detective did very good work. Tita Merello, as the singer who loves the criminal, although she is the detective's girl, was very good both as an actress and singing the tangos by Cobián and Cadícamo. Niní Gambier was a very pleasing heroine, and María Santos and Augusto Codecá played comic parts well.

Viento Norte was released on the 13th of October 1937, directed by Mario Soffici for Argentina Sono Film. It was regarded as the best film of the year. Enrique Muiño, Elías Alippi, and, after nearly twenty years of absence from the screen, Camila Quiroga were outstanding among the cast. Based on an episode from General Lucio V. Mansilla's book *Una Excursión a los Indios Ranqueles*, adapted for the screen by Alberto Vacarezza, it was the last film produced by Angel Mentasti, who died shortly after it was shot.

The film was set during the last years of the nineteenth century, when the Indians had not yet been annihilated, and it told of the love of an army lieutenant and a girl who meet again years later, when he is a Commandant and she a good wife and mother. Despite the years that have passed, their passion is reborn. As a complement, the film also showed a juvenile romance, some humorous moments and descriptive scenes of the couple's environment.

The music sheet of the tango "Niebla del Riachuelo," from *La Fuga* (Pampa Film / Warner Bros., 1937).

Enrique Muiño as the Commandant, Camila Quiroga as his old love, and Elías Alippi as a nice Don Juan headed a cast which was largely outstanding. Angel Magaña, Orestes Caviglia, Rosita Contreras, Malisa Zini, and Delia Garcés (making her debut) completed the cast.

El Escuadron Azul, released by the Sociedad Art Film Argentina (S.A.F.A.) on the 24th of November 1937, was Nelo Cosimi's last film as a director; he would only as work as an actor until his death on the 5th of October 1945. *El Escuadron Azul* was a new version of *Corazón Ante la Ley,* Cosimi had shot with great success in 1929; it was converted to sound months later, becoming the first sound feature film produced in Argentina. Although he had the collaboration of the Regimiento de Granaderos a Caballo General San Martín, Cosimi did not achieve the success of the original production.

The plot is about a lieutenant who is degraded because he is thought to have stolen some important documents, although he is later proved innocent. The lad turns out to be the son of the colonel with whose daughter he is in love, but this problem is resolved at the last minute, when the boy, and the audience, find out that she is adopted. Despite partial successes, the results were modest. Domingo Sapelli, Sara Watle, María Esther Podestá, Samuel Sanda, Adolfo Almeida and Raúl Castro made up the cast.

Tres Argentinos en París, which Manuel Romero directed for Lumiton based on his own script, was not only a great success when it was released on the 26th of January 1938; it was also the first time, for an Argentine film, that the outdoor scenes were shot in a foreign city, in this case Paris, France. Romero knew the city of Paris well, as he had made his first films there, and he perfectly matched the scenes shot there with sets that were specially designed by Ricardo Conord at the Lumiton Studios at Munro, Province of Buenos Aires.

The story tells of three small-time crooks who are willing to make sacrifices for the sake of the happiness of the daughter of one of them, even though she does not know who her father is. Florencio Parravicini, Tito Lusiardo and Hugo del Carril made up the leading trio. Irma Córdoba and Enrique Serrano also had short parts. The original music, composed by Enrique Delfino, as were the songs in the film, had a simple and lithe melody.

On the 8th of February 1938 Francisco Canaro presented a new production: *Dos Amigos y un Amor.* This film was the debut of both the star of the film, Pepe Iglesias, and its director, Lucas Demare, who was also the author of the script, based on a story by Félix Martinelli Massa.

Pepe Iglesias was then a very popular radio comedian, who would renew his success in films. Lucas Demare would become one of Argentina's most prestigious film directors.

The music of *Dos Amigos y un Amor* was by Francisco Canaro, who also appeared in the film leading his orchestra, and Lucio Lemore. The story was a conventional comedy that took place at a radio station, and had some melodramatic episodes. Pepe Iglesias, in his work for radio, had demonstrated more capacity, aptitude, and qualities than those demanded by this film. Juan Carlos Thorry, Francisco Bastardi, Norma Castillo, and Santiago Gómez Cou as the villain had the other important roles in this production.

After several years of acting successfully in comedies, Luis Sandrini decided to start his own film company, the Corporación Cinematográfica Argentina. The comedian decided to produce *Callejón sin Salida* as the first film of the new company. It was written, directed and acted by Elías Alippi; this was in gratitude to Alippi and Enrique Muiño, who had given him the leading role in their theatrical production of *Los Tres Berretines*, which he would repeat on film to start his successful career.

The film was released on the 30th of March 1938, and the results were notable, but it was not a great commercial success. Elías Alippi had a lot of resources to shoot this film, and took advantage of them all. It is the story of a man who loves a frivolous actress who abandons him when he loses his money; he falls into the clutches of drink and gambling, sinking lower and lower. The music by Hermes Peressini demonstrated an understanding of what was going on in the film unknown until then. Alippi, gave an excellent performance, and Maruja Gil Quesada was very good as the heartless woman. Ada Cornaro, Esther Paonessa, Rosa Catá, Sebastián Chiola and Elisardo Santalla completed the cast of the film.

A new film by Manuel Romero, *La Rubia del Camino*, released on the 6th of April 1938 (only 28 days after being shot), was a new hit for Lumiton. This comedy, directly inspired by others that came from Hollywood, was different from them because its soundtrack featured tangos by Francisco Lomuto. It was conceived to show the merits of Paulina Singerman, who until then had done comedy on stage.

La Rubia del Camino immediately made Paulina Singerman into a great film star. It is the story of spoiled millionaire girl who discards boyfriends as if they were rags. Running away from a ridiculous Italian count with whom she was about to be engaged, she manages to convince a truck driver, the hero of the story, to take her to Buenos Aires. The truck driver tames the shrew and they fall in love with each other. Paulina Singerman was very photogenic a good actress. Fernando Borel, as the gallant, was attractive and self-assured. Sabina Olmos, in a very short part, was outstanding singing a tango. Enrique Serrano played the comic part of the picturesque Italian count well. Marcelo Ruggero, Enrique Roldán, Mary

Dormal, Alberto Terrones and María Vitalini contributed to the film's success.

After several years' absence, Julio Irigoyen reappeared directing a feature film. His film company, Buenos Aires Film, was by then the oldest Argentine film company that was still active, as it had started its activities in 1913. Until the sound film revolution Irigoyen produced both features and industrial or advertising films. After a long time doing only advertising, Irigoyen went back to making fictional films, producing a long series of features at very low cost that were generally shown as fillers and that never achieved critical acclaim. His first film of this period, and his first sound feature, was *Sierra Chica*. It was distributed by an American company called Monogram, and it was released of the 12th of May 1938. It was about a crook on the run who hides in a peasant's house; the peasant tells him his own story to teach him a lesson: he too has been a criminal, and ended up in jail. The leading parts in this story were played by Rodolfo Vismara and Nelly Edison, backed by Mecha Midón, Arturo Sánchez, Totón Podestá, Ema Franco, the singer Enrique del Cerro and others. The film included scenes shot at the Sierra Chica Prison.

After three years of relying exclusively in the work of Manuel Romero, Lumiton started to expand in the field of film production. One of the founders of the company, and a pioneer of Argentine broadcasting, Enrique T. Susini, directed *La Chismosa*, a film made to show the actress Lola Membrives at her best in her sound film debut. The premier took place on the 8th of May.

The film was based on a tango by Arturo de Bassi and Florencio Iriarte, who had sung several years before with Membrives, and now did so again on screen. Susini conceived the plot, together with Luis Marquina, and it was nothing more than an extension of the tango's lyrics: A childless gossip takes care of someone else's daughter, and creates intrigues in order to see her made into a lady, but the truth comes out and the girl despises her. However, when she realizes all that this woman and her husband have done for her, she leaves her boyfriend and returns to them. The photography by Alfredo Traversa highlighted the beauty of Paraná River, the Tigre Delta, Córdoba, the Iguazú Falls and the Misiones landscapes, and was an excellent complement. The music was in the care of Georges Andreani, and Lola Membrives and Amanda Varela sang with good results. The actresses were backed up by José Olarra, Milagros de la Vega, Héctor Velarde, Rosina Gras, Mary Dormal, Héctor Quintanilla, Augusto Codecá, Luis Orellano and Germán Vega.

After appearing in some films, the singer and actress Amanda Ledesma became a star when she took part, with Floren Delbene, in *El*

Lola Membrives and Amanda Varela in *La Chismosa* (Lumiton, 1938).

Ultimo Encuentro. This melodrama was directed by L. J. Moglia Barth and was based on a story by August César Vatteone. Not without flaws, this production for Argentina Sono Film was released on the 26th of May 1938. It was the story of a criminal who falls in love with a young and rich aristocrat who was requesting contributions for an old-folks' home; she also falls in love with the crook, who, because of his past, comes to a tragic end. Moglia Barth interrupted the flow of the plot in order to allow Amanda Ledesma to shine as a singer. Floren Delbene, as the crook, was very good, and the secondary roles by Marcos Caplán, Chola Mur, and others, were well played.

El Canillita y la Dama was the second film from the Corporación Cinematográfica Argentina, founded by Luis Sandrini. This film, the first with Sandrini by his own company, included the debut of Rosita Moreno, who had achieved success in Hollywood, and especially after working in Gardel's last films.

Rosita Moreno was always loved by the Argentine audiences. Before she worked for Gardel, she had her debut onstage in Buenos Aires, at the end of 1933, and after that, she was to take turns between her work in Hollywood and many visits to Argentina, where she was always celebrated by the local public and artists alike. By 1938, her film career in Hollywood had declined notably, as Spanish-language films had been abandoned, and she was not successful in films in English. Argentina gave her the chance to continue her career and maintain the reputation that she had achieved working with Gardel.

Antonio Botta and Luis César Amadori wrote the script of *El Canillita y la Dama*, directed by Amadori, which became a popular success when it was released on the 8th of June 1938. It was the story of a news vendor who helps a girl escape from a fiancé forced on her by her father; she falls in love with a companion of the news vendor, and he,

Floren Delbene and Amanda Ledesma

hurt in his feelings, informs on her to her father. After some farcical situations everything turns out right. Luis Sandrini had the opportunity to show his acting ability, both in serious and comic scenes. Rosita Moreno was very pleasing, and had the chance of showing her ability as a dancer. Lalo Bonhier, Juan Mangiante, Sara Olmos, Miguel Gómez Bao, Armando de Vicente, María Esther Buschiazzo and Aurelia Ferrer completed the cast.

Lumiton presented *Mujeres que Trabajan* on the 6th of July 1938. Another success, it was written and directed by Manuel Romero. Mecha Ortiz and Tito Lusiardo headed the cast of this sentimental comedy. The film was Niní Marshall's debut on screen; until then she had been a radio comedian, with a very popular character called "Catita."

The plot was about a rich and idle girl who is forced to work as a salesgirl in a store after her father's suicide. The result was an agile and dynamic comedy, in which sentimental and farcical scenes blended with Alberto Soifer's music, that allowed all the actors to shine. Mecha Ortiz turned out to be an excellent heroine, naturally restrained and possessing an unmistakable personality. Niní Marshall, repeating some of her jokes from the radio, gave another pleasing performance. Alicia Barrié, Teresa Serrador, Mary Parets, Hilda Sour, Fernando Borel, and Enrique Roldán made up the rest of the cast.

Luis Bayón Herrera, until then a man of the theater who had occasionally taken part in films as a scriptwriter, started his career as a director specializing in comedies with an adaptation of *Jettatore*, a famous

Mecha Ortiz, Pepita Serrador, Alicia Barrié, Sabina Olmos, Alita Román, Hilda Sour, Mary Paretz, and Tito Lusiardo in *Mujeres Que Trabajan* (Lumiton, 1938).

comedy by Gregorio de Laferrere. Those cast was headed by Enrique Serrano and Tito Lusiardo. The release of this production from the Lumiton studios took place on the 10th of August 1938.

This story, about a gallant who invents a ruse to keep his girlfriend from being forced to marry an older man, is one of the classics of Argentine humor. The simplicity of the plot and the excellent performance of its actors made for a good comedy. Tito Lusiardo (as the hero) and Enrique Serrano (as the man who was supposed to be bad luck), were joined by Benita Puértolas, Alita Román, Hilda Sour, Pedro Quartucci, Juan Mangiante, José Alfayate, and Alimedes Nelson.

After his work on *Viento Norte*, Mario Soffici directed *Kilómetro 111* with Pepe Arias, who achieved success again after poor results with *Maestro Levita*. *Kilómetro 111* from Argentina Sono Film, released on the 31st of August 1938, was based on an original story written by Sixto Pondal Ríos, Enrique Amorín and Carlos Olivari. It was the story of a kind railway stationmaster who loses his job because he allowed some settlers to send their freight on credit and the settlers can't pay after a local bank manager refuses them the credit that had been promised them. The results were very good, although perhaps not as memorable as those previously achieved by Soffici with *Viento Norte*. The action was centered on Pepe Arias, although the film also has a secondary sentimental plot that was acted by Delia Garcés and Angel Magaña. José Olarra, Miguel Gómez Bao, and Inés Edmondson were the other principal members of a very good cast.

The Monumental Cinema showed a short cartoon called *El Mono Relojero*, based on a story by Constancio Vigil, at the premier of *Kilómetro III*. It was made by Quirino Cristiani, seven years after he presented *Peludópolis*. According to *La Prensa* "the technical part of the film was very good, and clearly says that we can expect a lot from the cartoonist, when he finds a better theme to develop." *La Vanguardia* wrote that "the good qualities of the film were vividly remarked on by the audience. It is the first work of its kind done in the country, and shows great promise for the future."

The release of *Madreselva*, on the 5th of October 1938, was a landmark in Libertad Lamarque's career. From then on, the singer and actress was the most popular artist in Argentine films.

The film was considered by many to be the best Argentine film of the year. The script was written by Ivo Pelay and Luis César Amadori, and directed by the latter. It was based on a popular tango that was written for a play in 1931 by Francisco Canaro (adding the lyrics to the music of his tango from 1915, called "La Polla." In the film, which had music by Canaro, Alfredo Malerba, and Hans Diernhammer, Libertad Lamarque sang, among other themes, the tango upon which the story was based although she could not eclipse the version recorded by Canaro with Gardel in 1931.

Madreselva was the first film to be produced by Argentina Sono Film at their own studios at Martínez, in the province of Buenos Aires. John Alton, head of cinematography at the studios, was responsible for the camerawork. It told the story of a girl who is forced to turn down the man she loves so as not to hurt her old father in the last moments of his life. The outcome was moving. Libertad Lamarque was rated a great success as both an actress and a singer in the leading role. Hugo del Carril was an adequate and restrained leading actor,

Libertad Lamarque in the cover of the first edition of the *Cin Argentino* magazine in 1938.

and also sang some songs in the film. The best performance was by Leo Rápoli, as the old puppeteer; his performance was touching, from the first scenes up to his character's death, next to his daughter and his puppets. Miguel Gómez Bao, Malisa Zini, Perla Mary, and Julio Traversa completed the cast.

Francisco Canaro enjoyed the popularity of the film *Madreselva*, as he had written the music of the tango that had started it all. On the other hand, as a producer he had recently experienced a boxoffice failure with the release of the film *Turbión*, which Antonio Momplet wrote and directed for the Río de la Plata Company, with dialogues by José Antonio Saldías.

EMI, the record company for whom Canaro recorded since the days of Max Glücksmann, tried to give him a hand with a celebration for recording of the musical themes from the film (*Milongón* and *Salú Salú*), pretending that he had made 4000 recordings. Although Canaro's discography is notoriously prolific, (301 themes recorded in 1931, for example), he would only reach 4000 recordings shortly before his death, fifteen years later.

Nothing helped and Canaro lost a very large amount of money; he subsequently had to restrict his film activity, mostly renting his studios to other companies. It was a very good, though conventional, story about gunfighters, featuring Francisco Petrone and Luisa Vehil.

Los Caranchos de la Florida, an adaptation of Benito Lynch's novel of the same name, made by Alfredo Volpe and Alberto de Zavalia and directed by the latter, was Pampa Film's first movie shot in its own studios. The outcome was quite good. Premiering on the 2nd of November 1938, the film adaptation followed the novel

Amelia Bence and José Gola in *Los Caranchos de la Florida* (Pampa Film, 1938).

quite faithfully: it was about the struggle between a father and son for the love of a woman; when a passionate conflict breaks out, both end up dead. José Gola, in the leading role, performed to some acclaim. Amelia Bence, as the woman who caused the conflict, gave a good performance, as did Domingo Sapelli as the father. The rest of the cast supported them well.

El *Viejo Doctor*, directed by Mario Soffici for Argentina Sono Film, was an artistic and boxoffice success when released on the 18th of January 1939, foreshadowing an excellent year for the Argentine film industry. The story, by Sixto Pondal Ríos, Carlos Olivari, and Enrique Amorín, was about the son of a humble and old neighborhood doctor; the son, who doesn't have any scruples, tries to get rich by becoming a doctor. This central conflict was posed by Soffici with moderation and nimbleness; he also inserted some comic episodes to tone down the drama. Enrique Muiño, as the old doctor, managed to convey emotion, and Angel Magaña, as his son, was expressive. Alicia Vignoli, Roberto Airaldi, Gloria Bayardo and Cirilo Etulián completed a very good cast.

Luis Bayón Herrera directed *Mi Suegra es Una Fiera*, a comedy produced by Julio Joly at E.F.A., which was released on the 24th of February 1939. It turned out to be a popular comedy, reuniting Olinda Bozán and Paquito Busto.

Olinda Bozán, Francisco Alvarez, and Paquito Busto in *Mi Suegra es una Fiera* (E.F.A., 1939).

La Prensa described it as a purely commercial film, the first film to be described as such:

> This film is a version of the play with the same name that is also an adaptation of the farce by the French authors Hennequin and Mithcel.
> The script keeps almost all of the characteristics of the stage original, with its arbitrariness, its conventionalisms, its dramatics effects, that evidently lose strength when moved to film. Some dialogues are too artificial. But this does not keep the film from being, due to its general characteristics, what is called a commercial production, this means that despite its defects it has very good chances of being accepted by the public, particularly in the more popular cinemas. It has quite a few scenes that have a sure comic effect and it does not matter that the resources used are not very legitimate. They have attempted to produce a successful film, which will earn money, more than an excellent film. This purpose, we must recognize, has been abundantly achieved.

This comedy was about an irascible dominant woman who finds, on the day of her daughter's wedding, that her son-in-law is about to rebel against her authority. She then decides to break up the marriage, making the man think that his brand new wife is his own daughter, the fruit of a forgotten affair. Several funny adventures are woven around this piece of news, with other characters taking part. They find that it was all an invention, and the liar loses her authority once and for all. Besides the very good work by Olinda Bozán and Paquito Bustos, the rest of the cast, headed by Alita Román, Sussy Derqui, Francisco Alvarez, and Héctor Calcaño, gave good performances.

Enrique Santos Discépolo (almost a Chaplin emulator in this case) achieved popular success as an actor and composer with *Cuatro Corazones*, released by S.I.D.E. on the 1st of March 1939. His work as scriptwriter and director of the film was not so well received.

The plot of this musical comedy (written in collaboration with Miguel Gómez Bao) presented a cynical and not very honest owner of a nightclub who is redeemed by an act of nobility, and a singer who lets himself be courted by a rich widow so as to help keep up the business. Discépolo's part in the movie was so big that the work of the rest of the cast was secondary. In this context, Irma Córdoba gave the best performance in the film, and Gloria Guzmán's comic qualities were exploited fully. Alberto Vila and Tania shone in their songs, and Eduardo Sandrini and Herminia Franco did well.

Luis Arata had obtained a great success with *Mateo*, based on a play by Armando Discépolo. Another film based on a play by Discépolo, *Giacomo*, was released on the 4th of April 1939, and was an even more important triumph in his career. According to *La Prensa*, Augusto César Vatteone directed what was a good film, and Arata's performance was vigorous. It was story of a noble and honest worker who loses all his money because of his love of a woman from the theater. He is old and insolvent, and

Irma Córdoba, Gloria Guzmán, and Enrique Santos Discépolo in *Cuatro Corazones* (S.I.D.E., 1939).

the family of a nephew humiliates him until a friend makes them believe that he keeps a lot of money in a trunk. When it is opened, all that they find are cuttings and memorabilia of the woman, and the old man is thrown out of the house.

The reconstruction of life in the early 1900s increased the success of the film. Luis Arata's work was original and colorful, making his tragedy impressive. Carmen Lamas, as the woman who makes him lose all his money, gave an attractive and prominent performance. Felipe Fernansuar, in the difficult role as the villain, Pascual Pelliciota, María Esther Podestá, Ernesto Villegas, Darío Dossier, Eduardo Santalla, Ana Jordán, and the young actresses Rayito de Sol and Chiche Gicovante completed the list of principal actors.

Based on a play by Jardiel Poncela, inspired on *La Dame Aux Camélias* by Alexandre Dumas Fils, *Margarita, Armando y Su Padre* was a great success for the Lumiton Company when it was released on the 19th of April 1939. Florencio Parravicini and Mecha Ortiz headed the cast of this film, with Francisco Mugica directing his first movie. The story had very little cinematographic action, but the director, Francisco Mujica, managed to keep the film interesting. Mecha Ortíz, Florencio Parravini, Ernesto Raquén, Carmen Lamas, Pedro Quartucci, Alita Román, and María Santos made up a good cast. The original music composed by Enrique Delfino, creating and sustaining the necessary atmosphere, was a decisive accessory to the film's success.

A new comedy by Tito Lusiardo, and a new popular success, *El*

Luis Arata and Carmen Lamas in *Giacomo* (E.F.A., 1939).

Sobretodo de Céspedes, was released on the 9th of May 1939. It was an E.F.A. studios production based on a play by Ernesto Marisili and Félix de Madrid, directed by Leopoldo Torres Ríos, which kept the original play's sense of honor. It was the story of a good man who gets hold of a special overcoat: When he goes out into the streets he comes back with the pockets full of wallets, jewels, money, etc., not knowing that a band of thieves deposited the fruit of their labors in it. Considering the modesty of his budget, Torres Ríos managed to do a worthwhile job. Tito Lusiardo's performance was supported by Delia

Poster announcing *El Sobretodo de Cespedes* (Cinematográfica Terra, 1939).

Codebó, Felisa Mary, Armando de Vicente, Francisco Alvarez, Rosa Rosen, Emperatriz Carabajal and Héctor Calcaño.

Using an original script by Antonio Botta and Luis César Amadori, Luis Sandrini achieved an important critical and box office success with *Palabra de Honor*. Released on the 10th of May 1939, this film directed by Amadori brilliantly combined comedy with drama.

It is the story of a decent ice cream vendor who covers several neighborhoods on his tricycle, who arrested and accused robbery in the factory he works for. In jail he becomes friendly with the heroine's father, and promises to give him some cash that he has stashed away at the thieves' house. After some comic scenes, the ice cream vendor recovers the money and returns it to the factory owner, who, in turn, is in love with the heroine. At the climax the thieves kidnap the girl, and an army of ice cream vendors sail out on their tricycles to rescue her. The story ends with the death of the hero; he rescues the girl, and falls painlessly when he sees her happiness. Sandrini's performance demonstrated his great talent as an actor; he performed well both in the humorous and dramatic scenes. Alicia Vignoli, Roberto Airaldi, María Esther Buschiazzo, Alfredo Fornaserio, and José Casamayor completed the cast.

Almost four years after his tragic death, Argentina Sono Film, presented *La Vida de Carlos Gardel*, directed by Alberto de Zavalía, on the 24th of May 1939. The script by Last Reason and Oscar Lanatta was not a faithful reconstruction of his life, but an invented biography, as was usual in the movies imported from Hollywood in those days.

Notwithstanding and beyond its false story, the memory of Gardel, still

Hugo del Carril and Delia Gareés in *La Vida de Carlos Gardel* (Argentina Sono Film, 1939).

fresh in people's minds, made the film a huge success. Hugo del Carril's performance came out well, in a really difficult part. His performance and his singing made him one of the most important persons in Argentine cinema. As the heroine, Delia Garcés (who would later marry the film's director) became one of Argentina's great stars. Elsa O'Connor, Miguel Gómez Bao, Juana Sujo, Santiago Gómez Cou and Mario Lotito collaborated well in other important roles.

After this success, the next Argentine release was a film meant to be shown as a filler in double features. The veteran Buenos Aires Films presented *La Hija del Viejito Guardafaro* on the 1st of June 1939. This melodrama directed by Julio Irigoyen was a bit confusing, as it presented two stories that apparently

Arturo Sánchez and Yaya Palau in *La Hija del Viejito Guardafaro* (Buenos Aires Film, 1939).

were not related. *La Prensa* described them this way: "The principal one refers to the daughter, or better, the granddaughter of the Punta Mogotes lighthouse keeper. This girl, a model of domestic virtues, is pestered by a man of the world who has left his home. One day the lighthouse keeper sees a situation of crude violence, and after a tough personal combat, strangles the bad man. He was precisely the seducer of the girl's dead mother, and in consequence, her father, although this circumstance was unknown to everybody. The bad man's wife, mother of a small son, tries to rebuild her life after some time has passed, as her doctor and counselor from the days in which she had been abandoned, asks, with generous affection, for her hand in marriage. Only at the end does one notice the link between the two stories in the plot." The results were modest. The cast included Arturo Sánchez, Yaya Palau, and Enrique del Cerro.

Niní Marshall's comic performances on radio gained her immense popularity; above all with a character called "Catita" that Lumiton and Manuel Romero had presented the year before in a secondary appearance in *Mujeres que Trabajan*. Her success in that film allowed her to start a very long film career, becoming the most popular comedienne in Argentina. *Divorcio en Montevideo*, released on the 7th of June 1939, was her second film and the first in which she headed the cast. It was very successful; Manuel Romero directed this film based on a script of his own and on contributions from the actress, who would take part in writing the scripts of most of her films. In this case the film presented a conventional story about a millionaire who decides to marry a manicurist, so as to receive an inheritance, and then to leave her. In this setting, Catita, as the manicurist's friend, centered all the interest on herself, with her wit and way of speaking. Sabina Olmos, as the manicurist, received praise for her work. That was not the case with Roberto García Ramos as the hero, as his aloofness did not win the public's sympathy. Enrique Serrano played the disagreeable marriage-maker, and Marcelo Ruggero, Hilad Sour, Pedro Laxalt and Mary Dormal completed the cast.

As a silent film in 1924, *La Cieguita de la Avenida Alvear* had been a very unimportant production. Julio Irigoyen, its producer and director, remade it as a sound film. Released on the 15th of June 1939, this new version had the same unhappy fate as the former. The plot of this Buenos Aires Film production was about the case of young doctor who cures a blind girl, with whom he falls in love, and tries to marry. The cast included Yaya Palau, Arturo Sánchez and Enrique del Cerro.

Ambición, based on a play Michel Allard, with Floren Delbene, Fanny Navarro, Mercedes Simone, and Alberto Anchart was the first Argentine film by its director, Adelqui Millar (also author of the script with José B. Cairola) after his experience making films in Spanish for Paramount. His most famous work was *Luces de Buenos Aires* with Carlos Gardel, which that was reissued together with his first Argentine film.

The plot of *Ambición* tells the story of a bohemian painter in the Latin Quarter of Paris who, in his poverty, is helped by the girl who loves him. But when he receives prizes and money he abandons her, and returns to Buenos Aires, becoming famous. When the girl comes searching for him, the painter does not understand that she loves him, but she recovers his affection with the help of some friends. Adelqui Millar's directing was

Poster announcing *Divorcio en Montevideo* (Lumiton, 1939).

Director Adelqui Millar, Mercedes Simone, Alberto Anchart,and cinematographer Gumer Barreiros on the set of *Ambición* (S.I.D.E., 1939).

good, and the film demonstrated that the country could count on artists and technicians capable of making a film that was as good as the foreign productions. Floren Delbene in the leading role was good, as was Fanny Navarro as the heroine. Mercedes Simone was outstanding, helped by a couple of songs composed by Rodolfo Sciammarella, that unhappily, were not made into records. Alberto Anchart, Carlos Perelli, Mary Parets, Rafael Frontaura, and Elsa Martínez completed the cast. Adolfo Carabelli, at the end of his long career, composed the music of the film.

At this time it was evident that Argentine producers were starting to attempt much more ambitious projects than those undertaken until then. Julio Joly presented *Nuestra Tierra de Paz*, directed by Arturo S. Mom. The movie was an evocation of Argentine history, and above all, of General San Martín, and was released on the 4th of July 1939, with great success. Since the days that Julián Ajuria had presented *Una Nueva y Gloriosa Nación*, the Argentine film industry (even though that silent film had been shot in Hollywood) had not undertaken such a great endeavor. *Nuestra Tierra de Paz* was a historical evocation of the May Revolution, and the person of General San Martín, showing broadly some of the most important aspects of his achievements. Pedro Tocci embodied San Martín (thanks to exact make-up applied by the actor Narciso Ibáñez Menta) both as the young soldier and as the old man at Boulogne-Sur-Mer. Elsa Martínez, in the double role as the wife and daughter of the general, performed well. The rest of the cast was not as prominent as the central characters. The music by Alejandro Gutierrez del Barrio was a great compliment to the film.

Lumiton started production in 1933 with the comedy *Los Tres Berretines*, which was originally a very successful play by Arnaldo Malfatti and Nicolás de las Llanderas put on stage by the Muiño-Alippi company.

The results were successful both for its producers and for the Argentine film industry. Seven years later Lumiton decided to repeat the experience with another play by Malfatti and de la Llanderas that had also been a great success on stage for the Muiño-Alippi Company. The play was called *Así es la Vida* and, for the film version, the producers assigned the director's job to Francisco Mugica, famous for *Margarita, Armando y su Padre*, and the same actors who had put it on stage, including Enrique Muiño and Elías Alippi. Enrique Delfino was responsible for the music, demonstrating once more his capacity for producing soundtracks.

The artistic and commercial results after *Así es la Vida*'s release on the 19th of July 1939 were exceptional for the Argentine film industry, affirming in the industry's popular taste and leaving behind all the problems that it had faced in the past. The adaptation by Luis Marquina made a memorable film: it told the story of a family over the span of thirty years. It showed the family's daughters growing up and getting married, its sons with their successes and failures, the arrival of grandchildren, and the deaths of the elderly family members. Enrique Muiño gave a moving performance playing a character who is transformed as the years go by. Elías Alippi, as the brother-in-law, gave a good performance. The acting of Sabina Olmos, in the leading part, earned her some of the highest praise of her career. Enrique Serrano, Arturo García Buhr, Niní Gambier, Hector Coire, and Pablo Vicuña had other important roles. The sets by Ricardo Conord and the photography by José María Beltrán were praised, as was the music by Enrique Delfino.

With its successes and failures, Argentine cinema was finally leaving behind its sad days when the public rejected it, because it was not up to what came from abroad. The most brilliant period of the history of Argentine films was beginning.

In this context, Pampa Film presented its production called *Prisioneros de la Tierra*, directed by Mario Soffici, and with Angel Magaña (who replaced José Gola, who died during its production), Francisco Petrone, Eliza Gálvez (later called Galvé), Raúl Lange, Homero Cárpena, and Roberto Fugazot, on the 17th of August 1939.

This film was not only a great success, it is considered one of the great films of all times, an honor that no other Argentine film had ever achieved. *Prisioneros de la Tierra* must be considered as among the best films, worldwide. Based on Horacio Quiroga's short stories "La Bofetada," "Un Peón," "Desterrados," and "Los destiladores de Naranjas," the script was written by Quiroga's son Darío and Ulises Petit de Murat. With the exploitation

Opposite: Poster announcing *Así es la Vida* (Lumiton, 1939).

LA PELICULA ARGENTINA QUE LLEGARA — *Lumiton* — A SUS MAS HONDOS SENTIMIENTOS

PRESENTA A

ENRIQUE MUIÑO
ELIAS ALIPPI

en

"ASI ES LA VIDA"

con

ENRIQUE SERRANO
SABINA OLMOS

A GARCIA BHUR
NINI GAMBIER
FELISA MARY
ALBERTO BELLO
ALIMEDES NELSON
HECTOR COIRE
PABLO VICUÑA
ALFREDO JORDAN
JOSE RUZO
FERNANDO CAMPOS
MIGUEL COIRO

★

Dirección de
FRANCISCO
MUGICA

HOY
ESTRENO

Adaptación cinematográfica de
LUIS MARQUINA

De la comedia de
LLANDERAS y
MALFATTI

Música de
ENRIQUE
DELFINO

MONUMENTAL
LAVALLE 780

PAMPA
FILM

PRESENTA

"PRISIONEROS DE LA TIERRA"

CON

FRANCISCO PETRONE · ANGEL MAGAÑA
ROBERTO FUGAZOT · HOMERO CARPENA
ELISA GALVEZ · RAUL LANGE

PEPITO PETRAY · FELIX TORTORELLI · MANUEL VILLOLDO

Argumento:
U. PETIT de MURAT y MARIO QUIROGA
Basado en varios cuentos de
HORACIO QUIROGA
Música de fondo
LUCIO DEMARE

Dirección
MARIO SOFFICI

La más recia y vigorosa de las expresiones dramáticas, en el escenario majestuoso de la imponente selva de Misiones.

Desde
HOY
en el

REAL CINE
ESMERALDA 425 · U.T. 31-3800

ALPR

of rural workers in the province of Misiones as the background, the plot presented a brutal overseer who mistreats the workers, an alcoholic doctor defeated by the environment, and his daughter who, attempting to escape from the violent overseer who desires her, meets a boy in the forest and falls in love with him. The boss then sends the boy to work in the harshest part of the forest, but the boy organizes an uprising and beats the overseer in a hand-to-hand fight. He then snatches away his whip and forces the overseer to drag himself to the river, throws him onto a raft and sends him downstream. The lad, now a criminal, tries to run away with the girl. Her father, suffering from delirium tremens and thinking that he sees monsters everywhere, attacks his daughter when she tries to help him, wounding her mortally. The boy, with nothing to live for, lets himself be killed by those searching for him.

Lucio Demare

Mario Soffici made the story strong and vibrant, using short dialogues without unnecessary details and good camera work. Francisco Petrone, as the overseer, played his part well and with restraint. Angel Magaña, as the young hero, gave a better performance than in his earlier works. Raúl Lange was notable as the alcoholic doctor, and Elisa Galvé demonstrated that she was a good actress. Roberto Fugazot, Homero Cárpena, and the rest of the cast performed very well.

One of the factors that helped make the success of *Prisioneros de la*

Opposite: Poster announcing *Prisioneros de la Tierra* (Pampa Film, 1939).

Tierra was the sound track composed by Lucio Demare. The pianist and composer had started working for films, helped by Francisco Canaro, in 1936, although he would mostly put music to his brother Lucas' productions. He formed his first orchestra in 1938, cutting many records for EMI, and would write the music for many films in which it appeared. It was with *Prisioneros de la Tierra* that Demare established himself as the best Argentine film composer.

After a very long career fighting for the existence of an Argentine cinema, José A. Ferreyra was reaching the end of his career, and he achieved a great success on the 30th of August 1939, when S.I.D.E. released *Chimbela*, based on an original script by Antonio Botta.

It told the story of a young lady who supports her family. She falls in love with a man who is running from the police after being accused of a murder that he did not commit. This was Ferreyra's last successful film. Elena Lucena was in the leading role, and sang some songs. Floren Delbene, Eloy Alvarez, Salvador Lotito, Nury Montsé Mary Dormal, Salvador Arcella, Raúl Castro, and Alejandro Beltrán were the supporting cast. The songs by Rodolfo Sciammarella and the music by José Vázquez Vigo were well received.

José A. Ferreyra retired after three more films, due to the throat cancer that would cause his death on the 30th of January 1943. Ferreyra's prolific work, and his battle for Argentine cinema, were not in vain. He also had the satisfaction of knowing that the tangos that he wrote for his silent films were recorded by Carlos Gardel.

By the end of 1939 one could say that the Argentine film industry was well established. Many years of efforts and frustrations were finally bearing fruit. While some companies were expanding, others were diminishing their production or closing. By then Argentina already had great stars and directors. There were comedies and dramas of a quality comparable to the best imported from overseas.

Hollywood studios had finally stopped producing films in Spanish and Argentine films were taking over.

Argentine cinema had entered its golden age.

The Resurgence of the Tango's Popularity

During the silent film years, many Argentine films were, directly or indirectly, based on tango lyrics. To prevent the failures that had occurred in the past, the producers tried to exploit the popularity of certain songs.

In those years, people could go to a secondary cinema, more than to see a movie, to hear their favorite tango orchestra. The most popular orchestras were those that managed to cut records. However, the sound film revolution was the beginning of a severe crisis. Besides the loss of jobs, it seemed that the public preferred jazz from the American movies.

Facing up to the situation, some tango orchestras started to insert fox-trots, shimmies, and other foreign dances into their recordings. The best prepared for this situation were some of the most popular orchestras. Their very popularity allowed them to surmount the crisis, and they did not want to lose the chance of tapping the fashionable rhythms. Francisco Canaro, Roberto Firpo, Francisco Lomuto, and Osvaldo Fresedo were some of those that incorporated new rhythms along with tangos.

The results were successful, although they could not be compared to the recordings made in the U.S.A. Francisco Lomuto, however, had a success comparable to the best records imported from North America with his own fox-trot, "Hay Que Aprender a Bailar," recorded in 1929. Lomuto, Canaro and Firpo had already recorded jazz some years before. On those occasions the orchestras changed their tango instruments for others that were more appropriate for jazz. By 1929 they were using jazz instruments, but still kept the bandoneons in all their recordings. Canaro was to use a trumpet well; Lomuto the clarinet; Firpo a trumpet; and Osvaldo Fresedo used drums, a xylophone and a harp in his recordings. All these musicians would stop playing foreign rhythms in the future, although they would keep using the instruments.

Argentine artists could not compete against the jazz that came from the United States, but there still was a demand for tangos, although less than in the silent film times. In 1936, Roberto Firpo formed a quartet with which he created a very personal way of playing tangos in a primitive manner, although far from the primitive tangos of twenty-five years earlier. He gradually set aside his orchestra, and disbanded it in 1944. Francisco Canaro founded the Don Pancho quintet based on the same ideas, and only for cutting records, but people thought that the quintet was Francisco Lomuto's, so he changed its name to Quinteto Pirincho. He would keep it up, together with his orchestra, until the end of his life.

The artistic director at RCA Victor was Adolfo Carabelli; he had his own jazz band and also recorded a few tangos after 1931. He also controlled the company's "orquesta típica" (tango orchestra). Carabelli hired many musicians as company employees for the exclusive purpose of recording tangos. His personality determined the sound of practically all the orchestras in those years, and RCA Victor decided that with so many musicians under contract, and for commercial reasons, one orchestra was not enough. So, besides the Orquesta Típica Victor, there now was the Orquesta Victor Popular, the Orquesta Típica Los Provincianos, lead by

Ciriaco Ortiz, the Orquesta Radio Victor Argentina, conducted by Mario Maurano, the Orquesta Argentina Victor, the Orquesta Victor Internaciónal, the Cuarteto Victor and the Trío Victor.

As the years went by, RCA Victor managed to uphold the quality and popularity of its orchestras, while other artists, such as Julio De Caro, who had recorded at Brunswick at the beginning of the thirties, never managed to regain the popularity that they had achieved in the silent movie days.

The closing of the Brunswick and Columbia Companies (that had merged with Gramophone to set up EMI, which edited the Odeon label in Argentina) meant the end of the opportunity to record for many orchestras, which were not "commercial" enough to go to RCA or EMI. Only Edgardo Donato and the Ciriaco Ortiz trio were popular enough to continue their activity at Victor, just as Rafael Rossi had at Odeón.

The ideas of the influential Julio De Caro were brought up to date by other musicians. The violinist Elvius Vardaro formed a sextet based on the ideas that De Caro had formulated some years before, but it was considered to be non-commercial and for that reason he was not able to cut records. However the sextet left one disc with the tango "Tigre Viejo" by Salvador Grupillo, and took part in two films, *Radio Bar* and *Muchachos de la Ciudad*. The bandoneon player Pedro Laurenz, who had left the De Caro orchestra with almost all his musicians in 1934, formed a group with himself as leader, re-elaborating De Caro's ideas. At the beginning, it was declared non-commercial, although it later managed to cut a few records. The great orchestras were considered commercial. The visual attraction of a lot musicians offered more possibilities than the sextets, which dominated the tango scene until at least 1934.

When Adolfo Carabelli left the artistic management of RCA Victor in 1934, new possibilities for a change in commercial viewpoints for the tango emerged. By then the tango was regaining popularity. The musical trend of the first sound films was passing, and the tango was again the what the public preferred. Luis Adolfo Sierra has said that about this, that around the middle of the thirties "the tango returned from the café tables and the cinema seats to the dancer's feet."

The situation was still difficult. The most popular artist was Carlos Gardel, who had managed to go on selling records successfully despite the Depression, and above all after making films. His death seemed to leave the tango facing an abyss. However, it was the orchestras more than the singers who managed to revive the tango.

This resurrection had its great protagonist in Juan D'Arienzo. He had become popular in the silent movie days recording for the Electra Company between 1928 and 1929, with a style that was predominant in those days, and that he would continue to develop. But in 1934, he changed abruptly, leaving the violin and taking up the baton, with the intention of attracting dancers, and with a style meant for that purpose. This style included strong and firmly marked rhythm, giddily accelerated, without respite in the permanent contrasts between "staccatos" and pronounced silences, with many piano solos, accentuating the melody with the right hand, or with a countersong on the fourth string of the first violin.

The impact of the style was very important, and D'Arienzo was signed to RCA Victor in 1935, achieving great impact recreating old favorites. The critics at the time considered his style revolutionary. Today it can be considered slightly monotonous and repetitious, but with time, D'Arienzo made his style a bit more flexible. He achieved

Juan D'Arienzo

even greater success, especially after 1940, when he was forced to re-build his orchestra, as his musicians had left him to try their luck on their own.

The popularity of his records allowed him to appear for the first time in films, in *Melodías Porteñas* and to compose "El Vino Triste" in 1938 with Manuel Romero for his film *Gente Bien*.

Seen from a commercial point of view, the style introduced by D'Arienzo was adopted as a model by the recording industry, so that all the orchestras in those days were obliged to speed up their rhythmical structure.

Based on D'Arienzo's achievements, the bandoneon player Aníbal Troilo (Pichuco) formed his orchestra in 1937, and started to record with it the following year. The orchestra was distinguished by the phrases, the variations and the embellishments by Pichuco's bandoneon, which took it to the first rank. But its most noteworthy feature was that achieved by the

Aníbal Troilo is surrounded by singer Fiorentino and the musicians of his orchestra at the time of its debut in 1937.

pianist, Orlando Goñi, who introduced a more elastic conduction of the group with "bajos bordoneados" and loose notes in the low register.

As Luis Adolfo Sierra said, "after accumulating success and experience with great responsibility, Pichuco introduced new concepts in the form of expression, and in the timbre of his group. He added 'cellos, and then a viola, permanently, completing the string section with four violins, while reinforcing the bandoneons with five players. He hired the best arrangers, who marked the stylistic evolution of the orchestra." Later, Troilo's orchestra would have a slower rhythmic accent, and more musical quality, without losing any of the musical characteristics that gave it its identity.

After many year of frustrations trying to form orchestras, the pianist Osvaldo Pugliese achieved success in 1939 (although he would only record after 1943, at EMI) with a way of playing that reconciled being perfectly adapted to the dance floor with a complex structure and advanced technique. According to Luis Adolfo Sierra, "He achieved the characteristics of his orchestra through audacious new proposals. The strength of its rhythmic accentuation lies on a singular overlaying of planes of sound, weaving a fabric of subtle multiple rhythms, in which different instrumental sections mark different divisions of time, in the midst of an inexhaustible richness of resources and effects, sometimes almost impossible to perceive. And the different themes surge from that conjunction of opposing rhythms, with admirable expressiveness in the original way that the soloists have of "saying" their parts.

The other orchestra that managed to distinguish itself at the end of the thirties was the one lead by Carlos Di Sarli from the piano, who, although he had already been successful, and had a discography from the days of silent films, achieved his definite establishment in 1938, and rejoined the RCA Victor catalogue the year after. Although in those first years he had to follow the predominant rhythmical concepts, and he would soon make them more flexible, his style was basically the same as the one that he had developed formerly, even when he had accompanied the singer Mercedes Carné at the Brunswick Company (without his name appearing on the label). According to Sierra: "Without worrying to much about harmonic problems, the Carlos Di Sarli orchestra versions are invariably adjusted to an established scheme, achieving its interest through a very precise and subtle range of tones, alternating in well achieved contrasts, the 'staccatos' and the 'legatos,' and the 'crescendos' with the 'pianissimos.' The use of strings almost in unison, doing without the bandoneons as principal voices, and the permanent presence of Di Sarli himself, with his inimitable conducting from the piano, and the 'contracantos' of the first violin, gives the orchestra its characteristic color." The most important thing, without doubt, was Carlos Di Sarli's style at the piano, with his left hand marking the rhythm.

By about 1940, the tango was, with the Argentine cinema, entering its most brilliant age. With Gardel gave, the solo tango singers did not achieve the success obtained by those that sang with the more popular orchestras in those years.

After Francisco Canaro, all the orchestras managed to feature their singers, giving them, more and more as the thirties went by, opportunities to shine rather than just singing a refrain in the middle of a melody. Some singers achieved a prominent place on the billboard, sometimes as prominent as the director of the group.

Another consequence was that each group played its own repertoire almost exclusively. According to Sierra, "it was very exceptional then for a success to reach a group other than the one that had been its original creator. So that the original concept of a success, in the sense that a work entered the repertoire of different performers, as used to happen before, when tangos were premiered in plays in the theater, or in reviews, had been completely reversed. Each orchestra played its own repertoire, and some of the versions, reached the same degree of success as if they were still in the times in which all the groups performed the tunes that the public demanded, not caring who had been their creators."

Argentine films, which in the silent film era had used some popular tangos as a base for making films, would not completely do without them in the sound film period. Tango musicians were the principal composers of the sound tracks. Fortunately, the work of many of the fashionable orchestras from those years was recorded in the films shot in Argentina. Apart from the critical or commercial evaluation that can be done on those productions, they have the value of providing information about numerous musical groups and the favorite singers from those times.

Conclusions

As this investigation on the origins of Argentine cinema ends, and reflecting on how events occurred, on how film shows started, and how the dreams of its pioneers finally came true around 1940, it is remarkable that much was achieved in very little time, leaving frustrations behind and overcoming financial, technical and artistic obstacles.

The decision, determination, and will of the pioneers that struggled to consolidate an Argentine film industry needed years of effort to overcome the obstacles that appeared when Hollywood films started to take over screens worldwide around 1910, and the even bigger difficulties brought by sound movies.

The period that produced the most evolution and consolidation in Argentine film history took place, basically, between the releases of *Riachuelo* in 1934 and *Prisioneros de la Tierra* in 1939, opening a new age, one of the best known and documented in its existence.

Argentine films had been until then synonymous with modesty, and lacking all kinds of elements. After 1940, film production in Argentina could count on technical and artistic elements comparable to those of any foreign production. Argentina produced great actors and great directors, who would do their best work in films that were to be celebrated by the public.

BIBLIOGRAPHY

Bravo, Enrique. *Señoras y señores … la radio está en el aire.* Buenos Aires: C & R Ediciones, 1998.

Byrón, Silvestre. "Los años veinte," in *La historia del tango,* vol. 6. Buenos Aires: Ediciones Corregidor, 1977.

Cadícamo, Enrique, and Luis Adolfo Sierra. *La historia del tango,* vol. 7. Buenos Aires: Ediciones Corregidor, 1977.

Couselo, Jorge Miguel. "El tango en el cine," in *La historia del tango,* vol. 8. Buenos Aires: Ediciones Corregidor, 1977.

_____, Mariano Calistro, Claudio España, Ricardo García Olivieri, Andrés Insaurralde, Carlos Landini, César Maranghello, and Miguel Rosado. *Historia del cine argentino.* Buenos Aires: Centro Editor de América Latina, 1984–1992.

Curubeto, Diego. *Babilonia gaucha: Hollywood en la Argentina, la Argentina en Hollywood.* Buenos Aires: Editorial Planeta, 1993.

Di Chiara, Roberto. *El cine mudo argentino.* Buenos Aires: author's edition, 1996.

Di Núbila, Domingo. *Historia del cine argentino.* Buenos Aires: Edición Cruz de Malta/Editorial Schapire, 1959.

Ferreyra, Fernando. *Luz, cámara … memoria: Una historia social del cine argentino.* Buenos Aires: Ediciones Corregidor, 1995.

Gobello, José. "Enrique Delfino y el tango canción," in *La historia del tango,* vol. 6. Buenos Aires: Ediciones Corregidor, 1977.

Heinink Juan B. and Robert G. Dickson. *Cita en Hollywood.* Bilbao: Ediciones Menajero, 1990.

Morena, Miguel Angel. *Historia artística de Carlos Gardel.* 4th ed. Buenos Aires: Ediciones Corregidor, 1998.

Nudler, Julio. *Tango judío.* Buenos Aires: Editorial Sudamericana, 1998.

Selles, Roberto. *Tango nuestro.* Buenos Aires: Editorial Agedit, 1998.

Sierra, Luis Adolfo. *Historia de la orquesta típica; evolución instrumental del tango.* 2d ed. Buenos Aires: Ediciones Corregidor, 1997.

Sredch, Enrique, *et al. Ser Gardel.* Buenos Aires: Ediciones PxP, 1990.

Tango: Los hombres que hicieron la historia. Contributions by Norberto Fontevecchia, Luis Adolfo Sierra, Boris Puga, Bruno Cespi, *et al.* Buenos Aires: Editorial Perfil, 1980.

Tango, 1880–1980: Un siglo de historia. Contributions by Norberto Fontevecchia, Luis Adolfo Sierra, Boris Puga, Bruno Cespi, *et al.* Buenos Aires: Editorial Perfil, 1979.

Ulanovsky, Carlos; Marta Merkin, Juan José Panno, and Gabriela Tijman. *Días de radio: Historia de la radio argentina.* Espasa Calpe, Buenos Aires, 1995.
Zucchi, Oscar D. "Edgardo Donato—a plena luz," in *La historia del tango,* vol. 6. Buenos Aires: Ediciones Corregidor, 1977.
_____. "Francisco Lomuto," in *La historia del tango,* vol. 4. Buenos Aires: Ediciones Corregidor, 1977.

Newspapers

Crítica
El Diario
La Epoca
La Nación
La Vanguardia
La Prensa
La Razon

Internet Sites

Todo Tango: http:www.todotango.com
Archivo Di Film: http:www.archivodifilm.com
Gardel Universal: http:www.geocities.com/gardelsiglo21

Magazines

Atlantida
Caras y Caretas
Cine Argentino
Radiolandia
Sintonia

INDEX